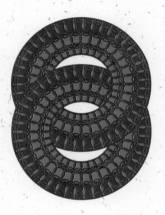

A Gradual Twilight

AN APPRECIATION OF JOHN HAINES

A Gradual Twilight

AN APPRECIATION OF JOHN HAINES

Edited by Steven B. Rogers

with an

FOREWORD BY DANA GIOIA

CavanKerry ✦ Press LTD.

FORT LEE, NEW JERSEY

LIBRARY OF CONGRESS CATALOGING-IN-PUBLICATION DATA

A gradual twilight : an appreciation of John Haines / edited by Steven B. Rogers.
    p. cm.
Includes bibliographical references and index.
ISBN 0-9707186-2-4
    1. Haines, John Meade, 1924—Criticism and interpretation.
I. Rogers, Steven B. 1951–

PS3558.A33 Z68 2002
811'.54—dc21   2001058290

Cover photo courtesy of John Haines
Photo of John Haines by Joseph Enzweiler
Cover and book design by Sylvia Frezzolini Severance

First Edition

Printed in the United States of America

CavanKerry Press Ltd.
Fort Lee, New Jersey
www.cavankerrypress.com

Let me live in my house by the side of the road,
And be a friend to man.

—Sam Walter Foss

For John Meade Haines
poet, essayist, conservationist,
and a true friend of man

CONTENTS

Traces

FOREWORD

The lessons of John Haines' life and work are mostly uncomfortable ones for contemporary readers. He has spent much of his adult life living in the Alaskan wilderness, often fishing and trapping for survival. He wrote initially mostly in isolation. His outspoken nature has kept him from securing tenure or even steady employment at any university. In a literary age characterized by middle-class professionalism and institutional security, especially among academic writers, Haines reminds one of the deep, historical connections between the artistic vocation and voluntary poverty. His creative and critical development came at a substantial personal price. He is a prophetic writer—in both verse and prose—one who views, appraises, and castigates his society. By spiritual necessity the prophetic writer must stand apart from his or her milieu and renounce the compromises that solicit its rewards. Renunciation, sacrifice, and dedication are central virtues of the bohemian tradition, which is perhaps why that life choice has so evidently declined in our prosperous society. But elective poverty permits the sort of freedom, candor, and purity that characterizes Haines' work. In a literary era dominated by institutional life, he stands out as both a singular and exemplary figure.

Haines' critical reputation tells a great deal about current American literary culture but very little about the author's true artistic stature. Haines is neither a famous nor popular writer. Although his poetry appears in some anthologies, his work is more frequently omitted, and it rarely appears on college reading lists. His essays are seldom cited in academic literature. He has never won a Pulitzer Prize, National Book Award, or Bollingen Prize. He has never served as poet laureate—not merely in Washington, D.C., but even in his own thinly populated state of Alaska. During the last decade's boom in poetry coverage by the media, Haines has remained nearly invisible. He has already had one critical collection published about his work—a serious and substantial volume that received virtually no attention from scholars or reviewers. Why does a writer of such seemingly modest reputation deserve another book in his honor?

The answer to this question will be made abundantly clear in this ample new volume. John Haines is a poet and essayist whose uncompromisingly honest and conspicuously individual perspective speaks deeply to many writers. The earnest intensity of his work may be too much for the casual reader, but most writers recognize it immediately as the enlivening energy of a real artist. Likewise Haines' impatience with received opinion and literary fashion probably scares off many conventionally minded literati, but his dogged independence and general suspicion of all intellectual orthodoxy is exactly what makes him an invaluable author to his admirers. Reading Haines' work is not a passive activity: it is a lively and engaged conversation, sometimes even an argument, which leaves the reader by turns provoked, informed, annoyed, surprised, and challenged. No alert reader finishes a book by Haines without somehow being transformed or enlarged by the experience.

Haines is not merely a fine writer but a necessary one—a poet and essayist who enlarges his readers by challenging their unexamined assumptions. More important, he challenges their assumptions not only about art and literature but also about life and the physical world. His vision is large, comprehensive, and earnest—ranging from poetry and painting to politics and the environment. One need not agree with everything he says to feel and appreciate his genuine significance. Like so many prophetic or provocative poets—from William Blake to D. H. Lawrence and Robinson Jeffers—Haines can be obscure, hyperbolic, cranky, biased, and infuriating. He can seem, by turns, exciting and confused, revealingly personal and hopelessly subjective. One can concede that he possesses a number of minor intellectual vices without losing sight of his penetrating intelligence, conceptual originality, artistic brilliance, and moral authority. He is earnest and ambitious. He may go astray among the foothills, but he finds and ascends the mountains. Living too long in the flatlands of contemporary literary culture, we often forget that the mountains exist. They seem so impossibly distant and formidable. But despite our neglect, they remain and allow a writer brave and hardy enough remarkable perspectives. Whether or not his own age acknowledges the fact, Haines is such a writer.

—Dana Gioia

STEVEN B. ROGERS

Stories I Have Listened To

Ever since I was a young boy I have often dreamed of going to Alaska, yet unlike so many others of my generation who have entertained similar aspirations, I have tried hard not to harbor the notion that I would find the wild and untamed frontier Alaska once was. My earliest impressions of Alaska date back to the 1950s, when I would religiously watch *Sergeant Preston of the Yukon* on television, and I read several books about the Alaskan and Yukon gold rushes. As a young kid I could often be found outside with a small garden trowel, searching for treasures buried in the urban lawns and parks near where I grew up. Or with one of my mother's aluminum pie pans sluicing for gold in the gutter in front of our house.

During frequent boyhood visits to my grandparents' Michigan farmstead, I would listen to my maternal grandmother tell stories about her two uncles, Horace and Wilbur Haydon, who, perhaps captivated by the romantic descriptions of gold fever in Jack London's *Call of the Wild* and *White Fang*, left Michigan in the final years of the nineteenth century in search of fortune and fame. They headed first to Seattle and then up the Inland Passage to Skagway, Alaska, on their way to the Klondike gold rush in the Canadian Yukon. Perhaps they would have eventually ended up in Alaska, but after their time in Dawson City they both headed back to Whitehorse, where they married Native American women, and they never returned home to Michigan. One of them, no one in the family seems to recall which, was eventually done in by his wife for reasons unknown, and the other drowned in Kluane Lake, situated halfway between Whitehorse and the Alaskan border. One of the sons, Jack Haydon, my grandmother's cousin, settled in Kluane, a small settlement at the far southern end of the lake, in the late 1920s, where he and his son, also known as Jack Haydon, ran dog teams.

It was in Kluane that father and son first encountered Bradford Washburn, the noted explorer and cartographer and leader of a National Geographic expedition to map the last uncharted areas of the St. Elias Mountains, those majestic peaks poised along the Yukon-Alaskan border, in February 1935. For a fee of five dollars a day Washburn hired the younger Jack Haydon, his six dogs, and a large sled to help transport the expedition up the newly discovered and charted Lowell and Hubbard glaciers. My grandmother had a copy of an old *National Geographic Magazine* describing the 1935 Yukon expedition led by Washburn, and each time I visited the farm I would sit and read, and then reread, the story of Jack Haydon's adventures on the glaciers of the St. Elias Mountains, always studying the black-and-white photographs of a young man and his six-dog sled exploring those unknown mountains and ice fields of the southern Yukon. Jack Haydon died an old man in Whitehorse, in the Yukon, not that many years ago. But I will always remember him as a young man in those black-and-white photographs. Even now I will pause to flip through the dog-eared pages of the magazine, and the thrill of that adventure so many years ago is still there. And the dreams of Alaska begin all over again.

Like some of my ancestors I am drawn to a quest for fortunes found and lost, and for distant frontiers real and imagined. I have always hoped that someday, perhaps, I would have an opportunity to strike out on an Alaskan journey of my own. Until I do, and I am certain that I will, I have had to live vicariously through the adventures of others.

When I was in elementary school I had a good friend, Carl Anderson, who moved with his family to Anchorage in 1963. I envied his good luck, and even though I knew he was living in a city, it was an Alaskan city, and I somehow imagined him in buckskins and snowshoes trudging his way through raging blizzards each morning on his way to his new school. On the weekends, I pictured him in a canoe or a kayak floating down wild Alaskan rivers. I am quite certain there were moose and bear and deer in his yard every day. I don't know if he ever did any of this, or whether he even tried. I never heard from him again after he moved away, and my mind soon turned to other thoughts and concerns. Then came the news of the devastating Good Friday earthquake that struck southern Alaska on March 27, 1964. Measuring 8.5 on the Richter scale, the quake was responsible for over 130 deaths throughout Alaska. There were rumors told around school that Carl and his family had disappeared during the quake and were feared dead. There were some who speculated that they had headed into the Alaskan wilderness and were never heard from again. I remember watching the television reports from Anchorage and Valdez after the quake, each time looking at the faces along the streets where huge fissures left gaping asphalt wounds, hoping that I might see Carl and know that he was still alive. I never saw his face, but I hope deep down that he is still alive somewhere up there, wearing buckskins and snowshoes and trudging his way to work each morning.

I came close to realizing my dream of going to Alaska in the summer of 1970, between my freshman and sophomore years in college, when my friend Greg and I packed up my 1966 Ford Mustang, a homemade ALASKA OR BUST sign duct-taped to the rear bumper, and set out from Milwaukee in late July for a long trip up to the Trans-Canada Highway, at Winnipeg. From there we headed westward across the Canadian prairies to the foothills of the Rockies. I had always hoped we would head north through Alberta, joining the Alaskan Highway at Dawson Creek, in British Columbia, and from there we would drive up through the Yukon, visiting the places I knew from my grandmother's stories. If we were lucky, perhaps we would continue our journey into Alaska, skirting the Tanana River on our way to Fairbanks, some 1,500 miles beyond Dawson Creek. After numerous detours of discovery on our way across Canada, our money and time ran out when we reached Lethbridge, Alberta, and we were forced to retreat back across Montana, the Dakota Badlands, and Minnesota, on our way home. Close, but not close enough to that distant and still elusive frontier. Then again, perhaps we never really meant to go as far as Alaska. We were gratified by the notion that we were headed toward Alaska; we were content just to leave Milwaukee behind and to be on the road to somewhere else. The ALASKA OR BUST bumper sticker was our cry of freedom, a symbol of fetters broken. Reaching Alberta and the Canadian Rockies was good enough for us. We enjoyed ourselves on the road, and after some unanticipated mechanical problems in the middle of nowhere in Montana, we were happy to return home in one piece.

There is always the danger of dreaming too much. Consider the story of Chris McCandless, a young hiker who, after graduating from college, gave away all his money, abandoned his family, and set off on a journey of self-discovery that eventually took him to the Alaskan wilderness in the shadows of Denali (Mount McKinley). Ever since he was a young boy he had wanted to escape into the bush, away from civilization. Perhaps we all do at one point or another in our lives. I know that feeling. Upon reaching Alaska, McCandless set off alone down the Stampede Trail with almost no food, very little protective gear, no map or compass, and almost no clue how he might survive in the unforgiving wilderness. A few years earlier a Romanian mountain enthusiast named Adam Popovich had attempted a solo ascent of nearby Denali without a tent, stove, water, or the appropriate survival gear despite numerous warnings by the National Park Service. Both he and McCandless were infected by a naïve hubris, a destructive arrogance, and neither could see the trees for the forest. Popovich was lucky he did not die; in his rush to make his ascent he failed to properly acclimatize and suffered a cerebral edema at 19,000 feet and was forced to turn back. McCandless was not as lucky. In his attempt to escape civilization into an uncharted wilderness (it was only uncharted because he chose not to take a map), he ended up starving to death in a derelict Fairbanks city bus 20 miles from the trail head where he began his journey. Being alone in the Alaskan wilderness can, for some, be a richly rewarding experience, but nature is unforgiving to those who do not show it the respect it deserves and demands. I guess deep down Greg and I both knew this; we were certainly not prepared to go into the Alaskan frontier wilderness we had been dreaming about since we were kids.

So, for the past thirty years, I have been satisfied to dream of Alaska through the books and reminiscences of others who have been there, for a brief moment or for a lifetime. Of course, I read Jack London when I was young. And there was Mardy Murie's 1962 memoir, *Two in the Far North*. While in graduate school in Tucson in the mid-1970s I read John Muir's *Travels in Alaska*, and I marveled at his 1880 discovery along the Alaskan-Canadian boundary of the glacier that now bears his name. I recalled the exploits of Jack Haydon farther to the north. I also read the further adventures of Bradford Washburn and his 1934 National Geographic expedition to southeastern Alaska's Mt. Crillon, not too far to the west of Muir Glacier, as well as his commentary on the 1964 National Geographic Mount Kennedy expedition to the St. Elias Mountains he had surveyed almost three decades earlier. During that expedition, James W. Whittaker, the legendary mountaineer and the first American to stand on the summit of Mount Everest, led his team, including the late Senator Robert F. Kennedy, on the first ascent of the mountain named in honor of a brother assassinated in faraway Texas the year before.

In 1978, after moving from Tucson to Washington, DC, I read John McPhee's *Coming Into the Country*, hoping his discussion of life in modern-day Alaska might better prepare me for what I would find when I finally got there. I quickly realized that Alaska was in many ways much as I had dreamed (and hoped) it would be, yet it was changing, and not necessarily for the better. I brooded that my chance to find the Alaska of my boyhood dreams was beginning to fade. Over the next decade, as I began a career in Washington and started a family, I had other things on my mind and I confess that I thought little of Alaska.

This all changed in 1990, with the premier of a new television show, *Northern Exposure.* Over the next several seasons viewers, including me, were entertained by the quirks and peccadillos of a ragtag group of modern-day homesteaders, adventurers, and bon vivants who lived in log cabins, trailers, prefab housing, even a geodesic dome, in the fictional Alaskan town of Cicely. Here moose and bear shared the town's main street with huge lumber trucks, and the locals relied on an odd blend of medical advice provided by a doctor from New York City and the local Native American shaman. After reading John McPhee, this is what I now imagined life in Alaska must really be like.

It was also around this time, in the summer of 1991, that I received an invitation to participate in a seminar at George Washington University as a Jenny McKean Moore Fellow in Creative Writing. Selected to lead the seminar was an Alaskan poet and essayist by the name of John Haines, the Writer-in-Residence at GWU for the coming academic year. Now I must admit that I was familiar with neither John Haines nor his work, but that he had gone to Alaska in the years immediately after World War II and there built a homestead where he lived and trapped for years piqued my curiosity. Discovering that he was a poet and writer of some repute intrigued me even more. What stories about Alaska might he tell? To prepare for the workshop, I went to a small literary bookstore in Washington, and to my surprise I found several of John's books on the shelf. I purchased a copy of his recent memoir, *The Stars, The Snow, The Fire* (1989), along with his first book of essays, *Living Off the Country* (1981), about his life in Alaska and the beginning of his literary career in a small isolated cabin on a hillside above the Tanana River. I also purchased two thin volumes of his early poems, *Winter News* (1966) and *The Stone Harp* (1971). I thought it important that I know something about the man and his work, but what I discovered in these essays and poems, and in the man I would meet for the first time just a few weeks later, has changed me in ways I am only now beginning to realize. For the first time I have truly opened my eyes to the unique beauty of Alaska and to the problems that now threaten what was once virtually untouched wilderness.

John Haines was born in Tidewater Virginia in 1924, and as the son of a career naval officer he frequently moved around the United States with his family. He never had an opportunity to put down real roots until 1947 following his own discharge from wartime naval service, when he and a friend set off to Alaska to find a patch of land to call their own. The friend quickly abandoned the adventure, but Haines settled at Richardson, on a hillside above the Tanana River almost 70 miles southeast of Fairbanks. Although he hoped to use the solitude at Richardson to focus on his art studies, he admits that his birth as a poet can be traced to his first real home, his homestead in Alaska: "I must have carried in myself from an early age some vague design of such a place and such a life. . . . From the first day I set foot in interior Alaska, and more specifically on Richardson Hill, I knew I was home. Something in me identified with that landscape. I had come, let's say, to the dream place" (*Living Off the Country*, 4–5). It was there that he began to write poetry seriously. In "The Hermitage" Haines writes:

> In the forest below the stairs
> I have a secret home,
> my name is carved in the roots.
>
> I own a crevice stuffed with moss
> and a couch of lemming fur;
> I sit and listen to the music
> of water dripping on a distant stone,

or I sing to myself
of stealth and loneliness.

No one comes to see me,
but I hear outside
the scratching of claws,
the warm, inquisitive breath . . .

And once in a strange silence
I felt quite close
the beating of a human heart.

I have also learned to appreciate the precarious existence of a man
and an artist whose very heart and soul are intrinsically tied to the
Alaskan homestead where he lived and toiled and about which he has
written so lovingly; a writer who has practiced his craft without the
perks and comforts of university tenure, without a retirement plan,
with little in the bank, who has made his living by his wits and words
alone. Despite these hardships, John Haines continues to create
poems and essays that capture the beauty of the natural world, to
identify the threats to that way of life, and to offer wisdom as one who
has patterned his life on the land that nurtured it.

The physical domain of the country had its counterpart in
me. The trails I made led outward into the hills and swamps,
but they led inward also. And from the study of things under-
foot, and from reading and thinking, came a kind of explo-
ration, myself and the land. In time the two became one in
my mind. With the gathering force of an essential thing real-
izing itself out of early ground, I faced in myself a passionate
and tenacious longing—to put away thought forever, and all
the trouble it brings, all but the nearest desire, direct and
searching. To take the trail and not look back. Whether on

foot, on snowshoes or by sled, into the summer hills and their late freezing shadows—a high blaze, a runner track in the snow would show where I had gone. Let the rest of mankind find me if it could. (*The Stars, The Snow, The Fire,* 19)

Where John Haines has gone in the past fifty years is woven among the words and images of his poems and essays, in the stories he has listened to and in those he has passed on to willing readers. I am still listening to the stories he tells about life in the Alaskan wilderness, and about those who have chosen to live there. I have never been to Alaska; perhaps I will never go. But now, at least, I believe I know something of the true Alaska. I have found some understanding of a place I have thought and dreamed about since I was a child.

WORKS REFERENCED

Haines, John. *Living Off the Country: Essays on Poetry and Place.* Ann Arbor: The University of Michigan Press, 1981.
———. *The Stars, The Snow, The Fire.* St. Paul: Graywolf, 1989.
Krakauer, Jon. *Into the Wild.* New York: Anchor Books, 1996.
———. "Club Denali." *Eiger Dreams.* New York: The Lyons Press, 1990, 64–66.
McPhee, John. *Coming Into the Country.* New York: Farrar, Straus and Giroux, 1977.
Muir, John. *Travels in Alaska.* Boston: Houghton Mifflin, 1915. John Haines wrote a preface to the 1987 Sierra Club reprint of this fine book.
Murie, Margaret E. *Two in the Far North.* New York: Knopf, 1962.
Washburn, Bradford. "Canada's Mount Kennedy: The Discovery." *National Geographic Magazine* 98, no. 7 (July 1965): 1–3. This issue also includes short essays by Robert F. Kennedy and James W. Whittaker.
———. "Exploring Yukon's Glacial Stronghold." *National Geographic Magazine* 69, no. 6 (June 1936): 715–748.
———. "The Conquest of Mount Crillon." *National Geographic Magazine* 67, no. 3 (March 1935): 361–400.
———. *Exploring the Unknown: Historic Diaries of Bradford Washburn's Alaska/Yukon Expeditions.* Edited by Lew Freedman. Kenmore, WA: Epicenter Press, 2001.

PART ONE

Contributions to
the Literary Landscape

THOMAS McGRATH

Working in Darkness

I think of the ones like the poet John Haines,
During those long years in Alaska,
Working alone in a cold place,
Sitting in darkness outside the pool of light:
Ice-Fisherman facing the empty hole of the page,
Patient, the spear poised, waiting for a sign.

And coal miners go out in the cold darkness
In search of fire and light.
In darkness they return to their homes.
The long years go by in the night that is under the earth
But they remember the sun.

And I think of my grandfather—how we planted potatoes
By the dark of the moon: each silvery wedge with an eye
To see on their journey and guide them quick to the sun,
As when, building the great ships, I hunted the signs
To weld the galvo or rivet the plates to the deck.

A kind of searching, translation of signs, a kind of hunting:
As when the bowman peers through the night-bound forest:
Reading the sounds of a shaken bush or a rattle of stones,
Patient and impatient driven and hungering, following
Through the cold day and the moon-patched colder night,
The wounded beast his calling says pursue
Though he have nothing to eat in the hunt but its bloody droppings.

MARION K. STOCKING

From A to Infinity:
A Half-Century of the Poetry
of John Haines

Auden once said that "the questions which interest me most are two. The first is technical: 'Here is a verbal contraption. How does it work?' The second is, in the broadest sense, moral: 'What kind of a gut inhabits this poem? What is his notion of the good life or the good place? His notion of the Evil One? What does he conceal from the reader? What does he conceal even from himself?' "[1] My early training in the old New Criticism inclines me toward the first approach. My subsequent career as a scholar of the Byron-Shelley circle convinces me of the importance of the second. Both seem appropriate for an examination of the work of John Haines, and the occasion of this celebration provides me with a welcome opportunity.

My appreciation of John Haines' poetry comes from years of reading, rereading, and reviewing his books, most recently the comprehensive collected poems, *The Owl in the Mask of the Dreamer*. And now I have before me *At the End of This Summer: Poems, 1948–1954*, poems that predate his first published poems. Fortunately, I have also his most recent book, *A Guide to the Four-Chambered Heart*.

My intent is to catalogue the qualities of the familiar Haines canon that make it so distinctive and so powerful for me. Then I hope to explore how the earlier book anticipates these qualities and how the later extends them. I'll follow Auden's lead: first the form and then the function.

---

1. W. H. Auden, "Making, Knowing, and Judging," in *The Dyer's Hand and Other Essays* (New York: Random House, 1962).

Haines' prosody is the product of a sure and sensitive ear. The lyric voice, the grace of cadenced song, can make the bleakest vision moving. Listen to the last stanza of "Water of Night":

> Over the drowned gullies,
> houses, fields of the earth,
> seething and rocking,
> water of night.

First we hear the rocking cadences (/xx/), supported by the rocking assonance (*drowned* to *houses*, *fields* to *seething*, *rocking* to *water*), symmetrically counterpointed against the lineation. The result is incantatory, hypnotic. Then we notice that we have been denied the closure of a verb. The intense compression of the syntax moves us rapidly from the spatial images of gullies, houses, and fields to the kinetic participles—"seething and rocking"—that leave us suspended in a poetic field of discharging energy. These paired participles echo back to earlier turbulences: "tumbling and foaming," "smoldering reef," "foaming wells," "sticking and sucking." Haines is capable of absorbing this rolling energy into the quiet concluding cadence of "water of night." By holding in a creative tension opposing emotional forces, syntax and diction collaborate to bring to moving closure a powerfully unsettling poem.

Despite the unparaphrasable complexity of much of Haines' poetry, his diction is usually lucid, close to the sensuous referents of the words. But he can charge this language with intense emotion (*seething*, *rocking*). At the other extreme, he employs as leitmotifs throughout his work a vocabulary of very simple resonant words that gain incrementally as they appear in poem after poem: *cold*, *ashes*, *dust*, *silence*, *stillness*, *stone*, *night*, *darkness*, *blood*, *leaves* (usually falling or fallen), *water*, *wind*, *ice*, *sun*, *fire*, *rain*, and, ubiquitous, *death*. If a Haines poem has a season—and most of them do—that season is almost certainly autumn or winter. (He takes off from where Keats' "To Autumn" ends.)

In combination with other images, these simple words can blaze with visionary heat, as "a lamp fueled with blood" and "deep fern-wood drowned in night." While each word recalls its objective source, Haines' diction, his imagery, and his syntax convey an imagination capable of tremendous concentration—compaction. In "Meditation on a Skull Carved in Crystal," here is what the dead see, dying:

> a grain of ice in the stellar
> blackness, lighted
> by a sun, distant within.

Each word carries the weight of its history and the weight of its literal referent, while projecting the imagination deep into outer and inner space. This is the extreme of the poet's power—beyond what any prose can do.

The inner form of a Haines poem often reflects this double-rooting—in the concrete and the visionary. Some poems are emblems, almost in the seventeenth-century sense (the enormous bison head in "The Head on the Table" as an emblem of "the whole journey of beasts on earth" filing soundlessly "into the gloom of the catalogues"). Parables and even allegory follow easily from emblems. But the most distinctive and original of Haines' architectural devices is the dream-vision, not much used since Shelley, in which the poet's meticulous observation of the seen, heard, smelt, felt world translates into an inner realm no less immediate, no less eloquent. The very title of *The Owl in the Mask of the Dreamer,* inverting as it does our customary habit of perception, expresses forcefully this intellectual challenge. For a brilliant example, see "The Sleep of Reason," which, by its title, associates itself with Goya's bitter dream-visions.

Above all, Haines' gift is lyric—the difficult lyric that forges its own bars and clefs and staffs and cadences. In the dark, in the declining season, on a doomed planet, the poet sings. And the great late sequences are organisms—families of delicately related short lyrics, combined to form visions of major scope and scale.

The audible and visible form of John Haines' poems reflects the insights and ultimately the character of the poet. His range is intimate and cosmic. He moves freely in space and time and from outer to inner weather. In "Panorama":

> We turn one ear to the flight of missiles,
> listen earthward with the other
> for fieldmice squeaking in the grass.

His sense of place is geographical, geological, and, ultimately, cosmic. "Will we ever again be at home / on earth?" he asks in "Victoria," which concludes among the "flung constellations":

> This rain of particles,
> random sparks catching fire,
> blowing out in the stellar drifts,
> each one seeking the other.

Literal space flows for Haines into the metaphorical:

> . . . the darkness
> growing across a landscape
> within you; . . .
>> ("To a Man Going Blind")

and

> There is a distance in the heart,
> and I know it well —
>> ("Ancestor of the Hunting Heart")

The poet's handling of space is multidimensional, but his treatment of time is even more complex. At one level he brings a historical perspective to his vision. "The Traveler" and "Stampede" in *Winter News* re-create thousands of years of invasions of the Arctic. Because of this sense of chronology, several of his poems condense some chapter of human history into a poetic sequence. His "Age of Bronze," he tells us, is a condensed history of Western art. "Water of Night" is an eight-chapter saga of civilization, from the auguries of the earliest peoples to today's sinister ash "blown down from chimneys."

The two corollaries of this intense sense of time "past, or passing, or to come" are elegy and prophecy. Because Haines was privileged to experience, in his homesteading in Alaska, a life of subsistence in harmony with an unspoiled wilderness, he has earned his bitterness of what in one lifetime has been destroyed on the planet. "The Oregon Coast"—with its opening recalling Longfellow's "forest primeval"—is an elegy for the "drenched / magnificence" before it was destroyed. The beautiful "Rain Country" is an explicit elegy for friends and a lost way of life, with its poignant lines:

> All
> that we knew, and everything
> but for me forgotten.

The elegiac tone is strong in "Diminishing Credo," in which Delacroix, participating through his art in the vitality of heroic history, came to see that "map of history vanished." The fuel for Haines' elegies is his passion for the friends, the way of life, the integrity of the wilderness, the high energy of art—all vanishing or vanished. The good life and the good place Auden enquires for would seem to have been there.

Projecting his insight into the future, Haines inclines to prophecy. In *Winter News* this takes the form of a foreboding. In *The Stone*

Harp two sharp little poems, "The Lemmings" and the prescient parable "The Flight," envision the imminent disintegration of social life. In the following volumes, the poet repeatedly extrapolates from the history of his time images of disintegration, dehumanizing mechanization, and extinctions. There is an Old Testament anger seething under some of these poems, fueled by a passion for the disappearing values. The line between prognostication and satire is, as Swift knew, invisible. In Haines' satiric poems there is a *saeva indignatio* very close to Swift's. His "Homage to David Smith" is bitterly ironic: he sees Smith's constructions as emblematic—his "gnawed shields, unfinished arrows," signs

> pointing inward to an iron self,
> or else toward the scrapyard
> to which we seem to be rolling—

"To the Wall" goes further in a Vision of Judgment excoriating the representative men of our unnatural day. His vision of the Evil One is precise and devastating.

How is one to conduct oneself among all this disintegration? Tragedy in every age has addressed this question: "what to make of a diminished thing" or—closer to the bone—how to survive, knowing what we know. The response suggests the measure of the poet. (In "Gerontion," Eliot asked, "After such knowledge, what forgiveness?" Forgiveness would hardly be a part of Haines' steadfastly post-Christian inquiry.) In one exceptional lyric, "Little Cosmic Dust Poem," he connects our expanded knowledge of cosmic time and space with the simplest of traditional responses. This lyric begins:

> Out of the debris of dying stars,
> this rain of particles
> that waters the waste with brightness . . .

It concludes:

> In the radiant field of Orion
> great hordes of stars are forming,
> just as we see every night,
> fiery and faithful to the end.
>
> Out of the cold and fleeing dust
> that is never and always,
> the silence and waste to come . . .
>
> This arm, this hand,
> my voice, your face, this love.

This eloquent song, with its embrace of Arnold ("Dover Beach") and Keats ("this living hand") is atypical among Haines' poems. For him more usually there seem to be two other answers—one outer, one inner. The outer one is through art. His many poems on artists testify to the power of art not only to express a social stance and a relationship to the universe, but to comprehend and survive disaster. At the one end we have the Inuit carving in ivory "a weasel the length of his finger"; at the other, the monsters spawned in Goya's sleep of reason. The art of the poet—the maker—has some power against ignorant destruction and even, in the elegy, against oblivion. In "Little Cosmic Dust Poem" perhaps "my voice" associates the poet with this power. At any rate, the lyric achievement of the poem itself testifies for the poet.

The other approach to the tragic question is really a deeper level of the first. It is the plunge into the eternal present of the dream-vision. The dream as a channel into the unconscious is one of the most powerful of Haines' distinctive resources. Within the domain of that vision everything—the nourishing, the deadly, and the nourishing-deadly—has meaning. The vision can comprehend the divided consciousness of the killer-for-food, the simultaneity of time and space, the paradox of the lamp fueled with blood. A simple example is the entrance into the spirit of Van Gogh, "On a Certain Field in Auvers"—ending with its blazing benediction:

> 'In the name of the poor,
> and of the holy insane,
> and the great light of the sun.'

At another level of composition (Frost: "There is nothing so composing as composition"), internalizing a reality preserves it alive: "Wilderness survives at the camp / we have made within us." At a vastly more complex level, "In the Forest without Leaves," perhaps the bleakest of the prophetic poems, the spell against oblivion is the emblematic birch tree, short-lived, like the rest of us, defoliated, burned, dispersed. Nevertheless:

> If and whenever we come again,
> I will know that tree.
>
> A birch leaf held fast
> in limestone ten million years
> still quietly burns,
> though claimed by the darkness.
>
> Let earth be this windfall
> swept to a handful of seeds—
> one tree, one leaf,
> gives us plenty of light.

Just as the distinction evaporates between the form and the content of the poet's work, so also does the line between the art and the character of the poet. Whether the poet in creating his poems is creating himself, or whether the poems are the natural flowering of an individual character (or some of both), the quality of the poems does appear to reflect certain strengths of character. It is probably arrogant for a critic in this age to venture onto this unfashionable ground, and it is certainly arbitrary to separate the inseparable, but I am going to try.

INTELLIGENCE

Haines has a fearlessly inquiring mind, probing into questions about the relationship of humanity to our best knowledge of the universe and relating this to the workings of the mind and spirit. In one of the mirror images that appear in his later poems, he claims this quality:

> Intelligence is what we find,
> gazing into rock as into water
> at the same depth shining.
> ("Meditation on a Skull Carved in Crystal")

Like Shelley he needs a worldview consistent with the sum of human knowledge—no matter how devastating to our aspirations and egos. "Good-bye to the Flowerclock" shows this pioneering spirit:

> It was time to push away
> the four walls of the years,
> to go to the end of the path
> and go beyond . . .

The recurring ellipses in his poem represent this intellectual pioneering beyond language, into the implications of the time/space continuum.

INTEGRITY

In the truest meaning of the word, Haines maintains throughout his career an unblinkered and unblinking course of exploration and synthesis. His poet's calling requires the forging of a unified vision. In another sense of integrity, he expresses strong feeling without sentimentality. His power of projecting himself imaginatively into an animal or bird stops rigorously short of pathetic fallacy. As early as *Winter News* we can see this in the three moose poems ("Horns," "The Moosehead," and "Victims"), which must be read together. Though he may allegorize a tree in "Poem about Birch Trees," he well knows that what he is encountering is "the blind face that is Nature." Even as a young man, the poet acknowledges without romanticizing the omnipresence of death. He very early achieves the ability to absorb what the scientist knows about the nature of the universe, to face the implications of this knowledge and the implications of the devastation of the planet, and to resist the human impulse to seek insulation through denial or through consolation in a self-created or inherited religion.

> To prayer and petition
> God speaks the simplest words:
> *sun, rain,* and *frost.*
> > ("Of Michelangelo, His Question")

PASSION

In *Winter News* the feeling for the natural world and the capacity to enter imaginatively into it flare in poems like "Horns," describing an encounter with a moose. The closest the reader can come to understanding and sharing this gift is in just such poems as this where the artist-poet's honed powers of observation are most apparent:

> I awoke and stood in the cold
> as he slowly circled the camp.

His horns exploded in the brush
with dry trees cracking
and falling; his nostrils flared
as, swollen-necked, smelling
of challenge, he stalked by me.

The immediacy of such lines extends, in later poems, to language that conveys the immediacy and the passion of the inner life. But it seems certain that the obverse of this passion, the icy rage against the suicidal stupidity of our time, is fired by the same fuel. He is Yeats' "cold and passionate man."

IMAGINATION

Born of the *image* and faithful to it, Haines' imagination moves inexorably from the outer to the inner, from the literal to the visionary. But rarely to the abstract. Of the simplest ingredients he forges the most complex, the most challenging concepts:

In place of the lamp
that was lighted,
a drop of blood inside the sun.
                    ("Meditation on a Skull Carved in Crystal")

The origin of this powerful poem is, I assume, the poet's gaze into the Aztec crystal skull in the British Museum. Between the gaze and the poem lies also the poet's research into the Meso-American culture that produced the sculptor. The absorbed observer and the enquiring mind were necessary to the process of creation, but it is the blazing imagination, working through meditation over many years, that brought us this poem that crystalizes a lifetime's insight. The poem is dated 1977–86. Many of Haines' poems carry such double dates, testimony to an artistry that cannot be hurried. Every word, every line, is given its full gestation time. The result is the strong harmony of words and music that, like all art, transcends time and space.

We come now to the new volume, appropriately titled *At the End of This Summer: Poems, 1948–1954*, with keen anticipation of new poems antedating his earliest published work. They may well represent, as Haines claims, "an early period of apprenticeship," but they are by no means juvenilia, having been composed between his twenty-fourth and thirtieth years. (It is humbling to recall that Keats died at twenty-six and Shelley at twenty-nine.) They follow the poet's first sojourn in Alaska and reflect the period of his formal art studies, his first marriage, and his discovered passion for words.

This passion for words has already developed into a distinctive lyric voice, where the precision of the observation manifests itself in prosodic precision. Although several poems illustrate a narrative gift ("The Riders," for one), the lyric impulse overrides the narrative as each story turns inward. To illustrate the technical accomplishment, here is the first stanza of "Journey on Water: A Prelude":

> When the noise of their paddles had ceased
> and the craft was quiet,
> borne unaided along the weedy shoreline
>   by the slow-moving stream,
> only the certain counting of water-beads dropping
>   singly from the blades
> of their extended paddles (it was as still as that): . . .

I admire intensely the flexibility and decorum of the accentual patterning of this rhythmic but unmetered verse. The first line echoes the anapestic regularity of the paddling, arrested by the inversion, *quiet*, at the end of line two. The third line drifts from *borne* to *shore* with only four light stresses (the others, stressed or half-stressed, for me suspend action breathlessly). I think of Keats' still air that "robs not one light seed from the feathered grass" ("Hyperion: A Fragment"). By this point I am enchanted enough to hear the music of the drops falling in the next two lines, my attention focused by the "certain counting" on the trochaic cadence sustained by *water*, *dropping*, and *singly*. The last line, six stresses long, prolongs the stillness to the point where the expository voice may enter (in iambs, in parentheses) to consolidate the experience in preparation for the main clause that opens the next stanza. I don't think I am projecting my reading into the prosody. I think the poet (studying Keats?) has achieved a mastery of the verbal technique that controls the pace, the attention, the ear of the reader so as to share physically and mentally an intense experience.

These early poems anticipate the later work in other ways. Although there are love poems here, and poems of spring and summer, from the first page ("Departure") we find falling leaves, deepening darkness, and "the flood of night." Here's the final stanza of this poem, that starts in a darkling landscape:

> And darker, the final bearing
> toward the wings
> that wait in gathered cloth for one
> who needs no eyes
> to see the drifting heartbreak
> of the smoky hills.

Here is a stanza that looks backward and forward in the Haines canon. It looks forward in its move from the outer to the inner landscape, an inner landscape charged with emotion. It looks forward in the prophetic vision of the winged figure, mysteriously but vividly "in gathered cloth." It looks backward in the vagueness of that figure and in the unfocused sentimentality of "drifting heartbreak."

We cannot know whether Haines in preparing this volume for publication revised any of the poems (as Yeats or Auden surely would have done). But we must honor him for retaining enough "drifting heartbreak" to allow us to appreciate the moral discipline that eliminated such language (such self-indulgence) from his mature work. The diction of these apprentice poems betrays a response that I can only call gothic: words like *descending darkness*, *tears*, *winding-sheet* (twice), *gloomy, mould, grave, bleeding, shroud*. "Procession," with its romantic-gothic file of ghostly children, has for me a historic value: it marks the terminus of the genre that flourished from Percy's *Reliques* through "The Eve of Saint Agnes" to—well—Walter de la Mare.

Several poems in this early volume anticipate the later lyric forms. Some are more tightly structured, with more formal repetitions, than the flexible later songs. But "Pictures and Parables" is a gallery of ten loosely related lyrics, anticipating the great sequences in *News from the Glacier* and *New Poems*. "Pictures and Parables," as its title suggests, is more of a miscellany, including little songs of personal choice, a simple portrayal of an encounter with a one-legged bird, a parable of a naked hermit, and an ambiguous religious meditation. Later sequences will be more organically integrated. What is missing from *At the End of This Summer* is the dream-vision, Haines' most distinctive means of translating the sensuous world into the unconscious.

In these early poems, space and time are superficially significant. Each of the four chapters bears the place and dates of composition. Washington and New York, Provincetown, New York again, and California sometimes color the poems that they nurtured. In poems of place like "Windsong" we sometimes can recognize the locale (Cape Cod), and we can certainly appreciate the accurate language, the melancholy music, and the search for significance that will combine to create the unforgettable lyrics of *Winter News*. But the melodramatic poem titled "Landscapes" appears to be drawn from John Martin or Caspar David Friedrich, complete with allegorical figures. The function of the natural world here seems merely to heighten an emotional response. The respect for the intrinsic integrity of the land comes in the books to follow.

Haines' sense of time—and the relationship of time and space—is developing in the early poems. In "Totem," the poet addresses an image in a museum and sees it not only as an emblem of a wilder, more "primal" time and place, but as an opportunity for his hands to " touch / the centuries," and ultimately as an ironic commentary on contemporary life. It looks ahead to the crystal skull in his most powerful work. "Interview," a dramatic monologue in which a seer addresses his interviewer:

> How old are you,
> friend? A half-inch of bright wire
> on a two-
>   billion-mile spool? . . .

anticipates the ironic voice and the temporal perspective that will distinguish poems to come.

The closest thing to elegy in the early poems is the elegantly formal "Poem for a Drowned Child." There are, however, hints of the prophetic voice to come. The ending of "Interview," for instance, begins the long look into the dark future:

>   I think of
> geological indications
> and wonder, as the age retreats, what
> moraines will your head-
> bones form at the terminals of Time?

It is premature to look this early for the consolations and terrors of art and philosophy and vision that distinguish Haines' mature work. At this stage the poet is still freely making choices and creating his songs and tales to express his growing view of the world. His technical skills developed before his experience of the world disclosed the full darkness of the path he was choosing. It is not, however, too early to look for the qualities of character that provide the bedrock of his major work.

The questioning intelligence that was to lead into the darkness of vision emerges in "Windsong," with its questioning refrain:

> How about the wind,
> what does that mean?

In "Night Falls Once" Haines is thinking through the questions that he will answer with further thought and experience, but they are the right questions about religion and love and time. The conclusion is acute, though the image is awkward:

> Night falls but that once, though
> A million dawns were stacked against the brain.

Despite the weaknesses of diction that sometimes require a stock response to carry the emotion, these poems bear witness to the integrity of character that distinguishes the poet's mature work. His ever-present awareness of death, for instance, is there from the beginning, along with his rejection of organized religion and its institutions. We see the firmness of ideas and clarity of convictions in the extraordinary poem "Admission," where the speaker appears to be the poet himself, addressing a lover colloquially and with painful candor. With icy self-analysis he is explaining their incompatibility—a disparity partly of taste but largely of the difference of ideas and opinions. "I have mine," the poet says:

> They are surely my own, and excepting
> Some heavenly revelation, it is
> Extremely doubtful that they will be

Changed or altered, save as they were
Formed, by experience and a ripening
Of conclusion.

Nevertheless, he assures his companion:

But for all this, we may have
Our moments . . .

They may sit together in the sun, and—in a passage of chilling self-recognition, even self-satire, the speaker admits

                                          I will
Remember to bend my head over and kiss
Your nose and cheeks and lips,
And move my hands over your shoulders
And neck. I will not forget to
Murmur something now and then into your
Dreaming ear, and I will try
Just as long and hard as I can to ignore
The busy singing of crickets in the grass outside.

A gentle reader may read this as a Browningesque dramatic monologue. Any way you read it, it is an achievement of extraordinary intellectual honesty. Yeats, I fear, would not have been capable of that "Remember" and "not forget to." Had Haines followed in this track we might have had (heaven forbid!) an American Larkin.

I look in vain in this early volume for the passion that smoulders and blazes in Haines' later poems. There is love, but it seems more like desire or affection, vulnerable to jealousy, egotism, and the turning seasons (see the extremely moving "On a Point of Departure"). In the little "Song" one cannot tell whether "my love" is a "fair girl" or the abstract emotion, but "she rides high / In a maze of cloudy passion." The clarity—of diction, of vision, of passion—is yet to come.

But the imagination is here, in the earliest surviving poems. It rises out of the images—in those few but significant passages where the observation is sharp and the language accurate. Here's a stanza of "Windsong":

> Over the long, sharp grass
> each grain
> of sand and every pebble on
>   the log shore
> hearing a different sound that is the same.

In "Similitude," the poet conjures first an allegorical image of a man flaying the ground with a blacksnake whip. He concludes without commentary by switching to the first person:

> And I know what it is to go
> into the woods in early spring
> with a heavy axe, choose a slender birch,
> and carefully balanced on
> my feet in the melting snow, swing
> and feel the sharp edge biting
> into the soft, wet flesh of the tree.

Here the image carries the imagination into the ambivalence that in *Winter News* appears as "Divided, the Man Is Dreaming." The ability to conceive and express a divided consciousness is one of the most valuable imaginative powers a poet commands.

The cover of *At the End of This Summer* is a Morris Graves painting of dark water with, on the surface, only a small glimmering of light. Deep below is a luminescent fish, at home in the dark, with a bright eye alert. It is a splendid image for this book with its darks and luminosities. *A Guide to the Four-Chambered Heart* could not appear more different. The stark black-and-white drawings, on the dust jacket and throughout the book, conjure up the gothic, not of the Romantic Revolution, but of the Goths and the woodcuts that extend from the medieval broadsides and dance-of-death sequences to the emblem-writers like Quarles in the seventeenth century. The elegantly produced volume contains three poems, all translating into concrete images the poet's landscapes of consciousness. The owl is gone, but the mask of the dreamer remains, an icon of a mental life. And the poet's wife, Joy, has illustrated each of these icons in clean if mysterious lines. At first I was troubled by the literalness of the illustrations; I tend to object to illustrations to poems as an intrusion on my imagination. But studying this book as a contemporary manifestation of the tradition of emblem-writers, I can justify it. Haines' early poems were sometimes vague in diction and thus in impact. Here, at the other end of the line, the images are sharp-edged and visible, but the roots of the images in the natural world have become remote. Look at the opening lines of chapter one, "The Chart," in the title poem:

> Pierced by an arrow aimed toward Paradise,
> the heartstem broken from a tree
> that stands in perpetual autumn,
> its leaves dipped in blood.

We are a long way from symbolism here (a symbol being a dynamic thing: the literal image plus the meanings that ray out of it). The figures here are purely allegorical, though the narrative drive of traditional allegory has given way to a static, or nearly static, representation. The problem is to understand what it represents. And from the first line the poet discourages translation or paraphrase. We can carry with us from our familiarity with early poems a sense of how the repeated autumns have consolidated into "perpetual autumn," and the "leaves dipped in blood" are an intensification through condensation of natural forces that we can understand. But nothing I am familiar with here or elsewhere helps me with the next stanza, once past the first line:

> A heart like all others, divided in four.
> Under the left shoulder a stained
> forefinger points to a hidden room
> where the dead parent lies,
> with a warning ghost at his head.

Here Auden's questions become truly relevant: "What does he conceal from the reader? What does he conceal even from himself?" Joy Haines' literal renditions do not help at all. The poet does not follow the exegetical tradition of the emblem books. We are on our own as we make our way through this strange and painful poem. There is the real heart—the four-chambered muscle. There is the emblem-heart—each of its chambers a room with icons: the stained forefinger, a mask in a frame, a sunken door, a sun "continually rising, sleeping and smiling, / the light of childhood and easier days." Perhaps these are four stages of the poet's life, perhaps not. Explication seems like a false route to the heart of this poem. I am doing better when I sit back and listen to the pure cadences, carrying me from stanza to stanza through this phantasmagoria of emblems, allowing the poet the privacy of his vision. If I had to guess, I'd conjecture that the ruthlessly self-examining and self-excoriating poet conceals very little from himself but chooses not to expose himself to the reader.

The second section, "The Wreck," is more accessible. It is explicitly a dream-vision, a succession of images that suggest a cataclysm in which a "fatal roadway" with "pavement stones upended, / ladders and gaping pits" and open-heart surgery are objective correlatives for some unnamed (possibly unnameable) trauma. The language is stunning:

> but the strung ribs spanning
> deep shadow, the marrowlights
> gleaming:

The meaning is clear in stanzas like these:

> As a surgeon might look down
> into the open heart he works on:
> his gloved hand stopped in its skill
> upon the stretched, blood-lighted
>
> tissue, he sees as in a red mist
> how his own heart ages and changes,
> desire and clear spring
> seized to a fountain of rust.

The lyric voice is sure: moving from the expository pace of the opening lines, through the pile-up of stresses that arrest the movement ("gloved hand stopped"), that weight the surgeon's observation, to the swinging cadences of the vision in the last line. The dance of the phonemes throughout is profoundly engaging (*tissue* to *mist*, *mist* to *rust*; the hiss of "tissue, he sees as in a red mist"; the surge of "ages and changes"). Here in the choking image of the "fountain of rust" is the imaginative compression of his strongest work.

The four sections of the "Four-Chambered Heart" sequence are complementary in tone and mode. After the surreal phantasmagoria of "The Chart" comes the violence of "The Wreck." Then in Part Three, "The Flowering Plum," Haines returns to the narrative mode, with the story of a tree that the narrator planted and nurtured in an urban land. Against the voices that judge the tree fruitless and unprofitable and call for its destruction are the voices of the children who protect it for its joy, "a warmth in its autumn shade," and because "sometimes it sings." This episode recalls "I am a Tree, Very Quiet are My Leaves" in *At the End of This Summer*, which also sheds its leaves but feels in winter its "strong roots / Beneath the snow." The final section, "Dead Leaves," extends the image of the poet as tree, then as the fallen leaf. It is impossible to read this without Shelley's "Ode to the West Wind" blowing through the memory. Indeed, Haines seems to be responding to that poem, with his "cold smoke from sinking bonfires" in place of Shelley's "unextinguished hearth." Perhaps he is responding to his own irrational youthful optimism. In place of the ending of "I am a Tree"—"I shall never stop growing"—he provides these bleak last lines:

> All memory gone, fiber and root
> of my flowering plum stripped bare;
> each tree a skeleton standing alone.

As the sequence conveys the mental traveler through a series of emblematic landscapes, it suggests no specific time or space—no Provincetown beach or Alaskan forest or asteroid belt. We are now in a time and space virtually abstract. What time there is seems to be the time of one human life. What elegy there is seems to be for the lost innocence of childhood. No prophecy but a vision of age and disintegration.

The two poems that complete *A Guide to the Four-Chambered Heart* add several dimensions to this dark vision. In "Orpheus" the poet addresses Orpheus as though he were present:

> To carry the dead and the loved,
> the lost and bewildered,
> through life and death in life,
> was your assigned calamity.

To bear one's stricken self for sixty years
is harder still. . .

But this poem ends differently from "Dead Leaves." Returning to
the sensuous diction and the expansive temporal sense of earlier
work, Haines arrives at a powerful conclusion:

Now, in the absence of any singing god,
let that other voice begin:

be it bellow, scream, or roar;
the plain music of crystal breaking,
chirp of frogs, thrash of leaves
in the twilight, mutter of sea-waves . . .

The unrehearsed, deliberate artifice,
older, deeper, and more lasting.

The music of these lines is masterly. And in such poetry I recognize
and celebrate the open-endedness, the unsentimental integrity, the
intellectual energy, the strong emotion, and the freshness of imagi-
nation that are the measure of this man.

The final poem, "The Telling," takes its structure from the
images of a palm reading, telling "of an inexplicable journey." The
images are clear but, indeed, inexplicable. The prophecy arises not
so much from the palmist's cryptic icons, displaced as they are by
shadows, but from the poet's conclusion (echoing Wordsworth):

In that improbable, fantastic place
I shall be planted somewhere
with trees and natural stones,
turned slowly round
in the hollow of obedient earth.

Clear enough. But the following stanza (which is on the last page of the book) explodes the whole quiet scene with an image so fantastic, so visionary, so brilliantly energetic, so public in its performance and so private in its origin, that it appears to augur a whole new poetic realm:

> And you, awake in the world,
> without a shadow and less
> than human, your ghost children
> driven before you
> down the cobbled mazes—
> mouth open,
> cropped hair in a fiery light,
> and your finally stricken heart,
> wondering and amazed . . .

Thus the book ends with one of Haines' distinctive ellipses, for three decades the sign of the imagination pushing out beyond language, beyond the finite. At the end he throws open a door into the heart and leaves the reader gazing, "wondering and amazed." Is it indeed a whole new poetic realm, or is it, strangely, a return to the gothic mode of the very earliest published poems? Is the winged and shrouded figure of "Departure" actually the tutelary spirit of these late poems? Is Haines, ultimately, the "nature poet" of a human nature more wild and dangerous than any Alaskan wilderness?

DAVID MASON

The Tenacity of John Haines

Nothing stains like blood,
Nothing whitens like snow.
—"In the Forest without Leaves"

Literary criticism has not yet come to terms with the poetry of America's western coast, and the reasons for this are complex. To begin with, most poets born on the coast, from Robert Frost to Gjertrud Schnackenberg, have been more closely associated with the East and its centers of literary power, Boston and New York. The best-known modern West Coast poets who come to mind— Robinson Jeffers, Theodore Roethke, William Stafford, and John Haines—were all transplanted from other locales (though Haines spent some important childhood years in California). One can fairly say that these poets *chose* the relative remoteness of their landscapes for private reasons, and, especially in the cases of Jeffers and Haines, forged relatively independent lives out of that remoteness.

Other transplanted poets of note include Kenneth Rexroth, Yvor Winters, Janet Lewis, Thom Gunn, Edgar Bowers, David Wagoner, Suzanne J. Doyle, and Timothy Steele; to list those born on or near the coast I would add Richard Hugo, Gary Snyder, Carolyn Kizer, Dana Gioia, and Robert McDowell. No doubt these lists are woefully incomplete, but perhaps this is symptomatic of the lack of critical consensus about West Coast writers. I raise these issues in order to suggest one context in which the career of John Haines can be considered. The publication of his collected poems, *The Owl in the Mask of the Dreamer*, in 1993, and *Fables and Distances: New and Selected Essays* three years later, as well as *The Wilderness of Vision*, an earlier volume of essays about Haines, provides me with an occasion to outline that career, reflecting not only on its singularity but also its relation to a part of the world rarely mentioned in our criticism. Having said that, I should add that the burden of Haines' recent writing transcends the limits of regionalism, as all significant writing must. Haines began as a nature poet, but has developed into a poet of significant intellectual range, whose principal subject is the place of the human in nature—of spiritual relations embodied in experience.

Born in 1924, to a somewhat nomadic military family, Haines first went to Alaska after naval service in World War II. Unlike a few other poets of his generation, he has not written directly about the war, but such bitter experience surely underlies his basic mistrust of dominant cultural institutions. After establishing his homestead on 160 acres of land southeast of Fairbanks, he left to continue art studies in Washington, DC, and New York. When he returned to the homestead in 1954, he lived by hunting, trapping and foraging—a period he has beautifully described in his memoirs, *Living Off the Country* and *The Stars, The Snow, The Fire*. He has since traded that subsistence life for the equally precarious one of a freelance writer and itinerant teacher. Few modern poets have been so committed to a life outside the conventional economy—few have been willing to take such extraordinary risks. Nothing could be further from the smug centers of literary power, yet Haines has fashioned a body of work that readers and literary historians cannot entirely neglect. He has even achieved the kind of success signified by literary prizes. More important, he has given us a genuinely northwestern sensibility, a voice that, at his best, is mythopoeic while resisting the easy mythology of popular culture—no small achievement for a man who published his first collection at the age of forty-two.

Despite his late flowering, Haines seems from the start to have taken seriously—perhaps too seriously—the artist's vocation. One notices, for example, a paucity of humor in his work, a lack of ornament, almost a painful sobriety. In at least one of his essays he seems aware of his own formal limitations, writing, "The practice of free verse, as we mostly know it, leaves little choice as to a suitable form, and consequently our poems all tend to look alike and sound alike" (*Fables and Distances,* 72). If one comes to poetry seeking *memorable* speech, Haines' poems often do little to assist the memory. One doesn't find the luminous rightness of line and diction available in the best work of Richard Wilbur, for example, and some critics have found it easy to dismiss Haines, incorrectly, as an untutored artist. The pleasures of Haines' verse may not be immediately evident to all readers, but they do exist. As Dana Gioia wisely wrote in his preface to *New Poems: 1980–88,* "Haines' poetry speaks best to someone who appreciates the deep solitude out of which art arises. The attention they [*sic*] require is not so much intellectual as spiritual. To approach this kind of poetry one must trust it, a difficult gesture in an era like ours where so much art is characterized by pretense and vapidity" (*New Poems,* xx).

The poems of Haines' first book, *Winter News* (1966), remind me of the fluid simplicity of Robert Bly's early work. Here, for example, is "Poem of the Forgotten":

> I came to this place,
> a young man green and lonely.
>
> Well quit of the world,
> I framed a house of moss and timber,
> called it a home,
> and sat in the warm evenings
> singing to myself as a man sings
> when he knows there is no one to hear.
>
> I make my bed under the shadow
> of leaves, and awoke
> in the first snow of autumn,
> filled with silence.

One cannot imagine the average New Yorker (if there is such a creature) having such patience with that silence. Perhaps it is an experience available only to those who already know it, the immense silence of a world in which no machines grate and no human voice other than your own fills the void. Even my own use of the word *void* is insufficient, because one learns, eventually, how full of life that absence of humanity can be. (I should add, however, that certain New York periodicals like *The Hudson Review* have long supported Haines' work; perhaps his appeal has always been broader than I suggest.)

In the midst of such silence, Haines composed some charming and ambiguous poems. Here is "To Turn Back":

> The grass people bow
> their heads before the wind.
>
> How would it be
> to stand among them, bending
> our heads like that . . . ?
>
> Yes . . . and no . . . perhaps . . .
> lifting our dusty faces
> as if we were waiting for
> the rain . . . ?
>
> The grass people stand
> all year, patient and obedient—
>
> to be among them
> is to have only simple
> and friendly thoughts,
>
> and not be afraid.

The poem charms me with the unexpected satire of its metaphor; it has the sort of broad appeal I alluded to earlier.

If the poems in *Winter News* derive largely from his home-steading experience, from being in nature, Haines' second book, *The Stone Harp* (1971), reminds us as well of his art school years. His purpose here is not always clear. I do not know what to make, for example, of the final image in "Dürer's Vision":

> The country is not named,
> but it looks like home.
>
> A scarred pasture,
> thick columns of rain,
> or smoke . . .
>
> A dark, inverted mushroom
> growing from the sky
> into the earth.

Without recourse to a specific illustration, the poem seems only vaguely apocalyptic, one of Haines' weaker efforts. I get more from "The Hermitage" (which is not about an art museum), collected in *Twenty Poems*, also published in 1971:

> I own a crevice stuffed with moss
> and a couch of lemming fur;
> I sit and listen to the music
> of water dripping on a distant stone,
> or I sing to myself
> of stealth and loneliness.
>
> No one comes to see me,
> but I hear outside

the scratching of claws,
the warm, inquisitive breath . . .

And once in a strange silence
I felt quite close
the beating of a human heart.

Here the forest found earlier in *Winter News* has again taken on alle-
gorical meaning, as it does in Dante. The "scratching of claws" could
refer to a sound the homesteader heard in his silent cabin, but the
poem transcends autobiography. Its sense of isolation is more uni-
versal than that which most of the earlier poems achieve.

By 1971, when he published *The Stone Harp* and *Twenty Poems*,
Haines had established a distinctive free verse technique and a range
of subject matter that, for all their successes, still allowed some crit-
ics to marginalize or neglect him. Here it might be useful to quote
from a letter that William Carlos Williams wrote to Haines on April
21, 1953: "The thing that makes you stand out as a poet," the doc-
tor wrote, "is your unaffected sense of rhythm and your intelligent
sense of how to make it an organic part of your composition." In the
next paragraph Williams added, "Measure is the secret of that
advance how to measure your verse (without strain) so that you can
control it consciously and with ease. Instinct is not enough for the
master of his craft. Free verse is not enough." Reading Haines' poet-
ry, one rarely forgets that one is in the hands of a craftsman, a makar,
as the Scots call their poets. *Cicada* (1977) and his volume of new
and selected poems, *News from the Glacier* (1982), won him new read-
ers, but did little to alter his reputation as a regional writer whose
region was far removed from most people's lives. He was poetry's
token Alaskan.

With the publication of *New Poems: 1980–88* in 1990, Haines
revealed larger ambitions. Very little in the book directly reflects his
Alaskan experience; instead, he has fashioned longer sequences of

meditative lyrics (something he had begun to do in his previous collection). Having established a good but limited range, Haines now steps off into fascinating visionary territory; the silence of his early work becomes the silence in which all human endeavor occurs, as in the beginning of "Days of Edward Hopper":

> These are the houses that stand,
> broken and entered; these
> are the walls written by rain,
> the sparrow arches, the linear
> stain of all that will one day
> turn to smoke in the mind.

I read these newer sequences surprised by a cumulative power I do not fully understand. This meditativeness is not simple-minded, but rigorously earned. What appeared to be naïveté in some of Haines' early poems now becomes harrowing allegory, especially in his concluding sequence, "In the Forest without Leaves." Here Haines tackles nothing less than the modern ecology, the precarious place of the human in nature. As if to prove to his readers how difficult it has been to develop and sustain this vision, Haines now dates the composition of his poems, some of which have evolved over decades. I find the practice mildly irritating, as if the poet were overly concerned with posterity, but Haines may have felt the need to counteract erroneous perceptions that his writing was effortless.

Images from science, philosophy, and art dominate the recent work, yet one of my favorite sequences in *New Poems* is "Rain Country," which moves me with its memories of specific people— Campbell and Peg and Bitter Melvin—who rejected the culture of the Lower 48 and the kinds of political power that still outrage the poet. Yet these durable characters have also gone away or died:

I write this down
in the brown ink of leaves,
of the changed pastoral
deepening to mist on my page.

I see in the shadow-pool
beneath my hand a mile
and thirty years beyond
this rain-driven autumn.

All that we loved: a fire
long dampened, the quenched
whispering down of faded
straw and yellowing leaves.

The names, and the voices
within them, speak now
for the slow rust of things
that are muttered in sleep.

There is ice on the water
I look through, the steep
rain turning to snow.

I have no comfortable jargon to describe the success of this poem, and my quoting only this final section cannot possibly do justice to it. Haines is utterly in command of his technique here. The few unpatterned rhymes—*now* and *snow*, *sleep,* and *steep*—quietly suggest life's partly-revealed forms. In the final section of *The Owl in the Mask of the Dreamer*, Haines builds on the strengths of these sequences, which thoroughly overcome the limitations found in some of his individual lyrics.

The two poets mentioned most often in his essays are Robinson

Jeffers and Edwin Muir, both of whom were born in 1887. They would appear to have little else in common. Contrast Jeffers' prosperous Pittsburgh upbringing and top-drawer schooling to Muir's stark Orkney boyhood and poverty in Glasgow. Jeffers moved from the city to his stone tower at Carmel, Muir from islands to grinding slum, finally escaping through education, starting to write poems at thirty-five, translating Kafka with his wife, and capping his career with *The Estate of Poetry*, his wonderful lectures delivered at Harvard. Both poets, however, developed mythic imaginations, describing human experience in classical and biblical terms. Both wrote powerfully about nature. Both assumed an audience of intelligent people who were not necessarily professors; perhaps in consequence, both have been neglected since their deaths by the sort of university-based critic who prefers the unreadable. In terms of their individualism, even their fundamental dourness, one can readily see their influence upon Haines. Perhaps he never developed Muir's example of writing in rhyme and meter because he began to write in a time when free verse still seemed liberating, rather than another kind of rote performance. I don't know. With regard to form, Haines' ideas appear to be both severe and catholic. As he says in one of the essays, "Great poetry has been written in formal measures and strict forms, in 'free' verse, and sometimes as intensified prose. I see no reason why this should not continue to be the case, unless we are going to insist on one or more kinds of orthodoxy and turn the entire thing into a subdivision of politics" (*Fables and Distances,* 81).

If comparison to Muir points up one kind of shortcoming in Haines' writing, a wholesale neglect of the folk tradition so important to the best Scottish writing, comparison to Jeffers indicates another. Haines' essay on Jeffers is one of the best pieces collected in *Fables and Distances*, revealing that Haines was long aware of the older poet and even made a pilgrimage to Carmel, though he avoided meeting Jeffers out of respect for his privacy. Haines notes that the commercial development of Carmel (something he would later observe in Alaska) never appears in Jeffers' poetry; an artist is more, much more, than a recorder of his environment. An artist must have both strong vision and strong technique, and Haines notes a rare quality in Jeffers' voice:

> When we read a poem these days we take if for granted that the poet is speaking to himself, to another poet, or to an audience of poetry readers or teachers of poetry. I don't say this is necessarily wrong, but it does place very definite limitations on the poetry. We have, for one thing, forgotten how to write in any voice but our own. We miss, I think, the dramatic voice that can only be used in the presence of an audience, actual or imagined. It would be difficult to name any major poet in whom this dramatic voice was entirely absent. . . . For Jeffers this sense of the audience was not only instinctive, it was, I think, essential to his poetry. We can never forget while reading him that he is speaking to a certain largeness in us, as to a congregation; his voice, at once personal and public, has that authority. (*Fables and Distances*, 56–57)

Though Haines has conceived some poems in voices other than his own ("In the Sleep of Reason" is an example), he is not really a dramatic poet. His larger sequences are meditative; character and narrative play a rather small role in them.

To be fair, he seems alive to these limitations, and the essays impress me again and again with the uncanonical breadth of his affections as a reader. He can also be severe. I, for one, rejoice in his dismissal of John Ashbery's *Hotel Lautréamont*. Haines could have become a hermit and written ever more hermetic verses in the manner of "Dürer's Vision"; instead he has decided to engage the larger world of ideas and political issues, to write as if writing mattered. I sometimes sense a too easy romanticism in his politics, as if it were self-evident that poetry should be subversive. His praise of Carolyn

Forché is so vague that I am not sure exactly where he stands with regard to her deeper aesthetic values, especially the nagging sense that her politics are a kind of self-aggrandizement. And in his review of *Expansive Poetry*, a deeply flawed and premature attempt to define the New Formalism, Haines sometimes confuses concern for poetry's audience with careerism, grabbing some awfully high ground for himself:

> [P]oetry is not in any useful sense a profession, and it is certainly not a competition, no matter what the behavior of individual poets might at times seem to indicate. It is something else: a complication of reality, a questioning of values and appearances, subversive to the extent that it asks necessary questions; a surrender, a dedication, as well as being at certain times and in certain instances a sacrifice—in which situation all questions as to career and professionalism become irrelevant. (*Fables and Distances,* 65)

I have already indicated that I believe John Haines when he talks about sacrifice, but plenty of poets leading more conventional lives have also made sacrifices for their art. The kind of poetry Haines describes here, albeit broadly, may be a summit tossed by Sturm und Drang, but it hardly represents the range of what is possible or desirable in verse. Passages like this go a long way toward explaining the absence of humor in his collected poems.

The same severity of character limits his charm as a literary memoirist. When at the end of "Within the Words: An Apprenticeship," he reveals that he knew Weldon Kees, Franz Kline, Willem de Kooning, and other New York artists, he gives us no anecdotes, no impressions of their personalities, as if mere mention of their names were sufficient. I commend his avoidance of cheap gossip, but the best raconteurs are interested at least partly in characters other than themselves.

These objections aside, I find *Fables and Distances* a rewarding book. He begins his preface by saying, "I have never felt it necessary or appropriate that a poet be limited to writing about poetry" (*Fables and Distances,* xi). One senses throughout the book a mind weighing ideas against experience, like a skilled carpenter eyeing fresh lumber. He sees the limits of human life, human knowledge, placing what faith he has in nature. Perhaps he would agree with the Irish poet Derek Mahon, who has written,

> An ordinary common-or-garden brick wall, the kind
> For talking to or banging your head on,
> Resents your politics and bad draughtsmanship.
> God is alive and lives under a stone.
> Already in a lost hub-cap is conceived
> The ideal society which will replace our own.
> ("The Mute Phenomena")

Haines' aesthetics derive, as any truly valuable aesthetic must, from the meeting places of life and art. He suggests that ultimately the greatest artificer is the one we know least about:

> There is a form that exists, independent of our will and invention, and one need not believe in either God or Plato to acknowledge a truth in this claim. To the extent that a poem corresponds in some degree to this living, timeless, but never more than partly revealed form, the poem will justify itself and outlive its moment of conception. We will call it apt, or fitting, or beautiful, like a house to be lived in. (*Fables and Distances,* 83)

Haines also writes splendidly about nature and nature writers like John Muir, showing a passionate and justifiable sense of ecological responsibility. Those of us who have even briefly glimpsed real wilderness can't help despairing when we see it whittled—or bulldozed—away. The millions who love the Northwest's beauty have all but destroyed it. Alpine meadows I camped beside as a boy now have to be guarded against trampling crowds, their delicate plants treated almost like works of art behind bullet-proof glass. It is sad and necessary and necessarily sad. Haines' anger about the indiscriminate commercial development of Alaska gives way, or partly gives way, to his recognition of the essential reality of change. It seems fitting that *Fables and Distances* concludes with a bitter-sweet memoir about his lost childhood loves.

For readers who discover John Haines' work and want some guidance in reading him, *The Wilderness of Vision* (1996) is the best available book. It contains good essays by its editors, Kevin Bezner and Kevin Walzer, as well as appreciations by other poets: Wendell Berry, Don Bogen, Dennis Sampson, Sam Hamill, Dana Gioia, and Donald Hall. Don Bogen's essay on the later poems is an especially useful extension of the impression (which I share) of Haines' fundamental romanticism: "Haines' work since 1980 has been an attempt to reconcile his Wordsworthian vision with an increasingly pessimistic view of the world." In his lucid readings, Bogen describes Haines' "drive to find an authentic vision in the face of cosmic annihilation . . . " (*The Wilderness of Vision*, 59–60, 69). Among the reviews reprinted here, Robert Richman's is particularly eloquent and just. Anthony Hecht, in a *Hudson Review* chronicle, responsibly clarifies his own aesthetic grounds for finding defects in *Winter News*. A much more dismissive review is Peter Stitt's of *Cicada*—a review that mixes critical justice with comments I find shockingly inappropriate, like the following:

> This attitude of breathless reverence at times calls to mind the group with which Haines is most generally classed—the Northwest school. The Northwest poets love Indians even more than the rest of us do, of course, and write lots of poems about their mystique. (*The Wilderness of Vision*, 220)

Here Stitt is the worst sort of snob, revealing his ignorance by dismissing subjects he apparently knows nothing about; his attitude toward the region is a common one. "These people are too naïve," the eastern critic seems to say, "too much in love with their vast tracts of empty land in which nothing useful or beautiful has been said." While it is true that Haines can on occasion seem the vaguest sort of mystic or animist, the truth is that a kind of animism underlies much American culture, and for good reason. We are, after all, a country in which wilderness has until recently been a real presence in peoples' lives—a fact that those who have known only domesticated landscapes cannot understand unless they use their imaginations.

The Wilderness of Vision also contains a good interview in which Haines discusses his intuitive approach to composition, which began as an effort "to pare down my eloquence" (19). It would seem a strange example to set before younger poets, this mode of negation, so spare in its affirmations. Perhaps some poets serve less as models for others than as examples of singular achievement. Perhaps Haines is, in both his life and his work, inimitable. As he writes, "Poetry, the making of a poem, is an act whose significance we can only grasp through the force of a great example; without that we have no true measure" (*Fables and Distances*, 81). Haines has set his example before us. He has brought a few extraordinary landscapes into American literature, and, more important, he has given us the acute attention of a shaping mind.

OTHER WORKS CITED

Bezner, Kevin, and Kevin Walzer, editors. *The Wilderness of Vision: On the Poetry of John Haines*. Brownsville, OR: Story Line Press, 1996.

HENRY TAYLOR

A Form of Patience:
The Poems of John Haines

I

Though there is more than one strong theme in the poetry John
Haines has written in the past fifteen years or so, among the
strongest is a profoundly satisfying elegiac evocation of the time he
spent as a homesteader in Richardson, Alaska, "some seventy miles
from Fairbanks," according to the biographical note on the jacket of
his first book, which appeared more than thirty years ago. Seeing
that locative phrase, I think of the first time I had a letter from him;
it arrived sometime in 1966, bearing one of the most desolate return
addresses I had ever seen: Mile 68, Richardson Highway, Fairbanks,
Alaska. It was not hard to imagine a postman trudging those miles,
and handing Haines his mail over the top of a chest-high snowdrift.

I will return to the poems of that first book, which do not give
exactly the same impression of those years as do the more recent
poems recalling them. In 1993, Graywolf Press brought out Haines'
The Owl in the Mask of the Dreamer: Collected Poems, and in 1997,
Copper Canyon published *At the End of This Summer*, a collection of
poems it seems fair to call apprentice work. As such gatherings will,
these compress an evolution marked, as most are, by periods of
important discovery and periods spent on false scents. The speaker
has aged, of course, and let the early experiences come into the per-
spective of those that have followed it. But looking easily back and
forth between Haines' earlier and later work, one notices how often
the more recent poems mention other people who were there in that
landscape, and in some cases may still be. The human population of
the earlier poems, by contrast, is very sparse indeed.

"Tenderfoot," first collected in *New Poems: 1980–88* (1990),
takes its title from the name of a place near Richardson, and imag-

ines the quiet that has settled on the log house, the dusk coming down, and two people who may still be there:

> Jessie, the Indian girl, stands
> at the doorway in silence,
> her thin face turned to the earth.
>
> No more than an aching shadow,
> her father bends at the sawhorse,
> cutting the last dry pole.

After a couple of lines giving other small indications of deterioration, the poem ends:

> The black mouths of the rain barrels
> are telling of migrations,
> the whispering rush
> of a lonely people toward the past.

Despite the presence of Jessie and her father, this poem still conveys some of the mysterious vacancy of the earlier work—a sense not merely of the landscape's emptiness, but of its being full of something foreign to the speaker's experience, and hard to define.

"Rain Country," however, the longer poem that immediately follows "Tenderfoot," contains passages evocative of energetic community, such as this one from the first section:

> Thirty-one years ago
> this rainy autumn
> we walked home from the lake,
> Campbell and Peg and I, . . .
>
> Bone-chilled but with singing
> hearts we struck our fire

from the stripped bark
and dry, shaved aspen;
and while the stove-iron
murmured and cracked
and our wet wool steamed,
we crossed again
the fire-kill of timber
in the saddle of Deadwood—

down the windfall slope,
by alder thicket, and now
by voice alone, to drink
from the lake at evening.

The poem is in six sections, the first three mostly retrospective without comment, the last three more focused on the gap between past and present. The fourth looks again at the moment described above:

It was thirty-one years ago
this rainy autumn.

Of the fire we built to warm us,
and the singing heart
driven to darkness
on the time-bitten earth—

only a forest rumor
whispers through broken straw
and trodden leaves
how late in a far summer
three friends came home,
walking the soaked ground
of an ancient love.

The poem moves from mere recollection to recollection tinged with awareness that memory is what remains, and that tenuously; this stanza ends the fifth section:

> Remembering, fitting names
> to a rain-soaked map:
> Gold Run, Minton, Tenderfoot,
> McCoy. Here Melvin killed
> his grizzly, there Wilkins
> built his forge. All
> that we knew, and everything
> but for me forgotten.

This reference to Melvin is the second in the poem, and complicates the impression given in the first; the poem's third section very briefly evokes four people, each by a single act or statement in a context briefly established; again, the ending of the section:

> Bitter Melvin, who nailed
> his warning above the doorway:
>
> *Pleese dont shoot*
> *the beevers*
> *They are my friends.*

Haines' relatively recent poems about his time in Alaska sometimes portray a man going over a set of memories, trying to fill some of them out, trying to keep them from escaping, coming to some sense of what it means to have done something so absorbing, so unusual, and, yes, so courageous, and then to discover years later that even the memory of having done it might perish, but for the potential durability of a moving poem.

In a slightly earlier poem, first collected in *Cicada* (1977),

Haines describes the selective way in which memory focuses an experience; the poem is called "To My Father," and opens with two stanzas about starting a fly-cast on the Blackfoot River—probably the one in Montana, though the poem does not say—and seeing, shining on the water, the "deep stillness of boyhood":

> And I remembered, not the name
> of the river, nor the hill
> in Maryland looming beyond it,
> nor the sky, a late rose
> burning that eastern summer;
>
> but the long, rock pool that whispered
> before us, and your voice
> steady and calm beside me:
> "Try it here, one more time . . ."

Recollection of patient love is scarce in Haines' poetry, yet that very quality is what Haines has brought to bear on his own experiences.

The search for specific details that might fill out a sketchy recollection is the point of departure for a section in Haines' memoir, *The Stars, The Snow, The Fire: Twenty-five Years in the Northern Wilderness* (1989). Haines briefly mentions this book in the preface to his collected poems, asserting that "there are pages" in it that seem, "except for their sentence structure, to be poetry and of a continuity with my poems in verse." In Section III of a chapter called "With an Axe and an Auger," Haines recounts a visit to an old man, a former colleague of those days, now in retirement in a "rain-swept city on Puget Sound." He is seeking information—for prose, poetry, or its own sake:

> There are some things I have wanted to verify, and so I
> ask him, remembering that once long ago he or someone else
> had told me. Whose cabin was it that burned down near

Birch Lake one winter night over forty years ago? And who was it that had that long walk across the ice on frozen feet before he found shelter again?

"Oh, that was Jim Chisholm," he answers. "He was a big drinker!"

The story of Jim Chisholm's frozen-legged walk has occurred much earlier in the memoir, in a chapter called "Stories We Listened To." There, it is a detailed anecdote related by Allison, one of three men—another is Haines—sitting around a table in the kitchen of a roadhouse in Richardson. Whether or not the old man on Puget Sound is Allison, we are not told; but we are shown, in this delicate bit of self-reference, one of the innumerable processes by which experience may become literature.

In the account of the visit to the old man, Haines moves easily between prose narrative and the kind of "poetry" he describes in the preface to *The Owl in the Mask of the Dreamer*. The distinction is not always easy, for prose narrative has its capacity for memorable stylistic elevation; but in Haines' case, it is possible, sometimes, to see a sentence leaning toward the kinds of effects that occur more often in the poems.

Near the end of the visit, Haines has a brief vision of the old man's last days, presented in an elegant paragraph. Its elegance, however, does not nudge it from the realm of prose:

These will be the last, calm and empty years, with a watered garden, a trimmed lawn, a little money in the bank. It will be enough finally to sit in the house day and evening, while the last strength goes, looking into the distance from whatever window he finds himself beside.

That seems quite difficult to improve; furthermore, the paragraph sends out no signals that it would be better in lines. Two pages earlier, though, as the old man gradually overcomes the doubts raised by his fading memory and his uncertainty how to place his visitor, there is a paragraph with a somewhat different sound:

> He accepts me now. I am someone he used to know, though I see that he is still trying to fit my name and face to a map. The landscape is half-obscured by mist, but somewhere within it there is a road by a river, high bluffs, and a mailbox on a post.

The flow of images is rapid, and certain rhythmical units suggest apt line breaks. Perhaps the strongest surge in the direction of poetry is the last verb. That it is singular requires the sentence, strictly speaking, to mean that the road is by the river, by the bluffs, and by the mailbox. To make the verb plural has a punctilious sound in this context, yet the singular form lets the sentence have the images both ways, even though only one way is grammatical.

II

We have for several decades been aware of Haines as a poet of wilderness solitude; it takes a little effort, now, to recall how unusual his subject matter seemed when it began to appear in the 1960s. In his first book, *Winter News* (1966), he presented, among other things, a kind of short poem whose style appears simple and straightforward, but whose effect is to arouse a strong sense of mystery. Such a poem is "Denali Road":

> By the Denali Road, facing
> north, a battered chair
> in which nothing but the wind
> was sitting.
> And farther on
> toward evening, an old man
> with a vague smile,
> his rifle rusting in his arms.

Some of these early poems are explicit about the relationship between the human hunter and the hunted animal, but few of them are anything but casually conversational with place-names. The original situation, as Haines recounted it during a reading in Salt Lake City in 1970, was that he and a friend were out hunting, and part of the day walked the road that runs east-west between Richardson and Denali. They saw the chair that someone had discarded, and later encountered another hunter, the somewhat spooky old man. The poem presents literal fact, even in the last line, for metal that rusts does so constantly, however imperceptibly.

Yet because some context has been withheld, and because nothing is known of the observer beyond the observations, and because the poem contains no main verbs, the facts hang in an atmosphere slightly shocked by their presence; the word *rusting* even suggests, momentarily, the unlikely notion that the old man might not have moved for a decade or so. In the early 1970s, as a young teacher of poetry, I allowed myself to imagine that, during composition, the last line of the poem might once have read "his rifle resting in his arms," and that Haines might suddenly have seen what could be done by changing a single letter. Haines has since assured me that he wrote *rusting* the first time.

In order for a snap of the fingers to have the effect even of a very small explosion, the immediate surroundings must first be filled with quiet and an unspecific suspense. This is one of the basic principles of a kind of poetry that flourished in the late 1960s and early 1970s, in association with Robert Bly, among others. It has been called Subjectivist Poetry and Deep Image poetry; both terms seem problematic, to the point that some practitioners would prefer not to be included by them, just as today there are middle-aged writers of metrical verse who prefer not to be associated with New Formalists.

Haines entered the sphere of Robert Bly at least long enough to respond to one of the poems in Bly's first book, *Silence in the Snowy*

Fields. Bly's "Poem Against the British" describes what seems to be a spring or summer breeze, and ends,

> There are palaces, boats, silence among white buildings,
> Iced drinks on marble tops, among cool rooms;
> It is good also to be poor, and listen to the wind.

Haines's "On the Road" begins,

> It is not good to be poor.
> It is good to listen to the wind,
>
> but not when you stand
> alone on a road at night
> with all your winter parcels,
> like a mailbox waiting for
> a postman who will never arrive.

The speaker describes the "carloads" of wind, and thinks of his home, and his wife waiting for the slippers he has bought:

> There is a light through the trees—
> it is only a simple place,
> with two souls strung together
> by nerves and poverty.
>
> It is not good to be poor—
> and there are no coins in the wind.

Haines' poem can stand independently of Bly's, but for those who make the connection, it might have a harder edge of impatience with sentimental views of being out in nature.

As far as Deep Image poetry is concerned, the variety of its manifestations is so large that it is easy to imagine a relatively calm poet, like Haines, resisting association with some of the more flamboyant surrealism the term also claims to include. In any case, poets and critics accustomed to working on a larger scale, or in traditional forms, were sometimes mystified at the limitations these poets seemed consciously to have chosen, but every pole has two ends, as well as an infinite number of points along its length. An old and honorable attribute of poetry is that it can produce memorable effects in the space of, say, thirty-five words.

If the literal facts of the case are given a slightly more energetic push in the direction of fantasy, the effect can be more powerful. "Winter News" begins with a report:

> They say the wells
> are freezing
> at Northway where
> the cold begins.

Northway's name makes it sound quite logical that the cold would begin there. It turns out that the town is actually south of Fairbanks; it is the southernmost settlement within Alaska on the Alaska Highway. The next two stanzas are directly factual in their treatment of the ordinary details of life in such a climate:

> Oil tins bang
> as evening comes on,
> and clouds of
> steaming breath drift
> in the street.
>
> Men go out to feed
> the stiffening dogs, . . .

The "oil tins"—small tanks such as those that supply individual dwellings with kerosene—"bang" because at dusk the air inside them contracts so sharply that the steel sides of the tanks snap inward, like the freshness-test bulge on a jar lid. The dog-feeding stanza ends with a comma; after the white space, there is this haunting conclusion:

> the voice of the snowman
> calls the white-
> haired children home.

Though the children are bundled up against the cold, their hoods allow some stray wisps of hair to escape, and the children's breath condenses in it. So the only leap of imagination here is "the voice of the snowman," which simply cannot be explained at the same level of literal fact that carries the rest of the poem. We can come close: the children have imagined it, perhaps, or an invisible parental voice comes from beyond the snowman. A moment's further reflection leads to the suspicion that the snowman must have been built when the air was warm enough for the snow to pack. Such justifications, however, are cumbersome and unnecessary, because the poem rises out of the literal into the fantastic with complete effortlessness. It gains authority when the "snowman" is seen not as some version of Frosty, but as the Man of Snow, a Snow Being that makes things happen in that place. I shall return to Haines' use of this kind of personification.

The second stanza demonstrates one of the risks that this kind of free verse runs more or less constantly: the sentence itself is not obtrusively laden with prepositions, but arranging it in short lines poses a problem with their placement, so that a relatively ineffective line like "and clouds of" can seem momentarily adequate. I have been able to speak this poem aloud from memory for many years, but I cannot locate the ends of all the lines without looking at it.

One of the reasons is my tendency to notice the iambic pentameter in such clauses as "and clouds of steaming breath drift in the street" and "the snowman calls the white-haired children home."

Years after he had published these poems, Haines wrote of them in his preface to *The Owl in the Mask of the Dreamer* that they were

> born of the isolation in which I then lived—that remote, largely self-contained world of the forest, of snow and animal life, of hunting and gathering—and into which news of the outside world penetrated even so. What I wrote then emerged with difficulty from a kind of spell, one that I was reluctant to break, knowing that once I did, nothing would ever be quite the same.

It is in the nature of this spell that the speaker's isolation is exaggerated, if indeed the later recollections are more trustworthy on that point. *Winter News* contains only one or two proper nouns; "Deserted Cabin" refers to "Campbell's Hill," but there is nothing in this book to suggest, as Haines' later writings make clear, that Campbell was someone Haines knew, and even talked with somewhat regularly. Such human forms as appear in *Winter News* are generic and remote—Eskimos, "Red Men," "shaggy tribesmen," the glimpsed forms of hunters, the ghostly presences of Gold Rush prospectors. The beings portrayed with lifelike energy are animals, as in "Prayer to the Snowy Owl":

> Descend, silent spirit;
>
> you whose golden eyes
> pierce the gray
> shroud of the world—
>
> Marvelous ghost!

Drifter of the arctic night,
destroyer of those
who gnaw in the dark—

preserver of whiteness.

Reading Haines' autobiographical prose, which makes it clear that he was moved to go to Alaska by some strong preference for the discomforts of solitude over those of urban community, one sees a young man returning to his house after an evening of storytelling, feeding his sled dogs, bedding down alone, and finding himself beyond the reach of whatever voices he was just listening to.

III

A second theme in Haines' recent poems, and one that has been less steadily treated over the years, arises from his having studied painting and sculpture before he began to write. In an essay called "Within the Words: An Apprenticeship," now collected in *Fables and Distances: New and Selected Essays* (1996), he writes of his struggles with the art supplies he took to Richardson in 1947:

It seems to me now that I tried a few sketches, perhaps a watercolor or two. But with the advent of early winter the sunlight departed and the nights grew longer. Moreover, the outdoor scene with its snowmass and its slanting and fugitive winter light, its mountains and its icebound river, struck me as so overwhelming and dominant in itself that my halting efforts to reproduce some of it on paper or canvas seemed to me more and more futile. After a few weeks I grew despondent and cast about for something else to do. . . .

I was attempting to set down, in what seemed to me the only appropriate form, something of what I was seeing and coming to know, far off there and alone in a strange country. I was at the same time attempting to clarify, for myself and for some future reader, something of that loneliness and its effect on me, a thing at once painful and strengthening.

A somewhat minimalist approach seems an appropriate response to a landscape that itself seems minimal. In *The Stone Harp* (1971), however, Haines found himself often in the "lower forty-eight," amidst the unrest of the late 1960s, occasionally hard-pressed to adapt his familiar methods to the matters at hand.

When the facts of an instance are cut down drastically enough, the poem may be more baffling than mysterious, merely puzzling rather than resonant. A poem that noticeably runs this risk is "Dürer's Vision," from *The Stone Harp*. It is brief enough to quote in its entirety:

> The country is not named,
> but it looks like home.
>
> A scarred pasture,
> thick columns of rain,
> or smoke . . .
>
> A dark, inverted mushroom
> growing from the sky
> into the earth.

David Mason, reviewing *The Owl in the Mask of the Dreamer* for *The Sewanee Review*, recently said, "Without recourse to a specific illustration, the poem seems only vaguely apocalyptic, one of Haines' weaker efforts" ([Winter 1998]: 106). Oddly enough, it is quite easy to locate the picture Haines refers to; doing so, however, raises almost as many questions as it answers. As reproduced in

Christopher White's *Dürer: The Artist and His Drawings* (New York, 1971), the drawing is titled "Vision in a Dream"; it is a pen and watercolor dated 1525, and Haines' description of it, especially in the second and third stanzas, is as accurate as one could reasonably ask. So it might be fair to say also of Dürer that his drawing is "vaguely apocalyptic."

What Haines has ignored, or perhaps not seen translated, is an inscription that Dürer wrote under the drawing, in which he explains exactly what he dreamed, and what he is trying to represent. The "thick columns" are not rain, but water unmixed with air, plunging earthward as if from gigantic faucets; one, the "inverted mushroom," has hit: "The first struck the earth about 4 miles away from me with terrific force and tremendous noise, and it broke up and drowned the whole land. I was so sore afraid that I awoke from it. . . . So when I arose in the morning I painted it above here as I saw it. God turn all things to the best."

It is impossible to tell from the poem, or from the poem together with the picture, how much of Dürer's "Vision" Haines understood when he wrote the poem, which nevertheless turns out to be more of a notation than a prophecy. Mason cogently calls it "one of Haines' weaker efforts," but it exemplifies the steadfastness with which Haines has been drawn to set down his encounters with the unknowable, even when the method at hand seems ill-suited to the task.

A gradual shift in Haines' way of working is partly indicated, as I have said, by the slow increase in his attention to other human inhabitants of his world. There is an almost exactly corresponding decrease in his dependence on a figure of speech that turns up somewhat more often than it is successful; this is a form of personification that is sometimes less developed than asserted. Plant life, especially, inspires this trope. Haines experimented with it before 1950; in "I am a Tree, Very Quiet are My Leaves," now available in *At the End of This Summer*, the effect is very much that of a self-conscious exercise:

I have grown old standing here—
I who have watched my withered leaves
Gathering at my feet
And the gloomy masses piling overhead; . . .

Six or eight years later, in *Winter News*, spring is hailed as the time "when the green man comes":

The man is clothed
in birchbark,
small birds cling to his limbs
and one builds
a nest in his ear.
("And When the Green Man Comes")

In "To Turn Back," which apparently means to revert to an earlier form of existence, Haines wonders how it is to be grass, and then invents a conclusion:

The grass people stand
all year, patient and obedient—

to be among them
is to have only simple
and friendly thoughts,

and not be afraid.

It is possible to read this as a gentle parody of Bly's early work, but Haines' work contains so many examples of personification by fiat that this one, too, has finally to be taken at face value. There are forms of writing—editorial, polemic—in which the invitation to disagree is strongly implicit, and sometimes even explicit. But the suspension of disbelief is not always willing when such an invitation occurs in a poem. There are some striking personifications in Haines' work, even a few that seem to work in spite of themselves. "To a Man Going Blind," for example, contains a surprising figure, almost a cartoon, and yet it is starkly memorable:

> Summer was more like a curse
> or a scar, the accidental blow
> from a man of fire
> who carelessly turned toward you
> and left his handprint glowing
> whitely on your forehead.

By contrast, "The Legend of Paper Plates" is strained and overinsistent on the "manhood and womanhood" of the trees that were the plates' ancestors:

> The land was taken for taxes,
> the young people cut down
> and sold to the mills.

There is a weird appropriateness to the way the use of this figure diminishes as more humans are portrayed, but some of its occurrences endure, as reminders of the artist's urge to enter as deeply as possible into the essence of the object of contemplation. In the latest poems in *The Owl in the Mask of the Dreamer*, there are references to painting or sculpture by Goya, Bosch, Rodin, Michelangelo, Hopper, Giacometti, and other artists, as well as poems spoken by fictional characters, such as an eighteenth-century scholar and a Roman governor. A couple of them present a view of art history; Haines says, in his note on the collection's title poem, "This poem is a concentrated history of the art of sculpture, from early times to the present. The last three stanzas refer to a famous metal sculpture by Alberto Giacometti." The poem relates the evolution of sculpture's relationship to the earth's materials:

The craft of an old affection
that called by name the lion shape
of night, gave rain its body

and the wind its mouth—the owl
in the mask of the dreamer,
one of the animal stones asleep . . .

By tinker and by cutting torch
reduced to a fist of slag,
to a knot of rust on a face of chrome.

As the poem moves to its conclusion, the evocation of the
Giacometti sculpture leads to a phrasing that recalls the earlier per-
sonifications, though here it is first of all a way of describing the art.
The poem's last two lines have about them a sense of contemporary
alienation, perhaps, but they also recall the lovers on Keats' urn:

So, black dust of the grinding wheels,
bright and sinewy curl of metal
fallen beneath the lathe:

Speak for these people of drawn wire
striding toward each other
over a swept square of bronze.

For them the silence is loud
and the sunlight is strong.

No matter how far they walk
they will never be closer.

Like most poets who have had the strength to stay with whatev-
er the urges are that drive them into writing poems, and into risky

ways of life, Haines has responded many times to mysterious promptings, to inspirations, that he has not come to clarify. But when the poems are clear, and not pushed too hard into being, they speak, with stark economy and memorable force, of how a hard life can be worthwhile. The irascible poems of the middle years give way to the more recent elegiac strain in a way that brings to mind Frost's remark, in his introduction to E. A. Robinson's *King Jasper:* that "Grievances are a form of impatience; griefs are a form of patience."

The Hermit-Seer

John Haines is one of the greatest living American poets, yet he has never quite achieved the fame he deserves. He isn't neglected, exactly: his poems and essays appear in excellent journals, his books from distinguished publishers; he has won major grants and awards, most recently from the American Academy of Arts and Letters and the Academy of American Poets; *The Wilderness of Vision*, a volume devoted solely to critical essays on Haines' poetry, is available from Story Line Press. But Haines' name does not resonate as strongly in creative writing schools as those of poets demonstrably less worthy than he.

In *Fables and Distances*, Haines' latest book of essays, he writes of one of his heroes, the Scottish poet and critic Edwin Muir: "He was a quiet man, not given to assertion, and this fundamental modesty in an age of town criers can be seen as a disadvantage." As with Edwin Muir, so with John Haines. Haines' quietness is not just of personality, but of principle. He has spent most of the last four decades in the Alaskan wilderness, shunning both the limelight and the tenure track; but even if he had stayed in the Lower Forty-Eight and become a full professor, it is hard to imagine that his work would have been much different from what it is. Haines—with Thoreau, Dickinson, and Jeffers—is one of the great solitaries of American literature. He shares significant qualities with all three— Jeffers' melancholy, Dickinson's power of observation, Thoreau's belief in self-reliance.

In 1996, Graywolf Press issued both *Fables and Distances* and an expanded version of Haines' collected poems, *The Owl in the Mask of the Dreamer*. These books are obvious springboards for a reconsideration of Haines' life work, and also help explain why Haines' popularity has lagged behind his achievement. Whether hunting for moose near his Alaskan homestead or considering the paintings of Hieronymus Bosch, Haines remains true to his basic theme: that each of us is alone in the world, with only the examples presented by nature and art to guide us. If we are to survive, we must constantly use our minds and hearts to draw whatever wisdom we can from our experience, and make whatever connections we can to people and places beyond the narrow confines of our lives.

This pattern of "Relentless Self-Scrutiny" (the title of James R. Wilson's essay on Haines) has been consistent throughout Haines' career. He is independent, courageous, and occasionally cranky, as mavericks tend to be. Consequently, Haines has very little to offer to those who turn to a comforting, all-embracing theory to explain life and art. Unfortunately for Haines, such people are legion in today's poetry world. Meter and rhyme are either the salvation or the annihilation of poetry; slammers and Nuyorican poets have either brought poetry to the people or dragged it into the gutter. Haines does not subscribe to any of these orthodoxies; to him, there are very specific things that make true poetry, and theories of stylistic purity are by far the least of them.

Haines explains his position in a letter originally published in *The Hudson Review* and reprinted in *Fables and Distances*:

> What does dismay me is a mentality, all too prevalent now, that insists on choosing of sides. According to this, if I respect Eliot, I am somehow disqualified from also respecting Williams. Or if I cherish the poems of Wallace Stevens, I must consign Robinson Jeffers to the dustbin. And so forth. But why must I choose among the poets whose work I love? Why can't I have them all, each for the sake of his or her own excellence? In fact I do have them all, and so does any reader who cares about the art and not some petty jurisdiction adjacent to it.

Haines' comments are plain common sense, and it is an indict-
ment of today's highly stratified poetry community that such
remarks may serve to marginalize him. Haines simply praises what
he finds genuine and refuses to praise what he finds precious, slop-
py, or false. In *Fables and Distances*, he defends Dana Gioia against
Greg Kuzma, and William Carlos Williams against Bruce Bawer; he
perceives Kuzma and Bawer's attacks as largely partisan, whereas in
the work of both Gioia and Williams he finds enduring qualities any
reader would be foolish to dismiss.

Haines can also be ruthless in his criticism, as in his assessment
of John Ashbery's *Hotel Lautréamont*:

> If you can believe that the late and increasingly realized pur-
> pose of this society is to popularize and trivialize the better
> part of the artistic and intellectual inheritance of Western
> civilization, then by an inverted logic an overpaid sports hero
> becomes a genius, and Andy Warhol becomes a great artist,
> and John Ashbery becomes the foremost poet of the day.

To read Haines' essays on poetry (comprising more than half of
Fables and Distances) is to be left in no doubt as to what attributes he
considers important to a poet: a wide-ranging imagination; an ear
for language; a painstaking devotion to craft, regardless of style or
school; a knowledge of, and interest in, the world beyond one's own
daily rounds; and a passion for justice, both social and political. This
last is crucial to Haines. More than once he quotes the novelist
Hermann Broch: "Political indifference is ethical indifference." At
one point, he makes his own addendum: "It might also be said that
in the end ethical indifference becomes esthetic indifference."
Virtually every great poet, he reminds us, has written social com-
mentary in one form or another. It is on this basis that he defends
the work of Carolyn Forché, a poet he might not otherwise be
expected to endorse: "Whatever might be its flaws as poetry, *The*

Country Between Us points in one direction for poetry; beyond craft, beyond provincialism, beyond self-absorption, into that universal human territory we all must enter."

Because he cares so much about the content of poetry, Haines tires quickly of those poets who, with their "rancor and peevishness," argue endlessly about its proper form. He is blunt about the New Formalism: "I doubt that the rescue of poetry from the prosaic mediocrity that afflicts it lies much in that direction. The typical poem today will be just as lacking in substance whether written in free verse, plain prose, or formal measures." Yet he deplores those who insist traditional verse is despicable: "I love the poems of Wordsworth, of de la Mare, and Yeats, and I would not like to think that this music has gone for good; for then poetry in English will be dead, no matter what improvisations might seem to resurrect it for a moment's excitement and distraction."

Haines himself writes exclusively free verse, although his style—short-lined, laconic, plain yet never easy—is so superbly honed and controlled that it can only be called "free" in the most technical sense. Critics such as Anthony Hecht and Richard Tillinghast take Haines to task for occasionally being *too* plain. "Sometimes a poem of his will sound, with lack of grace in its language, like an uninspired translation from a foreign language," Tillinghast wrote of Haines' first book, *Winter News*. But the plainness of Haines' language fits the plainness of the man—his need for the honest and unadorned. And, at his usual best, Haines achieves a graceful economy of language for which no one need make apologies. There are few contemporary poems, for example, as haunting as Haines' "Rain County":

> All that we loved: a fire
> long dampened, the quenched
> whispering down of faded
> straw and yellowing leaves.

The names, and the voices
within them, speak now
for the slow rust of things
that are muttered in sleep.

Even Tillinghast admits Haines has "a real tone of voice . . . and a presence that gains in force the more one reads him." Robert Richman goes further: "Among poets of his generation, Haines has an ear second only to Louis Simpson's." While arguments can be made for the excellent ears of other contemporary poets, Haines indeed is one of the great living masters in this regard.

The revised paperback version of *The Owl in the Mask of the Dreamer* contains more than twenty poems not in the original hardcover edition—mostly uncollected poems from the 1960s. These newly included poems represent something of a transition for Haines, away from the Alaskan-themed poems of *Winter News* toward the broader focus of his later work. Whatever the topic of Haines' poetry, however, the thrust of his work remains the same—the solitary seer, searching for comfort and wisdom in a world which offers those things, if at all, in a veiled, almost coded way. God, in Haines' world, is

distant and half-forgetful,
who goes on reading
from a book
that has turned to stone.
("St. Luke")

Images of shadow, cold, darkness haunt the newly collected poems only slightly more intensely than in his other poems. To these things, Haines is drawn as a moth to flame:

It is time, the great hunger
has fed itself, the heart filled

as it can never be,
hunting the air of summer.

            ("Autumn")

His intense, almost Proustian qualities of memory permeate many of these poems, adding to their poignancy and almost unbearable sense of lost time. The short poem "The Book," in its entirety, exemplifies this:

> A shadow grew up around me,
> and a quiet voice spoke from it,
> full of the wonder
> of a dark and faraway place.
>
> And it was my father,
> bending over me out of the shadow
> of years, reading to me
> as he used to
> from a book that I loved.

Dana Gioia has written of the significance of the North in Haines' poetry: "(I)t is not only a specific geographical area, but also the spiritual wilderness where the solitary imagination must confront existence without the comforting illusions of society. His North is a prophetic mountaintop from which the poet looks down on the corruption of the city. In this sense Haines is fundamentally a moral and political poet." *The Stars, The Snow, The Fire* is the title of one of Haines' essay collections, and that title could stand as the epigraph for his entire body of work. He is the lone figure in a wintry landscape, searching for the stars for direction, building his own fire to ensure his survival for one more night. He does not ask us to share his solitude so much as he tries to make us realize our own, and to help us find sustenance based on that knowledge. We are mortal, but the earth endures, and the earth is what we share. Its laws are immutable, and we disobey them at our peril.

As a critic of poetry, Haines attempts something similar: to make us see that poetry is a continuum, not a series of revolutions in which the True Form of Poetry is carved in stone for the multitude until the next revolution comes along. What is true in Wallace Stevens is what is true in Keats, despite their wildly different methods of prosody. To discard old forms out of hand is foolish; to reject new ones without thought is stuffy. What poets share is vastly more important than how they differ, and to lose sight of this is to lead poetry to the guillotine.

Hermit-seers are never popular. Tiresias was blinded, John the Baptist decapitated; Thoreau spent a night in jail, and might have spent longer had Emerson not come to bail him out. Nevertheless, their names endure. John Haines has forgone the sort of lionization John Ashbery could not live without. But he is known and cherished by those readers who still believe that poetry can mean something, and that poets can exhibit something akin to moral and intellectual force. It is, at the very least, an even trade.

ROBERT DeMOTT

"Close to Religious Aspirations": Notes on John Haines' Poetry

It is in the nature of every poetical work that stands midway between two cultural epochs that it is bound to be concerned with the search for a new faith. . . . Whenever poetry draws close to religious aspirations, it seizes on mythological concepts, and it does so not by intention but because this is in the nature of things.

—marked by John Haines in his copy of Hermann Broch, *The Spell* (1940)

Strict adherents of the poststructuralist persuasion in contemporary American literature, who revel in decenteredness, erasure, infinite verbal play, formal pyrotechnics, hybrid genres, thematic emphasis on race, class, or gender, and/or texts devoid of realistic signifiers (in which Nature, for example, is seen as merely another ideological construction), might not find much beyond its stark, unsentimental tone and escape from the bourgeois self to interest them in the poetry of John Haines. If volume eight of the new *Cambridge History of American Literature, Poetry and Criticism, 1940–1995* can be considered an accurate sign of the state of current academic discourse, then the diminished status of all kinds of poetry, especially nature poetry, in these hybrid times is already an established fact (Robert von Hallberg's survey of poetry is 248 pages, only forty pages longer than the survey of literary criticism and theory by Evan Carton and Gerald Graff). Perhaps more to the point, in the 894-page *Columbia History of American Poetry*, John Elder's chapter, "Nature's Refrain in American Poetry," covers twenty pages (with no mention of Haines). In the current lexicon of post–World War

II writing, John Haines seems to have been erased by the new millennialists.

In this move Haines has not entirely been an innocent or unwitting victim. Indeed, in his caustic review of Paul Hoover's Norton anthology, *Postmodern American Poetry*, he has shown the degree to which he strenuously opposes consideration of the poem as a language "object" and is suspicious of the "gibberish" of a "poetry cut off from normal discourse and apparently content to speak to itself alone" ("Turning Inward," 69). Haines' distaste for what he has called repeatedly the "narrow" postmodern stance in poetry is a sign, at one level, of his conservative temperament and opens him to charges of antediluvianism and reactionary nostalgia from the critical left. A writer highly suspicious of intellectual specialization, especially what he called in a conversation with Arthur Coffin the "professionalization of Letters" ("Interview with John Haines," 49), Haines has continued to act in the untrendiest of ways by cultivating in his early, formative life, for example, isolation over community, self-sufficiency over networking, nature over society, calling over careerism, propensity for belief over nihilism, intellectual amplitude over narrowness, character over personality, poetry over fiction or drama. If these are the moves of an unreconstituted individualist, they are also moves which have been forged from a deep set of personal convictions, a poetics of independence:

> But poetry is not in any useful sense a profession, and it is certainly not a competition, no matter what the behavior of individual poets might at times seem to indicate. It is something else: a complication of reality, a questioning of values and appearances, subversive to the extent that it asks necessary questions; a surrender, a dedication, as well as being at certain times and in certain instances a sacrifice—in which situation all questions as to career and professionalism become irrelevant. ("Formal Objections," 65)

On one level, on a more somber occasion, perhaps, John Haines' objections to many current poetry projects (and the paradoxes invoked by his assessments) could become fuel for a rigorous critique of his own stance as a poet, charges of failure of critical judgment indicating something weirdly amiss turned against him. But as George Steiner reminds us emphatically in *Real Presences*, "anything can be said about anything," and such debated and debatable cultural issues boil down finally to "a politics of taste" (7)—Haines' and everyone else's included. But happily, there is a more honorable and productive route to follow. So on a second level—the one that concerns me in this short essay—it is precisely Haines' traditional sensibility that engages my attention. His spiritual predilections, including his environmental consciousness, which is borne out of his resolute belief that "there is no life apart from Nature," provide a pathway to considerations of his own art, and provide a kind of matrix for understanding his often sacral view of poetry. Haines' poems can be said to issue from that linked, related experience of his total ecological/aesthetic/spiritual life, what he has called an integrated "place of conviction" (*Living Off the Country*, 85), an arena of relatedness, rather than the other way around. "If you believe that there is no spiritual value in the world," he told Matthew Cooperman in 1996, "that things are mere objects, and there can be no barrier to the penetration of the 'secrets' of nature, and to the exploitation of so-called 'resources,' then, in a real sense, the world is reduced to prose, and poetry becomes impossible. I think we must keep alive that sense of the ultimate mystery, or what can only be called sacred—sacred because it is finally beyond explication and beyond possession" ("Wilderness and Witness," 117).

If John Haines has never become part of America's "canonical master narrative," as Alan Golding names it in *From Outlaw to Classic* (xiv), not to read Haines would be the new apologists' loss, for his life's work in poetry is a sustained effort at entering, however briefly and lyrically, and against huge odds, a condition of "belief" concerning the world outside the ego. Beginning with his first book, born of his formative Alaskan homesteading experience, *Winter News* (1966), with its dreamlike opening invocation to his muse, the night-hunting Great Horned Owl, and extending all the way through "Night," the concluding poem in his recent collected volume, *The Owl in the Mask of the Dreamer* (1993), his body of work, his total imaginative tapestry, is consistently enlivened by his own individual version of "theory," his own informing agenda, so to speak, specifically several intricately conducted figures that create a certain coherent, cumulative force in his work. These include but are not limited to the divided self, the myth journey, the role of wilderness, the intersection of nature and culture, the political consciousness, and the deep prominence of the iconic image. There is also the musical repetition—the orchestration—of defining diction which takes to itself the properties of ideas (Haines has more than once bemoaned contemporary poetry's "lack of ideas")—such words as *wind, snow, silence, shadow, stars, darkness, dusk,* and *empty,* just to name a few operative and laden ones—are all woven tightly in the painterly, spatial fabric of his poems ("Discussion of 'At White River,'" 123). In this rare (for Haines, that is) domestic, but nonetheless symbolic, action presented in "The Weaver," the central image of the artist figure creates a resonant new order out of quotidian chaos:

> And her batten comes down,
> softly beating the threads,
> a sound that goes and comes again,
> weaving this house and the dusk
> into one seamless, deepening cloth.

The poem captures "one of those moments," Haines says, "in which it is possible to feel that something deep and essential in existence, eternal and unchanging, is somehow contained, illuminated, held briefly; an insight not to be explained or deciphered, a moment of pure being" (*Living Off the Country*, 134). To speak of Haines' religiousness, then, is not to speak of an exact creed, a specific orthodoxy, or the importation of an institutional set of values. Of these he has generally been skeptical, as in this early poem, "At the End of This Summer," where he writes:

> Let the inhuman, drab machines
> patrol the road that leads nowhere,
> and the men with Bibles
> and speeches come to the door,
> asking directions—
> we will turn them all away
> and be alone.

To speak of his religiousness is, rather, to speak of something far more lenient in its implication (even when the reference is overtly religious, as in "Christmas, 1962," in which Christ figures only as an "astonished refugee" giving "the strange, unshackled / gift of himself." More likely, to begin to understand the religious spirit in Haines' work is to see moments of illumination or insight arising from, or enacting a communion with, a "spirit of place, a presence asking to be expressed." It is the kind of situation evoked in "The Sound of Animals in the Night," where he writes,

> we come and go by the flare
> of campfires, full of ghosts
> with huge, wounded hearts,

or "Listening in October," where outside the house,

> . . . into the towering
> darkness . . .

> There are silences so deep
> you can hear
> the journeys of the soul,
> enormous footsteps
> downward in a freezing earth.

The poem creates a sense of both awe and awesomeness, a proper intuitional response to the moment, given its time and place.

In such poems as these, Haines wishes to reach a level of "authentic" communication, which uncovers "the significant shapes that lie behind appearances"; indeed, he sees the writer's function as one of initiating his audience to a world "beyond the private self" (*Living Off the Country,* 19–20). Thus, Haines' sense of morality is not so much the value-laden and normatively disputable properties of good and bad, associated with the human social community, but the implicit and necessary rightness of the artistic quest, the unstinting "commitment" to the ethical writerly life, by which, quoting from Wordsworth, he claims, "we see into the life of things" (*The Owl in the Mask of the Dreamer,* 4). In "Rain Country," one of his recent longish meditative poems, Haines writes of this private morality, this inflected sense of witnessing:

> Shadows blur in the rain,
> they are whispering straw
> and talking leaves.
>
> I see what does not exist,
> hear voices that cannot speak
> through the packed
> earth that fills them.

The passion of Haines' quest, then, the intricately traced figure in his poetic canon, is animated and quickened—if not directly informed—by a persistent apprehension (but not, I think, glamor-ization or trivialization) of dark sources, mythic gestures, natural mysteries, shadowy presences, and, in short, intimations of other-nesses in their myriad guises and forms. "You are here," he writes in a 1976 poem, "Alive in the World,"

> alive in this place,
> touching with sight
> things that are smoke tomorrow.

"It's important to keep in mind," he claimed to Robert Hedin in a 1989 *Northwest Review* interview, that

> Life itself casts a shadow, literally and symbolically. . . . very old human adventures—presentiments, imaginings, spiritu-al journeys—are in one way or another continually being re-enacted, even when, as is the case most of the time, appearances are deceiving and the meaning is kept from us. Only perhaps when the immediate and the temporal disap-pears, is put aside for a moment, do those other shapes become visible, and the true significance . . . is revealed to us. (*Fables and Distances,* 228)

Haines' participation in and enactment of the "myth-journey of humankind" (*Living Off the Country,* 70), in which he metaphorical-ly embodies the quester's role and sees beyond the temporal frame-work to the larger issue or form, are deeply personal, deeply felt, but not necessarily autobiographical in a narrowly confessional way. Efforts to make Haines into a contemporary shaman—all magical purpose and mystical effects—seem to me somewhat misguided because they undercut first of all the profoundly skeptical tone of much of his writing, and secondly the aesthetic dimension of his speakerly role and voice. In his 1975 essay "The Hole in the

Bucket," Haines has issued this qualification regarding the poet's "task": "to invest the 'I' of the poem with significance beyond the ordinary, to make of one's own predicament a universal case. Or to say it another way, it is to allow something besides the self to occupy the poem, to matter as much as the self" (*Living Off the Country*, 67).

To push beyond the "inadequate art" of a personality-driven poetry is to see something larger than the self in the view normally at hand, to push toward the center of the *"time-ghost* in things," the universal experience (whether psychological, political, or ecological), with its aura of tantalization. Haines accomplishes this in "Into the Glacier," where the speaker moves

> Deeper and deeper,
> a luminous blackness opening
> like the wings of a raven—
>
> as though a heavy wind
> were rising through all the houses
> we ever lived in—

or where the speaker moves toward a residue of mystery, as, for instance, in "The Fossil," in which he says:

> Sometimes in our sleep
> this gray, carnivorous shadow
> comes drifting and feeding,
> like the toothed smile
> at the lips of living men.
>
> A lighted spine lashing
> uphill in the evening traffic,
> home to the clay beds
> where night after night
> the heart's wide nets are cast.

CONTRIBUTIONS TO THE LITERARY LANDSCAPE

Perhaps even more to the point, Haines' speaker is willing to brave the center's infinite questions, which is for him the way to enter imaginatively the original condition of things, as in this lovely poem, "To Live among Children":

> To live among children,
> to listen, an ear to their trouble;
> the voices, demanding or gentle,
> small hands plucking
> the threads of a sleeve:
>
> ask to be told once more
> a story repeated by the shadows
> looming at cribside.
>
> And what had those shadows to say—
> vague and nodding,
> dense with the mystery always
> towering in the distance?
>
> That little has changed
> since that hour we too listened
> to a voice speaking in the oak leaves.
>
> And think of the answers we give:
>
> Why the continents drift,
> what wind carves the rock
> into cities, or blows the people
> on their polar journeys;
>
> what legendary shoulder continues
> to hold up the sky,

or why the mountain train
never seems to end.

All of our history come to that moment
when we look
at a shadow flying past:

What bird, what beast was that?

The fleeting moment, the shadowy distance, the winged image, the "mysterious prompting" as Henry Taylor calls its many manifestations (16)—these constitute some of the loci of Haines' spiritual attention, his visionary orientation. To live among those questions generated by such experiences is itself a way of being, and a kind of understanding that our life on earth must accommodate "an intuition of some greater, larger design in existence" (Honors Class Lecture). The traces of a prior life within and without draws Haines' eye time and time again, not toward nihilistic erasure alone, but toward a kind of humble, earned wisdom, such as is contained in the lesson of the Cumean Sibyl, who, Haines writes, "in responding to questions, wrote her answers upon leaves that quickly blew away and were lost." This "great symbolic" story, he adds, never ages: "The artist, the poet, the thinker, and indeed all of us in one way or another, are, it seems to me, in eternal search of those lost leaves and the answers written upon them. The study of nature is a part of that search, as is the study of art, or literature and language; a pursuit of the truth as we have known it in the past and are compelled to recover" ("The Nature of Art," 14). This tension between compulsion and humility can be seen in "Yeti," where Haines writes:

In this world we think we know,
something will always
be hidden, whether a fern-rib
traced in the oldest rock,

or a force behind our face,
like the pulse of a reptile,
dim and electric.

Or again in "The Eye in the Rock," one of Haines' signature Montana
landscape poems, where on "A high rock face above Flathead Lake,"
the speaker discovers a painted aboriginal eye, which in a character-
istically Hainesian paradox, both sees and is seen:

Over the lake water comes this light
that has not changed,
the air we have always known . . .

They who believed that stone,
water and wind might be quickened
with a spirit like their own,
painted this eye that the rock might see.

Haines' poetry—often thematically uncompromising, tonally
austere, and stylistically spare as it is—and his conception of the
poet's office, clearly harks back to an old, established aesthetic, a tra-
ditional linguistic emphasis and expressive sensibility of the kind, as
Don Bogen has noted, that we frequently associate with Roman-
ticism and its varied perspectival descendants (59). By invoking this
canonical lineage, I don't want to give the impression that Haines
is a literary dinosaur, hopelessly out of step with his own times.
Rather, I prefer to think of him as a maverick, less out of step with
his times than energetically working in that grand tradition of hew-
ing against the American grain. In his introduction to the Graywolf
Press reprint of Edwin Muir's *The Estate of Poetry*, Haines has writ-
ten in a self-revealing way: "Poetry for men like Muir and Jeffers,
as it was for Wordsworth and for Yeats, had in the end little to do
with celebrity and professional cheek, and everything to do with an

attitude that, as Muir well knew, lies close to the religious experience. Those for whom poetry is more than a career will know what I mean by this" (iii). Without pressing the category too far toward priestly exclusivity or elitist privilege, Haines is proposing a kind of bardic function, which emphasizes "poetry's traditional high purpose," its sense of calling, spiritual questing and seeing, or serious "vocation" (Honors Class Lecture). Part of that inheritance is his sense of the abiding "closeness of word and thing," which has been "central" in his writing, as he claimed recently in a symposium on "Writers and Their Faith" (Lythgoe, 7). To speak of "this essential connection" between nature and language reveals a Romantic stance more closely associated with attitudes about art, philosophy, psychology, and being consonant with the earlier writers Haines has repeatedly valorized (Wordsworth, Emerson, Eliot, Stevens, Jeffers, Williams, Muir, Broch, for instance) than with his thoroughgoing avant-garde or experimental contemporaries, John Ashbery, for example, whose *Hotel Lautréamont* Haines lambasted in *The Hudson Review* for its capitulation to superficial impressions, and for its jazzy, television- and media-inspired contemporaneity, its flat, depthless surface. The art of collage, Haines suggests—to put the best face possible on Ashbery's project—still signals the utter lack of a "search for which an entire life must be risked" (*Fables and Distances,* 40).

Risking life, of course, has long been Haines' habit and it seems an essential aspect of the lifelong "myth-journey." I am not speaking only of his youthful gambit in trekking off to Alaska in 1947 to build his homestead off Richardson Highway outside Fairbanks, or his decision—not totally self-willed—to stay out of the permanent academic loop, but the fact that his poems gain their special quality of voice and authority from the immediate presence of threatening situations, as in the dramatic "Horns," where the speaker encounters a rutting bull moose, at once Darwinian threat and totemic beast:

I fell asleep in an old white tent.
The October moon rose,
and down a wide, frozen stream
the moose came roaring,
hoarse with rage and desire.

I awoke and stood in the cold
as he slowly circled the camp.
His horns exploded in the brush
with dry trees cracking
and falling; his nostrils flared
as, swollen-necked, smelling
of challenge, he stalked by me.

Wary of uncomplicated transcendental, paradisal views, Haines'
poems acquire their special tinge of sadness from that nervous, edgy
sense of psychological risk, denial, skepticism that are imminent in
his poetical landscape, in the choices his speaker(s) make and are
made to make. In his otherwise quirky and often cranky Western
Writers Series monograph on Haines, Peter Wild says, rightly, I
think, that he "willingly assumes the hazard" (32). One wrong move
of the hand, we think, and even Haines' long sought for center, that
elusive core (even the one without exact answers), dissolves, as in
"On Banner Dome" where he writes:

The sunlight is never warm
in such a place; to sleep there
is to dream that the ropes
that hold you to earth are letting go,
and around the straining tent
of your life there prowls and sniffs
a fallen black star who overturns
stones and devours the dead.

The search for spirit, the voice that is great within us, whatever or however we choose to call it, however, seems among the predominate elements in Haines' work. In a revealing essay, "Within the Words: An Apprenticeship," Haines clearly marks his position, in the sense of his being called toward writing, despite its traps, snares, and pitfalls:

> Let me . . . say . . . I believe, against most current thought and practice, that poetry is neither a profession nor a career, nor can it in any genuine sense be understood as a choice, but comes as it were, to the chosen, as a gift or, it may sometimes be, an affliction. In the true instance it becomes an obsession, something that cannot be refused. If this is not the case, then in all honesty I believe that it would be better to have done some more practical and humanly useful thing in life. (*Fables and Distances,* 3)

In this statement, which is part justification and part manifesto, Haines lays out the nature of his calling, a special focus, a wide lens, that has allowed him to speak obsessively—but clearly, forcefully, and unsentimentally—about present events not only in the natural world (for which, perhaps, he is best known as a poet and memoirist), but also in the political and social world, especially in those chilling poems from *The Stone Harp* such as "Tar" or "A Dream of the Police" that strike resonant, prophetic chords this late in our history. And at times, the natural and political intersect, as in section XIII of "In the Forest without Leaves," when the speaker laments wholesale environmental degradation, embodied in the thoughtless destruction of the "tree of life," for which there is

> . . . no one left to tell
> of your heartwood
> peeled down to a seed of ash,

> your crowned solitude
> crushed to a smoldering knot . . .

In addition Haines' preoccupation with generative originations also has allowed him to turn back to other sources, intimations, and awarenesses—not mystical, but mythic in their dreamlike dimension and portent. "To the extent that it was possible for me," he says in "The Writer as Alaskan," "I entered the original mystery of things, the great past out of which we came" (*Living Off the Country*, 9), so that we see throughout his poetry certain creatures, events, things, people acting as psychic markers, sign posts, totems, "pathway icons," as they are called in Priya Mookerjee's book *The Wayside Art of India*, which Haines has recently quoted as an example of an older, unified art method (*Fables and Distances*, 121). In the interest of tallying our current diminution, Haines concludes his essay "Within the Words" this way:

> We have lost much of the ancient material of poetry, nearly the whole of its mythological background with all of its natural and supernatural transformations and embodiments—dragons and demons, metamorphic types, and so forth. That we can no longer look into the night sky and see there gods and heroes, whole constellations of beast and actors, means that the world as imagination has been reduced in scope and value. It is in part the mission of poetry to keep these and all related things alive, to renew their character and their meaning, and in so doing keep alive the language we speak to ourselves and to others, and keep fresh also the heart and the spirit from which the words must come. (*Fables and Distances*, 15)

Reading this statement, it is easy to think of his poem "The Head on the Table," where the speaker muses over an ancient bison head

"cushioned on the museum table" and elevates it from mere taxo-
nomic categorization by considering this older perspective:

> The ear thinned down to a clay shell,
>
> listening with the deep presence
> of matter that does not die,
> while the whole journey of beasts on earth
> files without a sound
> into the gloom of the catalogues.
>
> The far tundra lying still,
> transparent under glass and steel.
> Evening of the explorer's lamp,
> the wick turned down
> in its clear fountain of oil.
>
> In the shadow made there,
> a rough blue tongue passes over teeth
> stained by thirty thousand years
> of swamp water and peat.

In an arresting recent essay Bonnie Costello suggests that
"Fictions of nature as a primal Other or even a numinous presence
are receding as poets turn to the indissoluble mixture of gray and
green in which we live" (571). Though Haines is nowhere men-
tioned in her essay, it strikes me that his poetry meets Costello's
challenge of the diminished or vanishing thing by treading a very
fine line between ultimacy and the here and now. Keeping the
related things alive and energizing matter that does not die
through vision and language is part of Haines' "elegiac" mission, a
sustained effort "to renew the alphabet, the grammar of speech and
thought . . . so that something of the heart-healing beauty and mys-

tery can still be felt" (*Fables and Distances,* 190), remembering that for Haines the recovery of such "wilderness" is not merely physical and topographical (or ecological, for that matter), but is instead defined as "a condition that lives in the universe" (*Living Off the Country,* 52). Haines' awareness of sacred qualities in an otherwise fallen life, in Nature's otherwise "blind face," where the relative insignificance of individual humans in the cosmic scheme of things is painfully, perhaps tragically, apparent. Articulating an awareness of what Ihan Hassan has called "the harsh claims of spirit on our existence" (25), is not only honorable but necessary and honest, because it befits the teacherly role Haines envisions as being among the poet's duties.

Carrying the news of loss is not his sole purpose, of course, for Haines does not traffic in the slick commerce of nostalgia (though he does feel keenly changes in cultural epochs). His attempt is "to reconcile what are two separate and yet inseparable histories, Nature and Culture. To the extent that we can do this, the 'world' makes sense to us and can be lived in," he claims in "On a Certain Attention to the World" (*Fables and Distances,* 127). That is, Haines reaches toward a "real presence," which not only underwrites his whole poetics, but joins world and mind (Steiner, 20). Recognizing the breach that exists between those forces—journeying into it in poem after poem—without being able to heal it absolutely, but only to suggest a possible route for eventual belief, a tentative shape for the right habit of heart and mind—defines the particular tension Haines achieves in his best poems. This conundrum, this paradox (unresolvable) motivates several long meditative series poems he has written recently, "In the Forest Without Leaves," "Days of Edward Hopper," and especially "Meditation on a Skull Carved in Crystal" (prefaced by a quotation from Martin Buber: "After is the wrong word. It is an entirely different dimension. Time and space are crystallizations out of God. At the last hour all will be revealed.") In this latter poem its form partakes of a mournful search, a soulful bereavement into what might sustain us in the face of death, "the last confusion" (*The Owl in the Mask of the Dreamer,* 189). Not for nothing John Elder writes that the "poet's task in an age of global catastrophe is one of creative grieving" (726).

What saves us—or almost saves us—in such vast bleakness, what keeps driving Haines' poetry—even aesthetically in so far as such grace is ever possible—are those momentary apprehensions, glimpses, coexistences with a sacramental dimension. Like Hermann Broch's quotation which serves as an epigram to this essay ("I think Broch is right on the money" regarding poetry's religious sensibility, Haines told me in a letter), a quotation from nineteenth-century Swiss historian Jacob Burckhardt's *Reflections on History* serves as a telling epigram for *The Owl in the Mask of the Dreamer:* "Yet there remains with us the feeling that all poetry and all intellectual life were once the handmaids of the holy, and have passed through the temple." If poetry has fallen away from its primary, originating condition in the lives of most people and in the lexicon of many postmodern critics, there is a delicious irony here in Haines' choice of epigram, for at the very least it highlights the paradoxes of his own resolute lifelong search: "Life, art, and religion are one," he says emphatically (*Fables and Distances,* 122). Perhaps the best way to think of Haines' religious spirit, then, is to see it as a record of those moments when an animated awareness of a larger, nonmaterial presence intrudes, or becomes tangible, within the field of his experience. These are Haines' own versions of Rudolph Otto's numinousness (Studebaker, 97). In Haines' turn toward the mythic, sacral dimension of experience, where resonances are struck up in the imagination of the receptive listener/watcher, the world can be transformed at any moment, and a pathway opened to another order of existence. "I stood there in the moonlight," he says in "Horns,"

> and the darkness and silence
> surged back, flowing around me,
> full of a wild enchantment,
> as though a god had spoken.

As though, not quite, on the edge of: in Haines' best work such liminal and boundary moments tend less toward the elevated rhetoric and privileged epiphany of the typical romantic nature lyric, but rather are often muted, intimated, and understated, not an unusual angle of repose given the deceptive plainness of Haines' poetical style. The implications, however, seem clear—God, if that eminence can be given a name, can appear at any time, as in Section V of "News from the Glacier": "West of Logan Pass," where, Haines writes, a group of mountain goats "came down, / out of the cliffs above us." Except

> . . . one old billy
> who stood alone on the ridge,
> his beard in the wind,
> watching the watchers who
> waited and stamped their feet.

The isolated moment is a product of what Haines has called, in his essay "On a Certain Attention to the World," a kind of "veneration," as if within such objects and creatures, seen rapturously, "something of the impenetrable mystery might be sensed and named, and before which one might be, not designing or dominating, but quietly attentive" (*Fables and Distances,* 120).

There is a huge, abiding lesson in that last sentence. Despite what many have wished, it is probably a good thing that John Haines has not yet become part of America's "official verse culture," as Jed Rasula names it in *The American Poetry Wax Museum* (466–67). While Haines' prayerful bearing might not suit the most theoretical of today's literary critics and cultural tastemakers, it might, however, go a long way, especially for the attentive and sympathetic reader, toward pointing a way out of the current dilemma surrounding the "death of poetry," the end of nature, the loss of crucial belief. "His poetry reminds us that, however tenuously our proper connection to the world may be, we have not completely forgotten it," Kevin

Walzer claims. "That the realization is fleeting is only a reminder of how important it is—and how significant is Haines' work as a poet" ("An Elegist's Dreams," 81). "We must read," then, George Steiner reminds us in *Real Presences*, "*as if*" (18).

WORKS CITED

Bogen, Don. "Faithful to the End: John Haines' Poetry Since 1980." In *The Wilderness of Vision: On the Poetry of John Haines,* edited by Kevin Bezner and Kevin Walzer. Brownsville, OR: Story Line Press, 1996, 59–69.

Carton, Evan, and Gerald Graff. "Criticism Since 1940." In *The Cambridge History of American Literature. Vol. Eight: Poetry and Criticism, 1940–1995,* edited by Sacvan Bercovitch. New York: Cambridge University Press, 1996, 261–471.

Costello, Bonnie. " 'What to Make of a Diminished Thing': Modern Nature and Poetic Response." *American Literary History* 10 (1998): 569–605.

Elder, John. "Nature's Refrain in American Poetry." In *The Columbia History of American Poetry,* edited by Jay Parini, with associate editor Brett C. Millier. New York: Columbia University Press, 1993, 707–27.

Golding, Alan. *From Outlaw to Classic: Canons in American Poetry.* Madison: University of Wisconsin Press, 1995.

Haines, John. *Living Off the Country: Essays on Poetry and Place.* Poets on Poetry Series. Ann Arbor: University of Michigan Press, 1981.

———. *The Owl in the Mask of the Dreamer: Collected Poems.* St. Paul, MN: Graywolf Press, 1993; enlarged paperback edition, 1996.

———. *Fables and Distances: New and Selected Essays.* St. Paul, MN: Graywolf Press, 1996.

———. "Discussion of 'At White River.'" *Fifty Contemporary Poets: The Creative Process,* edited by Alberta T. Turner. New York: Longman, 1977, 120–25.

———. "Introduction." *The Estate of Poetry.* By Edwin Muir. St. Paul, MN: Graywolf Press, 1993, i–v.

———. Lecture to American Literature Honors Tutorial Class. Ohio University, Athens. March 11, 1999.

———. Letter to the author. June 15, 1994.

———. "The Nature of Art." *Amicus Journal* 18, no. 1 (Spring 1996): 14

———. "Turning Inward into Poetry." Review of *Postmodern American Poetry,* edited by Paul Hoover, *New Criterion* 13, no.10 (1995): 68–71.

Haines, John, with Arthur Coffin. "An Interview with John Haines." *Jeffers Studies* 2, no. 4 (1998): 47–56.

Haines, John, with Matthew Cooperman. "Wilderness and Witness: An Interview with John Haines." *Quarter After Eight* 3 (1996): 111–27.

Hassan, Ihab. "The Expense of Spirit in Postmodern Times: Between Nihilism and Belief." *The Georgia Review* 35, no. 1 (1997): 9–26.

Lythgoe, Michael H. "Writers and Their Faith: Christianity in Contemporary Poetry." *The Writer's Chronicle* 31, no.1 (1998): 5–15.

Rasula, Jed. *The American Poetry Wax Museum: Reality Effects, 1940–1990.* Urbana, IL: National Council of Teachers of English, 1995.

Steiner, George. *Real Presences.* New York: Cambridge University Press, 1986.

Studebaker, William. "Dreaming Existence: Mysticism in John Haines' Poetry." *The Wilderness of Vision: On the Poetry of John Haines,* edited by Kevin Bezner and Kevin Walzer. Brownsville, OR: Story Line Press, 1996, 92–99.

Taylor, Henry. "A Form of Patience: The Poems of John Haines." *The Hollins Critic* 35, no. 5 (1998): 1–16.

von Hallberg, Robert. "Poetry, Politics, and Intellectuals." In *The Cambridge History of American Literature, Vol. Eight: Poetry and Criticism, 1940–1995,* edited by Sacvan Bercovitch. New York: Cambridge University Press, 1996, 9–259.

Walzer, Kevin. "An Elegist's Dreams." In *The Wilderness of Vision: On the Poetry of John Haines,* edited by Kevin Bezner and Kevin Walzer. Brownsville, OR: Story Line Press, 1996, 70–82.

Wild, Peter. *John Haines.* Western Writers Series 68. Boise: Boise State University, 1985.

DONNA REDHEAD SANDBERG

Individualists and Idealists:
John Haines and Vincent Van Gogh,
An Analysis of "On a Certain Field in Auvers"

When Haines wrote *New Poems*, a hundred years had passed since Vincent Van Gogh took his own life in 1890. By 1990, the magnitude of Van Gogh's contributions to modern art has been acknowledged.

> And we hope that with
> a hundred years of practice
> we have learned to speak
> the appropriate words:
>
> 'In the country of the deaf
> a one-eared man was king . . .'

Haines' line from "On a Certain Field in Auvers"—"'In the country of the deaf / a one-eared man was king . . .'" recognizes the force of Van Gogh's explosion into the twentieth century even though Van Gogh himself thought some other artist would become a sort of nexus between antiquity and modernism. Van Gogh "accomplished a revolution in his paintings without ever abandoning the values of the great traditions in art."[1] He said in his letter #197, "I feel that my work lies in the heart of the people, that I must still keep close to the ground, that I must reach far beneath the surface of life, and progress through a great deal of anxiety and effort."[2]

---

1. W. H. Auden, "Making, Knowing, and Judging," *The Dyer's Hand and Other Essays* (New York: Random House, 1962).
2. A. M. Hammacher, *Van Gogh 25 Masterworks* (New York: Harry N. Abrams, Inc., 1984).

When describing an old-timer who had returned to Alaska to work an old claim, Haines said, "he had that authority derived from the strict honesty of experience." In Haines' life, honest experience becomes the simplicity inherent in survival: butchering moose or chickens, skinning pelts, planting a garden, building a cabin, breaking trail, hauling water, cooking his own food from what he managed to grow or kill, and the smells that go with all of this, of a way of life foreign to city dwellers. This is the healthy peasant life Van Gogh dreamed of—to live simply and honestly, to survive by one's own labors—yet seemed unable to firmly achieve. His plan had seemed healthy enough: "And it is something—something good to be out in the snow in the winter, out in the yellow leaves in the fall, out in the ripened grain in the summer, out in the grass in the spring; it is something—always to be with the women reaping the grain and the peasant girls; with the great sky above in summer, and beside the black hearth in winter. And to feel that it has always been and always will be. So what if then you may have to sleep on straw and eat rye bread—in the long run it will be better for you."[3] John Haines said of his life in the wilderness of Alaska, "Nothing I have yet done in life pleases me as much as this. And yet it seems only half-deliberate, as if I had followed a scent on the wind and found myself in this place. Having come, I will have to stay; there's no way back. I may not always be here in these woods . . . but what I have loved will always be here" (*The Stars, The Snow, The Fire*, 82–83). Van Gogh also chose to follow a dream, a dream of artists living and working together in harmony in a yellow house in the beautiful natural surroundings of southern France. Instead, he discovered within himself a progressively worsening mental state and an inability to generate and maintain those relationships he so desired. "Some things make sense only in the light of their personal necessity, and what that necessity is to be we choose for ourselves," said Haines, who believes "Nature will cure everything given sufficient time, and

3. *The Complete Van Gogh*, Letter 413.

CONTRIBUTIONS TO THE LITERARY LANDSCAPE

neither the earth nor the cosmos requires our presence in order to fulfill itself" (*The Stars, The Snow, The Fire*, 8–9).

When attempting to create a haven in Arles, Vincent found himself struggling to maintain the yellow house and ended up at the Night Café instead. In the midst of human passions, survival can come in many shapes, like an empty yellow chair "where the pipesmoker calmed his fury." Van Gogh's bouts with growing mental instability can be described by Haines' line, "punishing wind that blows." Such a wind "blows" through the mind and soul of any individual who is "different." Neither Van Gogh nor Haines have made the majority of their choices based on comfort or expectations, but on a deep, penetrating love. The kind of love it takes to be different. Van Gogh chose to live with the lower classes, close to nature, and to unite in a celebration of creativity with other artists. As Lex Runciman said in his review of Haines' *Other Days*, "For John Haines: to live in Alaska, off the land, with the land, is a 'way to touch the world once more'—in its largest sense, an act of love."[4] Haines said, "I remain dissatisfied with my own thoughts and feelings, puzzled sometimes too by the reactions of others, often fellow writers, who seem to pay only verbal allegiance to ideas." Van Gogh's experience with other artists also did not bring the joy for which he had hoped.

When Haines says, "The one-eared man was king," perhaps he acknowledges not only Van Gogh's ultimate triumph as an artist but also a misunderstood inner energy of sacrificial unselfishness, tenderness, compassion, and humility that originally filled Van Gogh with a longing to become a minister like his father and grandfather. He never seemed to lift himself up as being worthy of honor or praise and truly desired to help others. Van Gogh would even give his own blankets to relieve the suffering of the poor mining peasants, but he received no recognition as a minister from fellow clergy. The society of Van Gogh's time weighed good speaking ability more heavily than genuine

4. Lex Runciman, in *Western American Literature* 18 (Spring 1983): 70–71.

unselfishness when determining ministerial qualifications. By recognizing Van Gogh's personal integrity within a skewed society, Haines also "hears" some of what Van Gogh "heard" in the midst of rejection. Haines said "God speaks the simplest words: / *sun*, *rain*, and *frost*" ("Of Michelangelo, His Question"), and describes the role of the artist: "It seems to me that one important function of the poet, of the artist, is to discover, to reveal, and to complete that vision, the bits and pieces of which are all that most of us ever see and can seldom identify."

But why, personally for Haines, does Van Gogh become the "King"? Did Vincent's love for people and acceptance of life at its lowest levels make him the king? Van Gogh was misunderstood and rejected, first by his own father, by the ministry, by the traditional artists of his time, and also by the women he loved. Even among the impressionists Van Gogh suffered some rejection. Was there a depth to rejection in Van Gogh's life Haines recognized? Who has known more rejection than the Catholic Savior Haines grew up with, the one who was "despised and rejected of men," who "came to his own and his own received him not."[5] "In the country of the deaf" means more than literal deafness; it incorporates that deafness inherent in rejection. A man with one good ear will hear more than a man with two bad ears. If hearing is akin to understanding, it is more than ears in the "country of the deaf" that cannot hear. Human beings tend to reject what they cannot understand. The morning of July 29, 1890, Vincent's last words were, "La tristesse durera toujours." (The sadness will always remain.)[6] Haines writes:

> On this one day in July
> we speak the rites for all
> torn and departed souls.

Van Gogh's death "one day in July" becomes symbolic of "all torn and departed souls" in Haines' poem; the artist and the poet in

5. Isaiah 53:3 and John 1:11.
6. Quoted from by Elisabeth du Quesne-Van Gogh, 1913. *The Complete Van Gogh*, 52.

the process of their search finally become "no one." Perhaps Haines is familiar with the scriptural basis for this experience: "I tell you the truth, unless a kernel of wheat falls to the ground and dies, it remains only a single seed. But if it dies, it produces many seeds." Although written to describe the process a person's ego must undergo to achieve true spirituality, the poem aptly applies to the life of any creative and gifted individual; the ego must become subservient and devoted to the art, to God. It must die to truly live. Haines has a recurring theme of death in his work. As Richard Tillinghast put it, "The grim Alaska life seems to fit Haines' own bent of mind-grave, terrible, with an eye always on death."[7] Haines said,

> For death is a shadow priest
> leaning at his slotted window;
> no more than a voice, sabbath-
> darkened, whispering of penance
> and absolution:
> Death the confessor.

And:

> Believe in the angel beside you,
> his patient and willing gesture:
> (death with a letter
> to be delivered)
> Believe in the cross, whose wood
> is tinder, whose nails are rust:
> (Death with a fiery pencil
> will pierce you)
> Believe in the light blown forward
> from the darkness behind you:
> (Death with a windy lantern
> will find you)

7. Ibid., quoting Richard Tillinghast, "The Prizewinner, The Real Thing, and Two Others," *Poetry* 109, no. 2 (November 1966): 118–22.

Van Gogh's painting "Pièta" depicts a dead Jesus held by his mother at the foot of the cross. In Haines' poem, death finds a one-eared king in the land of the deaf. The king's last words spoke of enduring sadness, yet the language and sound in the last stanza of "On a Certain Field in Auvers" is reminiscent of religious rites, of incantation, a litany that repeats "of the, of the" similar to when preachers baptize believers in the death and resurrection of Jesus Christ speaking, "In the name of the Father, and of the Son, and of the Holy Ghost." Haines ends the incantation, "and the great light of the sun" reminiscent of Van Gogh's "Sower with Setting Sun" painting where the sun's great light dominates everything.

> In the name of the poor,
> and of the holy insane,
> and the great light of the sun.

In the consummate poem "On a Certain Field in Auvers," Haines has written a tremendous tribute to Vincent van Gogh and to all gifted but unrecognized souls who transcend the small rooms of life. With an incantatory form, Haines achieves a similar sense of awe, of religious intensity, and of transcendence common in language used to evoke worship. Who else deserves this honor but the one who is the "holy insane," "the king"? Out of the debris of dying stars there results "this arm, this hand, / my voice, your face, this love."

MICHAEL H. LYTHGOE

"The Night of Painted Iron": John Haines' Poems on Paintings and Sculpture

Poets have been writing about works of art since Homer described the shield of Achilles in the *Iliad*. Homer described a fictional shield. He created a shield, if you will, with his poetry, for the sake of his epic. The art of Homer's poetry, and its continuing translations, keep the shield of Achilles alive in our imagination. A number of John Haines' poems are ekphrastic poems. Before he published poetry, he was a student of art and won recognition for an abstract piece of sculpture called *Visitation* at the Corcoran Gallery in Washington, DC. He is better known for writing poems grounded in solitary landscapes—from Alaska to Montana to Virginia. Yet his work in the last twenty years has drawn significantly on his early background as a painter and sculptor, and on experiences derived from encounters with paintings and other works of art. John Haines treats poetry with the respect one gives to sacred rituals. Art for him is mysterious, magical, like a spell. His poems give us silences, spells, and visions. He gives voices to dumb metals which have been molded to convey lives of living flesh and blood. As he studied the paintings, and the painted iron sculptures of other artists, he started to write ironlike lines.

Donald Hall, writing on Haines' poetry for *The Nation*, observed: "He writes with a hard instrument on a hard surface, making no disposable verses" (*Death to the Death of Poetry*, 114). In fact, Haines' concern for making art that will endure seems also to distinguish the art he admires most in others. To make a lasting artifact—this is his aspiration. His choice of words and his subjects reveal his own *ars poetica*. As a poet, Haines is drawn to the black-smith, the welder, the metalworker, the stone mason, the miner. Beginning late in the 1970s, he began to return to visual art for inspiration to form poems on the page.

Sculpture has been featured in more of Haines' poems than paintings. He has written several poems on Rodin and Michelangelo. Human suffering is the connection between the works in oils and metals. His poem on Eugène Delacroix is called "Diminishing Credo." He tells us in his notes, Delacroix may have been the last great fresco painter at the turn of the century, when the "black hours" watched "the painted vistas / closing, the hour of the hero strike / and wane?" Photography was beginning to influence art; balloons were taking flight. New technologies were also having an influence on the artists. Haines' lines lament the passing of the painter who was both a romantic and a realist. Delacroix could bring animal torsos alive on canvas. But Delacroix also suffered as an artist. Haines keeps such an observation from being seen as banal or trivial, overly romantic if you will, by his spare prosody, his elevated themes. The best of his poems on art are expansive; they open up dramatic narratives and introduce myth or fable.

As early as 1969 Haines wrote poems titled with the names of artists, "Ryder" and "Paul Klee." But nature and family themes were more evident during this period until he wrote "In the Museum Garden," between 1970 and 1972. The place where this poem is set is unclear. It could have come from visits to art exhibits at Stanford University, or, perhaps, San Francisco. What is clear is that Asian art sparks Haines' imagination. His poems frequently read like meditations and dreams derived from his observations on the wilderness. In the second section of the poem the narrator sees "galleries, / steeped in the glory of echoes." The narrator also observes "a dragon," and "the stone horses, stolen from China . . ." Here is the third section of "In the Museum Garden":

We halted before a mountain
towering in silk, climbed a pathway
footworn by the steep passion
of the anchorite; high on a bench
of hand-quarried stone we rested,
dreaming in a shower of blackbirds.

The art reveals mountains. In art, the mountains are symbols conveying a sense of eternity, strength, gravity. The natural elements and earth's materials are the stuff of Haines' poems. He is inspired to write by what he sees in the landscape, and by the painting of an Asian landscape on silk. The "grave echoes in stone" will return in other images and visions of Haines' work. There is also a connection to the aesthetics of the ancient artist who made the art Haines is now writing about. But Haines makes something new—while bringing back to life the work of an ancient artist, a kinsman of his spirit.

The title poem from his collected poems, "The Owl in the Mask of the Dreamer," brings together the materials of sculpture; metal begins to replace stone or clay in the artistic shapes. It was written, Haines tells us in his notes, as a "concentrated history of the art of sculpture, from early times to the present."

By tinker and by cutting torch
reduced to a fist of slag,
to a knot of rust on a face of chrome.

The final three stanzas refer to a famous metal sculpture by Alberto Giacometti.

Speak for these people of drawn wire
striding toward each other
over a swept square of bronze.

For them the silence is loud
and the sunlight is strong.

No matter how far they walk
they will never be closer.

Haines' poems have a dreamlike quality that allows him to enter into works of art, the spirit of a "sinewy curl of metal / fallen beneath the lathe." The lines of this poem inspired, on the surface, by a piece of sculpture, can also be read as lines on the life he has known in the forest of Alaska. He remembers the silences of isolation and his memories bring back a bright sunlight that lasts for six months. There is also a suggestion that art, as life, is a journey. This is in part a memory poem. But as Haines looks at art, he always seems to see history, and history is about human suffering, war and death. His description of the materials used in the art he focuses on shows also his compulsion to listen. He hears the past in the present, the speech of stones, the "loud silence" of a shadowy people sculpted in wire. He is also compelled to see and speak of the toll of time, the rust on materials made to endure. Haines writes dark images, mysterious, even in sunlight.

In a June 26, 1999, letter to this author, Haines said: "The one piece of sculpture at the Hirschorn (Washington, DC) I can recall of David Smith's was a metal construction in the outer court, rather an abstract cannon on wheels. I don't recall the name of it, but it did inspire the poem I named for him." Haines may have been thinking of *Agricola*. He says he met Smith in New York City in the early 1950s, but did not know his work at that time. Later, Haines read about the artist. He writes, "Why some things happen when they do remains a mystery. All one can do is remain alert and act on the inspiration when it occurs."

We cannot always be certain of the exact piece of sculpture or the single painting that inspires Haines' poems. He has said he attended a major exhibition of Giacometti's work at the San Francisco Museum of Modern Art around 1990. He had read a biography of the artist before he saw his work. He made some notes at the time for poems he says he has yet to complete. Giacometti served as an influence on other artists who inspired Haines to write poems, including "Homage to David Smith":

> We are made of angle iron and crossbrace,
> we live and we die
> in the sunlight of polished steel,
> in the night of painted iron.
>
> All that surrounds us and by which
> we will be judged—
> these incompleted circles,
> perforated diaphragms,
> gnawed shields, unfinished arrows—
> will be taken as signs
>
> pointing inward to an iron self,
> or else toward the scrapyard
> to which we seem to be rolling—
>
> great studded wheels grinding
> over the pavement
> leaving behind us crushed glass,
> pieces of flattened tin.
>
> And riding the space-drawn carriage,
> as if they were weighted
> and bent in a terrible heat,
>
> five fixed and glowing figures
> who are not men.

When Haines writes poems on art, he does not, for the most part, write a gloss on a specific work of art. He is more likely to write a poem from a mood or a vision the work inspires. The object is often (as we saw in the poem for David Smith) not named. The material used in the sculpture is important. The artist who shaped the materials is important. The poet pays tribute to the sculptor or the painter (Picasso, Van Gogh, Dürer, Bosch), or writes about a painter's times ("Days of Edward Hopper"), the artists' struggles ("Of Michelangelo, His Question," "On a Certain Field in Auvers"), or an artist's entire body of work (Marsden Hartley's seascapes). Nonetheless, the vision of "five fixed and glowing figures / who are not men" is the final image in the poem for David Smith; it is a scene from a forge, perhaps, or an apocalyptic vision, a time of final judgment. The poet sees "gnawed shields, unfinished arrows— "signs" which imply an "iron" person. Is this a man of steel? We cannot tell for sure, but we are told the artistic scene (the iron men) could be rolling toward a "scrapyard." This is a kind of hell—"bent in a terrible heat."

Poems like "Homage to David Smith," or "The Burghers of Calais," allow Haines to bring the art of the past forward, and see it again in a new light. As Homer wrote about the shield of Achilles, so Haines writes about a bronze sculpture by Rodin. "The Burghers of Calais" was commissioned as a national monument, and was the first big commission Rodin won. It honored the leading citizen of Calais who surrendered and who was followed by five others, one at a time. These other five citizens actually remained unnamed, unhonored, for years. Heroes all, the Burghers were led by the richest man in the community—who sacrificed himself so that his community would be spared death by starvation.

> Someone has paid for the rope
> that binds these shoulders; frayed
> and shortened, it was sold
> by the yard, allotted in anguish.

And somewhere the fire that seared
the cradle to pour the metal
of shirts for these massive limbs,
these bared and planted feet,
cramped hands gripping the icy keys.

Flesh that is iron, stone
that is flesh. This one clutching
his face, who will not look up,
as if from the mire at his feet
he would raise his beaten homeland.

And he who turns to look once more
homeward, half-eager to catch
one farewell signal of smoke;
and he who measures the distance
still to walk, implacable, resigned . . .

This excerpt from "The Burghers of Calais" may reveal the most about Haines' aesthetics, but also a good bit about his own, solitary life as an artist. Haines remembers seeing the Rodin Garden of sculpture at Stanford University early in the 1980s. The bronze piece by Rodin is in Haines' mind representative of the displaced and the refugees of today. The figures by Rodin are resigned, implacable. Haines' poem suggests the artist should go on working, writing or sculpting, making art, even as his city goes up in smoke. One could read the scene in terms of the Balkans.

Haines concludes *The Owl in the Mask of the Dreamer* collection with poems inspired by Goya's "Black" paintings, more allusions to Rodin, and a piece on Michelangelo's immense reclining female figure of *Night* in the Medici Chapel in Florence. The dark notes of these poems on art also echo the tones of Goya's etchings from his series "Disasters of War." The figure of death moves through these poems. There is also an ambivalence about the hereafter. In "Stalled Colossus," Haines writes:

> you stand alone, facing
> the stone forehead of heaven,
> like a mountain
> no one can hope to climb.

These words seem hopeless. Yet the final poem, "Night," asks for the spell not to be broken in the sleeping stones. The "one sustaining solace" is "my night that has more night / to come." The narrator asks not to be wakened. Somehow the agony of the artist-poet, of Michelangelo who created art for the Church, inspires Haines to find a solace in the calm of a death-dream free from a "hunted world." With rare exceptions there is little color, simply lights and darks, shadows, some sunlight, and long periods of darkness in Haines' poetry. The darkness, as Haines has grown older, has looked more foreboding. But the darkness of peace or sleep can also be the passage out of a "hunted world." Art can cast spells (as in "Magic"), and give solace in life. Let the spell be unbroken, says the poet.

Haines was moved by primitive art to write "The Eye in the Rock." Art for him is the stuff of sacred rituals, mysterious, and magical. He has heard stones speak; he has received "news" from glaciers. We do well to listen to what comes from his spells and visions. One can profit from the silences he describes in his verse. While he has given voice to mute stones, so has he given voice to dumb metals conveying lives of flesh and blood. He has looked on paintings and painted iron sculptures, and strived to write ironlike lines; dreaming visions of human sufferings, his poems recall heroic history and disasters of warfare. He has given us poems that bring back to life the art of the past by reviving in words the blood and bone shapes in bronze.

His poems on Van Gogh and Picasso and Rodin may be the most accessible, but his poems on art and artists are all worth a second reading. They reveal something of the creative process, something of the artist struggling to interpret life into lasting forms. These efforts are not easy, nor are they often easy to understand. But life as Haines has lived it has not been easy. So the poet writes to make his lines last. He works his words with an affectionate craft, molding phrases, bending his lines, creating poems of angle-iron and crossbrace.

We know from *At the End of This Summer* (1998) that Haines' early efforts in making poems were complimented by William Carlos Williams. It is instructive to consider Williams' influence on his style. Haines' style is spare, and similar to Williams' own short, flat lines describing scenes in *Pictures by Breughel*. Williams also influenced the aesthetics of Georgia O'Keeffe with his view of composition: "No ideas but in things." In fact, with Haines, the *ideas* inspired by things are very important. So we may be right to assume that some of Williams' views on art rubbed off on the young Haines. Williams was part of the so-called Stieglitz group, and would have known O'Keeffe. William Carlos Williams once said to Edith Heal: "When I spoke of flowers, I was a flower, with all the prerogatives of flowers, especially the right to come alive in spring."[1] This helps explain O'Keeffe's romantic need to identify with a part of nature as she painted her flowers and bones. But it also seems to explain how consciousness and unconsciousness can merge, in a poem by John Haines on owls, mountains, or a work of sculpture; or, how the creative imagination works in a painting by Paul Klee.

One early poem written in the Carmel Valley of California between 1952 and 1954, "Two Horses, One by the Roadside," reminds us of why William Carlos Williams saw promise in the

1. Helen Vendler, editor, *Voices and Visions: The Poet in America* (New York: Random House, 1987), 175.

young John Haines, and how Haines, even then, was beginning to blend ancient art into his modern poems:

> Reminds me of a picture
> I saw once of a stone horse
> standing alone on
> the plains of China,
> part once of the
> gateway to a palace.
>
> Wind, frost, and many wars
> had chipped their souvenirs;
> the features marred,
> there still remained the
> essential form,
> rooted, as though of the earth.
>
> It gathered that lonely
> country about it, a mark
> to measure the silence of time.
> And I remember a smile
> was carved in its face,
> the smile of a secret—the dreams
> of emperors, perhaps.

Haines' poems on art and artists were written initially as a way for him to understand other artists and works of art. He was moved to write by the creative spirit of those he studied and learned to admire. Ancient poets first compared their lines to a painting or a shape made of clay when they started to write down words, instead of simply singing stories or reciting tales in verse. Now we can read in a poem a tribute to, or a description of, a painting by Van Gogh—and revisit works of art in the poetry of John Haines. We can imagine again a sculpture created by Michelangelo. Let us take this opportunity to celebrate the poetry of John Haines, reflecting on how the visual arts inspired some of his best poetry. Haines has given us lines to last as stone mountains endure on earth, and in ancient paintings. His poetry takes a long view, rooted as it is in our lands, and in our history. Haines' poetry captures terrain marred by wind and frost. His words give voice to bronze sculpture, oil paintings, and the silences of our natural world. He writes lines aspiring to last longer than hard nights. Let us appreciate his gifts: a body of poetic works, visions, pictures of smiles, secrets carved in stone statues designed to inspire dreams. John Haines gives us poetry as a bellows feeds the blacksmith's fire. His art is a breath, a spoken word, but words imagined in forms to outlast wars—as if inscribed in stones, or made of iron forged in fire, shaped, and painted to resist Time's rust.

PART TWO

Interview
and Short Glimpses

RAYMOND CARVER

The Cougar

For John Haines and Keith Wilson

I stalked a cougar once in a lost box-canyon
off the Columbia River gorge near the town and river
of Klickitat. We were loaded for grouse. October,
gray sky reaching over into Oregon, and beyond,
all the way to California. None of us had been there,
to California, but we knew about that place—they had
restaurants
that let you fill your plate as many times as you wanted.

I stalked a cougar that day,
if stalk is the right word, clumping and scraping along
upwind of the cougar, smoking cigarettes too,
one after the other, a nervous, fat, sweating kid
under the best of circumstances, but that day
I stalked a cougar . . .

And then I was weaving drunk there in the living room,
fumbling to put it into words, smacked and scattered
with the memory of it after you two had put *your* stories,
black bear stories, out on the table.
Suddenly I was back in that canyon, in that gone state.
Something I hadn't thought about for years:
how I stalked a cougar that day.

So I told it. Tried to anyway,
Haines and I pretty drunk now. Wilson listening, listening,
then saying, You sure it wasn't a bobcat?

Which I secretly took as a put-down, he from the Southwest,
poet who had read that night,
and any fool able to tell a bobcat from a cougar,
even a drunk writer like me,
years later, at the smorgasbord, in California.

Hell. And then the cougar smooth-loped out of the brush
right in front of me—God, how big and beautiful he was—
jumped onto a rock and turned his head
to look at me. To look at *me*! I looked back, forgetting to shoot.
Then he jumped again, ran clear out of my life.

JOHN MCKERNAN

Homage to John Haines

People return from the Far North

With stories of running water
With glossy photos of green grass   With baseball hats

With bracelets of bear claws
With medicinal powders and oils that glow in the dark
With paintings of 12-day sunsets

With new shoes and old gloves
With a chip of an igloo packed in dry ice
With three-foot stuffed crows
In polar bear rib-cage bird cages

You continue. . . . You continue to set forth
To the farthest north   Before you will ever arrive
With your sketch pad   With your India ink
With a red baton peeled from the horizon
With your sculptor's eye and a potter's hand

You may return to us   some day   Your calm voice
Showing us another more faithful world
You will teach us   How to build with air
From the quiet   Deep down inside things
Urging us   To tug open the inner doors filled with silence
And resurrect the eternal frontier   Stretching to the stars

MATTHEW COOPERMAN

Wilderness and Witness:
An Interview with John Haines

MC: You've lived in Alaska on and off for over forty years. What impelled you there in the first place?

JH: What was at first instinctive deepened into something else, thought upon and acted upon. I learned as I went, and in the process grew, as a man and a writer. But at first it was simply intuitive. I acted out a felt need to settle myself somewhere, and I had always been drawn to the woods, to the wilderness—to that world I had glimpsed as a boy standing on the streambank with my father, whether it was Maryland, Virginia, or the east slope of the Olympic Mountains in Washington State. It was only later, after my first venture to Alaska in 1947, and I had returned to school in Washington, and then to New York, where the writer in me began to be more focused and I became immersed in reading, that the further dimension of the thing began to show itself. Certain books influenced me, of course, certain writers; and perhaps it was William Carlos Williams, in his feeling for this place, America, what it had been, what it had become, who helped me clarify my own intuitions.

MC: There is, of course, a long tradition of American writers in the wilderness. Do you see your writing career as an articulation of the frontier experience—of, if you will, an "errand into the wilderness"?

JH: It's interesting how certain texts, at certain times in one's life,

This interview originally appeared in *Quarter After Eight* 3 (1996). It is the product of a prolonged conversation between that journal's editor and John Haines, beginning in Athens, Ohio, and continued, by mail, over several months in 1996.

help to clarify and add to the choices one makes on that more instinctive level. I had read, of course, the early north country adventures, the gold rush narratives, the stories by London and others, as well as a more general background in "outdoor" reading, from childhood on. It was later that I came to read more thoughtful and insightful books like Williams' *In the American Grain*, and Lawrence's *Studies in Classical American Literature*, as well as much serious American literature generally, and I mean the novels and the short stories, and so forth. And, of course, at a later time, I did read Thoreau and a number of other early American nature writers.

It's odd at times to recall the incidental things that may have influenced one's life, often events and details we will have later forgotten. When I was a boy in Washington, DC, I heard a priest one Sunday morning recite a poem called "The House by the Side of the Road." I've forgotten the author of the poem, and all I can remember of it is this refrain:

> I shall live in my house
> By the side of the road,
> And be a friend to man

And, in fact, many years later I built my house by the side of a road, and perhaps in some way sought to be a friend to humankind.

MC: Do you see your work emerging out of the particular locality or "place" of Alaska?

JH: Well, there is that specific locality by which many writers are identified, and for me that seems to have been Alaska, inevitably so, given the initial surprise of my work appearing as it did in the early 1960s from a source so unexpected. And there is the wider, the more general place, the nation, the continental mass on which the nation is based, and the particular period in which one lives. And there is this more abstract, historical situation we call Western civilization, its effects, its sources, its rise and decline. And then there is one's place as a writer in the story of our literature, our culture. In a valid sense, I think you cannot separate all of these into isolated instances; they all connect, and one's true place may be found at some intersection of time, place, and art. But it is true, all the same, that the place of one's origin, that physical place on the map, or where one has spent a sufficient time in one's life, has its indelible imprint.

MC: Ironically, for a writer so supremely identified with "place," you have no set home. Or said otherwise, your larger "home" in the wilderness of Alaska has implied a certain exile, displacement, or transience. How has that paradox affected you?

JH: My early life as a sort of migrant, being the son of a naval officer, certainly conditioned me as someone who needed to *place* himself. At the same time, that early life allowed me to absorb a sense of our continental space—of the continent as a whole—and as we become more aware of what we call a global humanity, I think this larger sense of things is important.

On another plane, I see my withdrawal into the wilderness as one more attempt to understand what it means to be here in this place, America, and in a true sense to settle myself in that place. I could have made no more natural choice than Alaska as it was then, in that postwar period, still a frontier.

As for my "displacement," as it were, from Alaska and the home I had made there, I had valid reasons at the time for leaving it and returning to this other world I left behind initially. My development as a writer seems to have required that return, and later, much later, a return to the Richardson homestead for a period of some years. To a considerable extent, I again reentered that part of my past, changed of course, and how could I not be. In the meantime, Alaska had changed, and is changing, and is no longer the place I found in that postwar year of 1947.

I have often regretted selling the homestead so many years ago, and especially considering the neglect I found it in when I went back in 1980. On the other hand, I do not regret the years I spent teaching in Montana, in Ohio, and elsewhere. I don't regret the year I spent in England, nor the time I gave to a household of children in California in the early 1970s. Somehow, all of this has contributed to the work I've done, the person I've become.

Naturally, there have been periods of confusion and depression, wondering where I was and what was the meaning of it. But eventually, through the work itself, the writing, and the good luck I've had in meeting the right person, the right situation, at the right time, the journey, so to speak, has clarified itself.

MC: This journey, then, outside of academia for the most part, has been a good, or even necessary, condition for your work?

JH: There are, as we say, trade-offs. As much as I have envied at times the settled circumstances of many of my colleagues and fellow poets, I have sensed also the dangers in that. It is perhaps not always best for the artist, the poet and the writer, to be too secure in this world, and especially not in our world today. A certain complacency and dullness may set in; we become too used to our comforts and certainties, and may increasingly find it difficult to locate anything new to write about. I believe I've seen this in more than one career among my contemporaries. I think the poet in us may at times gain from having our certainties disrupted and our life suddenly thrown open to the winds of chance. Crisis has a way, danger has a way, of focusing one's attention on that most important thing—the theme, the subject—that is of most concern in creative life.

Much of the great work of our time has come from writers in situations we might consider intolerable: war, poverty, imprisonment, exile, etc. Yet in many instances the artist, the poet, is reborn, forced, as it were, to face life again on some basic terms. But again,

I would not posit this as a rule; only to say that it does at times, and in outstanding instances, seem to have been the case, and may illustrate a fundamental law of existence. I know that some of my own best work has come of that sometimes momentary, sometimes prolonged, entry into a sort of no-man's-land, that blind alley or stopping-place many creative people have known, and from which I've been rescued by the creative act itself.

MC: In his somewhat infamous article "Can Poetry Matter?" your friend, the poet Dana Gioia, speaks about the sometimes insidious effect of the university upon the writer, both on his subject matter and his audience. What do you think about the massive proliferation of creative writing programs in America in the last twenty years, and what are the challenges to the young writers within that academic community?

JH: I wasn't aware that Gioia's article had become "infamous," though it certainly stirred a good deal of commentary, and all the better for that.

I have, if you will, and not entirely by choice, maintained a certain independence—at a price, of course. Had I been more aware of the academic situation, of the politics of this or that, I might have ended in a tenured position somewhere long ago. I don't doubt, from what I have observed of some of my contemporaries, that that in itself might have come with a price. I tend to be outspoken, and my experience in academe has led me to conclude that one must be very careful in speaking out on a subject or issue that lies outside one's professional field, at least while one is young and seeking tenure. Unfortunately, what may begin as professional prudence often ends in closed mental doors: a habitual silence when, as is the case at times, one's voice raised in protest might make a great difference. I admire a figure like Noam Chomsky, for example, a rare man. Yet I know, from observation and from talking with colleagues from time to time, that many of them do think and know very well what the issues are and where justice lies; yet they remain silent. This can be typical of the institution, whether it's the university or the corporation: the almost unconscious acquiescence in policy and the stilling of one's own private reservations or principles.

MC: Sounds like a pretty negative characterization to me.

JH: It should be understood that I came into maturity in a very different cultural atmosphere from the one we've grown used to in recent times. I mean in respect to literature especially. I would hazard a guess that my career, so to speak, would not have been exceptional, say, forty or fifty years ago. Our writers and poets came from all sorts of professions and walks of life, whether from a kind of urban bohemia like cummings, or from that more general life as represented by people like Williams and Stevens. It's true also that when I first began teaching the system was more open. Few people at the time seemed concerned over my lack of a terminal degree; it was the work that mattered, and I found myself welcomed on that account alone. It is possible to see the increasing professionalization, or certification, of letters in our time, when set against the background of the history of literature, as an aberration, one more consequence of the industrial system.

But I would agree with Dana, that it is not that the university is a bad place for a poet to be; it may be a bad place for all poets to be. Among other effects, there are the inevitable small politics that intrude, with the all too common result that some degree candidates, not always the most talented, may be preferred in the programs while others may be hurt in the process. I've seen this in practice, and it is not a pleasant thing to witness.

And then there is the other side of it, and I should say that I have benefited enormously from having taught in a number of programs over the years, with many lasting friendships among students and colleagues. In the best of circumstances I have enjoyed very much the collegial atmosphere, and in a lonely world that is no small thing. Perhaps the ultimate question is just how far we can go in this institutional incorporation of the arts and still retain that necessary independence and personal discipline. There may come a time when the poet, the writer, must stand up and speak out, even at the risk of professional retaliation and loss of position. I feel that at the present time few tenured poets in this country would be willing to risk that, a fact that does not bode well for the future of the art, nor for society. We should never forget that the university in Germany capitulated to Hitler and the Nazis with hardly a murmur of protest. A terrible lesson—and I see little reason to believe, given the general character of institutions, that things would be much different here in a similar circumstance. That is, silence is most apt to be the response.

So it's a pretty mixed business, and there are no easy answers. I suspect we were better off when only a few writing programs existed. There are too many of them now, and their value has accordingly been compromised.

MC: Perhaps it's a consequence of the solipsism and professionalism of creative writing programs, but in "Within the Words," from *Fables and Distances* you talk about the reduction of visions and resources for the contemporary poet; about the "loss of much of the ancient material of poetry . . . nearly the whole of its mythological background with all of its natural and supernatural transformations and embodiments." Could you explain this loss, our challenges?

JH: I wouldn't hold university programs responsible for what has become a general condition for modern peoples, and by that I mean mainly the loss of genuine spiritual life. I'm also uncertain that I could offer a satisfactory explanation for what is a pretty complicated matter. But I do think we could state the fundamental problem in this way: If you believe that there is no spiritual value in the world, that things are mere objects, and there can be no barrier to the penetration of the "secrets" of nature, and to the exploitation of so-called "resources," then, in a real sense, the world is reduced to prose, and poetry becomes impossible. I think we must keep alive that sense of ultimate mystery, of what can only be called sacred—sacred because it is finally beyond explication and beyond possession. In certain respects the ancients were wiser than we are. In giving to forces of nature names and faces they acknowledged its intimate presence among us, to be honored, feared, and obeyed; and when offense was given to one of the gods, to expect some kind of punishment. I really don't think that the essential terms for our existence have changed all that much.

MC: So how, then, if not lost, do we realize those terms?

JH: There are good reasons to believe that humanity must periodically be returned to original sources, whether we do so willingly as individuals, conscious to some degree as to why we do it, or are driven to it by circumstances of nature and history—by the collapse of civilizations, or the breakdown of society, by warfare or pestilence, etc. But sooner or later that return to something like primal condition will occur. The history of civilizations makes this utterly clear. The question, in our case, is when this will occur, not if—what form will it take, and how lasting may be the consequences. There is little doubt in my mind, anyway, that it will happen. Nothing lasts forever. For whatever good it may be to us, we need to see things whole.

It seems to require some drastic event in the world, in society or in one's personal life, to bring about the new thing. We saw this after WWI, with the sudden surge of energy in the arts, as if that event, as terrible as it was, brought with it new insights and released an energy pent up, as it were. A similar creative energy was released following WWII, as I have every reason to know, having been in some small way a part of it at that time. The Great Depression of the 1930s similarly brought some major talents to focus on that period and its social disasters. I'm not certain why this has to be so, but it appears to be a general and consistent truth, one apparent throughout history. The true artist will always rise to the occasion, and it is as if something latent in us is waiting for that specific moment when it will be called on to speak, to witness. Without the Greek wars, no Homer, no Sophocles. In the face of nearly universal affliction and catastrophe, the true artist must affirm what is most basic and valuable in human existence, and draw from that the necessary lessons.

MC: In a similar vein, could you talk about the definitional problems of the terms *nature* and *wilderness*? I'm thinking of your comments in "On a Certain Attention to the World" (*Fables and Distances*), and the inherent paradox of nature as increasingly absent and present—lost in an actual and archetypal way, but found as a trope or commodifiable object.

JH: Among my comments on the nature of Nature, so to speak, on wilderness and the wild, I've tried to point out the inevitable distortions and contradictions in our views and arguments. In my "Reflections on the Nature of Writing," I've said, and I believe it, that "strictly speaking, there is no life apart from nature." However, we seem to insist on putting nature out there somewhere, to be protected or exploited, to be looked at and learned from, and we are aware of a certain detachment or separation in doing this. On the one hand, our humanity, our developed or cultivated place in the nature of things, does separate us from that other nature: the wilderness, whether we mean the jungle, the woodlands, the grasslands, or the desert. At the same time, Nature as *the* force in life, is with us, within us, and never abandons us entirely. As we know all too well, we can hold on for so long, but we will all age and die, and nature in that greater sense will claim us, as it has claimed species and races, cities and civilizations. In this sense, there is no escape from Nature. None. And as aroused and outraged as I am at times over the destruction of so much of this earth and this continent of ours, I know that in the long run nature will return to claim its country again, and in the true sense, triumph. Driving the expressway, dining in a good restaurant, or watching a good movie, it's hard to keep this in mind, and best perhaps that we can't; but it is there nonetheless, and I am very much aware of it. You can clearcut the ridges, the mountainsides; you can burn off the high plains, flood the lowlands, and poison the seas, but the potential in nature is always there. To the extent that we befriend nature, preserving what we can, we help ourselves and our descendants.

But here again we have to acknowledge that larger Nature, the cosmos, the universe, which is too vast and potential to be permanently disturbed by our intrusions. We need to recall the ordeal of natural forces throughout millions, or billions, of years; the desolation left behind by ages of volcanic eruption, the flooding of continents, the breakup of landmasses, submergence and drift, and so forth. Nature is active, will remain so, and from the point of view of a remote god, it is all the same, and humanity but a momentary intrusion on the stage. Nonetheless, for our own sake, and the preservation of what is most to be valued among us, we owe that immediate nature around us a debt, and we should love it and keep it. Either that, or Nature, in its most fundamental sense, will find ways to punish us.

MC: If the abstraction of monotheism has killed off those gods, or if we have killed off nature itself, how do we regain our connection to the natural world?

JH: It is easy to overemphasize the so-called "death of nature." One thing has always impressed me when flying over the continental

INTERVIEW AND SHORT GLIMPSES

USA, from north to south and from east to west, and that is how much of the land itself remains open and unsettled. The cities and towns are still concentrated, and, when compared to the land, restricted. It's easy to forget this when driving, say, the DC Beltway, the Santa Monica Freeway, or even downtown Anchorage. Yes, there are clearcuts, vast dumps and landfills, and scarred countryside; but the place itself, North America, still has enormous space, a fact that does not excuse our continuing to spoil that which is close to us, within reach of our machines and our unrestrained appetites, nor relieve us of the responsibility to care all the more for what remains.

As to how we regain that closeness to nature, that is, I'm afraid, largely an individual matter. It is a problem for the artist, the poet and creative thinker; it is a problem for all of us in one way or another. But to save, to preserve, those more obvious and inspiring aspects of nature—I mean the woodlands, the wildlands—is surely a vital step, and I think most of us realize this. We must use this earth to live on it, but wisdom tells us that nature, however we define it, is finally in command, and we will never be able to change that, for all our schemes and manipulations. Indeed, to "conquer" nature is essentially a form of blasphemy. We might add that nothing truer has ever been said concerning our modern predicament than Jung's remark that "the gods have become neuroses."

MC: One of the things I'm impressed by in your work is an abiding sense of witness—to the natural world, to history, and to the political forces at play in contemporary life. It also strikes me that what I'd call the "poetry of witness" has become a sort of style or explicit agenda. I'm thinking of, for example, Carolyn Forché's most recent book, *The Angel of History,* or better, the reaction to it. What's your sense of this witnessing?

JH: Every poet is a witness to something; merely to be in the world is to witness. In a more specific sense, there are writers who have deliberately, consciously, through force of circumstance, borne witness to specific events. And there have been others, perhaps equally talented, who have turned aside or chosen not to speak. I think we are talking, for the moment, about certain real events in our time—social, political, etc.—all too well known. But at any time in human history these events—wars, uprisings, pestilence, etc.—have been present. How one responds to them, or doesn't, may determine the permanence of the writing. There are certain things in our time impossible to ignore. But the way in which one responds is not predictable and may not be immediately apparent. I mean, for example, you may have an Emily Dickinson in seclusion, writing what appear to be very private poems; and on the other hand, a Whitman, very much the public voice in expression. These are two extremes, if you will, and one might say that most poets fall somewhere in between.

I'm aware of Forché's work in this regard. Some years back, in an essay/review called "Something for Our Poetry," I discussed a book of hers as well as the problem of political poetry generally. I was not, am not, entirely convinced by her efforts and the claims made for the work that has come of it. Certainly she is not the first poet among us to have, in one way or another, seized on some drastic event elsewhere in the world and adapted her poem to it, or used it to intensify what might otherwise have lacked a real substance. In such a case one can count on an immediate sympathy transferred from the event, or the place, and critical estimates tend to be clouded accordingly.

But I am skeptical of this practice of, say, flying off to El Salvador or eastern Europe, spending enough time there to soak up some of the atmosphere, the names and details, then return to the relative safety of this country and publish work that supposedly speaks for that place and its horrors. That is too easy. The real thing is not to be acquired or spoken to in this way. To someone who has lived that time and place, who knows it as part of his or her very being, and is motivated to write about it, or otherwise convert the material into art—to that person, that writer or poet, we can listen, and should lis-

INTERVIEW AND SHORT GLIMPSES

ten. But we should be alert to the difference and not praise indiscriminately the incipient self-promotion of writers who use the miseries of others to appear to have a subject, or be grounded in that subject. There is a difference, a very big difference, not always easy to define. There is, I think, such a thing as colonialism of the word, and there are literary and cultural activities that are very much a part of our colonial habit of mind. But again, one cannot establish rules. It is up to a responsible criticism to attempt the necessary distinctions.

As for my own work, I have borne witness to that which has been, in one way or another, a part of my life, whether that has meant contending with the immediate facts of existence in that early homestead life, or the political events very much present during, say, the 1960s and early '70s; or living among children, taking part in their lives; or in the case of matters not so obvious or immediate, like reflecting back on a certain phase of my life as a student of painting and sculpture. All of these elements, and others like them, can be said to form the fundamental substance by which any of us can identify our life and time, and to which we owe a certain responsibility in the accuracy of our witness and feeling as writers.

MC: Silence seems to be a component of your witnessing. Could you talk about silence and how it *voices* itself through your work?

JH: We're talking, I think, about the stilling of outside voices and distractions, of a retreat into what is basic in one's being. I think of that early life I lived, and how it required that many things be reduced to essentials. In stripping away all ornament and *talk* from my poems, I was able—and with, for a period, the example of classical Chinese poetry before me—to concentrate my writing on those essentials. But one need not retreat into the wilderness to find that stillness, or silence. And not every poet would find it suitable or nourishing. It seems to have been an instinct in me to seek it, and the rest has grown from that.

MC: So, too, your work demonstrates a certain minimalist compression, both in language and image. Has the condition of landscape in Alaska necessitated a kind of poetic distillation?

JH: I don't like the word *minimalist*, to be quite frank, and I would not apply it to myself. The compression is there, of course, and in my view ought to be there as one more element that distinguishes verse from prose.

We could say that the life I chose to live many years ago, but not necessarily the landscape, forced me to rid my writing of all ornament and excess, and concentrate what I felt and saw to a rather extreme degree. For someone who, when young, was inclined to be expansive and philosophical in his verse, this concentration was a major feat. As for the landscape, that was a factor, of course. What the land embodied and yielded, in terms of life and art, was at the center of things. Certainly, if I had chosen to settle in the desert or some other remote area, I might well have found that necessary concentration, but the poems would have been very different. What constitutes place, in the true sense of it, cannot fail to influence, at times dictate, what the writing will be, in substance and form. But many other factors were involved: the reading I was absorbed in at one time or another, the poets whose example I took to heart, whether from the classical Chinese or modern European poetry; and a certain inner disposition that seemed to require me to rid my style of all excess and get down to the bare bones of things.

MC: Let's talk about the relationship between verse and prose. You speak, in the preface to your *Collected Poems*, about the continuity between your verse and prose, and of the more inclusive term *Dichter* that the German includes in the definition of poet. How does your work comprise the activity of a *Dichter*?

JH: What I like in that word *Dichter* is what I take to be the underlying conception of what it is to be a poet—of what the art, at its highest, is or can be. It's become too easy to talk about "vision," for example, but its presence or absence may be the determining factor.

I think we are talking about the writer, the poet, as spokesman, as speaker to the people, or as prophet. The form may be, nominally, prose, as in, say, Mann's *The Magic Mountain*, or Broch's *The Sleepwalkers*. Yet the impulse, the voice, the pacing, the insight is, at times anyway, that of poetry, and the formal distinctions between verse and prose become irrelevant. We are, for the moment, in the presence of something else; a certain authority, an unmistakable mode of truth. There is, evidently, in some countries a tradition for this, in Germany, perhaps in Russia; but we, to an extent, lack it, though one might say of someone like Melville or Faulkner, that he, at times, embodied it. It's true enough, anyway, that at some point verse and prose divided, and it might be said that the novel is the form that the epic has taken in our time.

MC: In a recent public lecture you spoke of how often your essays and memoirs read like poetry; that they were conceived as sentences and paragraphs, and yet something insistent pushes their utterances into poetry. What is it that pushes language back and forth from prose to poetry, poetry to prose, or said otherwise, what is it that distinguishes poetry from prose?

JH: Other than in a strictly formal sense—that is, between verse lines and stanzas on the one hand, and sentences and paragraphs on the other—that which makes the difference between poetry and prose would be difficult to define precisely. I am aware of it as, at times in a passage of prose, a sudden focus and intensity, a shift into another voice, if only briefly. In a long story by Chekhov once I came on a passage that spoke to me immediately as poetry, in its concentration and emotional power, and I have often recited those brief phrases to myself and others as one example:

For whom do they call
and who hears them
on that plain, God only knows.
But there is a deep sadness
and lamentation in their cry,
a scent of hay and dry grass,
and belated flowers . . .

                              (from "The Steppe")

To say again, it is that sudden concentration of emotional inten-
sity, clarity of image, none of it predictable; but if we are attuned to
language we will recognize it, or so I feel. For a very long time it was
poetry as verse, as song or chant, that dominated what we have called
imaginative literature. Perhaps because of its cadence and its formal
repetitions, verse was congenial to memory at a time when few peo-
ple had books. And then the novel appeared with, say, Cervantes,
and others, and came in time—in the nineteenth century, certainly,
as much of the twentieth—to dominate the field, to be *the* major
form of literary expression. For a time, in the first half of our centu-
ry, during the days of High Modernism, both poetry and the novel
shared equally in importance. I'm speaking of that literature I've
come to know in my life as a reader and writer, and while I feel that
what I've just said is broadly true, I know also that it is easy to over-
simplify something that is more variable and complicated than we
mostly realize.

To the extent that I can refer to some of this in my own work, I
would say that I have felt the activity of writing, whether in verse or
in prose, to be part of the same essential continuity: concentrated as
verse in one instance, expansive as prose in another. I have, at times,
when reading aloud from some of my prose, felt that sudden shift or
concentration I have referred to, and which I recognize as essential-
ly poetic. A few years ago, while revising an essay called "Shadows,"
I became aware that the brief prologue to that essay was in fact a

prose poem and could stand on its own. I tried putting it into verse lines, just to see what it would look like, and I think if I had persisted in it I might have turned it into a poem in verse, using a fairly long line. But I soon realized that the sentence and paragraph form I had chosen was the right form; that what I had to say fell naturally into that prose cadence, and I left it that way.

It's interesting to consider the argument between poetry and prose in the case of a figure like Hermann Broch. Broch wrote poems in verse and often in his novels he alternated prose and verse. But he became a great writer, a true poet, only in his novels. It is significant that his grave in Connecticut is marked with a stone on which is cut this simple memorial: "Hermann Broch, Poet and Philosopher." Whoever designed that gravestone understood something essential of the man and his work.

MC: In the essay "You and I the World: Some Notes on Poetic Form," you talk about your interest in process: specifically, of the evolution of forms necessitated by the challenge of free verse. Today we see that challenge in everything from prose poetry to the New Formalism. What is the "state of the form," if you will, as we near the Second Millennium?

JH: Well, we might put it this way. On the one hand, we have a universal free verse that seems as if it might be written by anyone, and little of it having any distinctive character. To my ear, at least, it is prosy, flat and dull, and is written by people who seem not to hear the language as something to be spoken aloud, carried in memory, with its cadences, its aural spaces and silences. It is writing meant for, born of, the printed page, almost a visual product, and I have little doubt that the use of computers has contributed to this in recent years. I'm talking about the poem as printed on the page, or on the screen. It may *look* interesting, but you cannot hear it. Put this against the poem as it was composed by poets in earlier times, aloud, to be sung or chanted, and passed on in that aural form. Ezra Pound said something I find still worth thinking about: "Poetry rots when it gets too far from music." A true insight.

A related problem is that current poets have inherited a free verse model, in terms of line break and stanzaic form, without the background in traditional poetry—without a true understanding of where this "free" form came from, why it emerged, and what it meant at the time. When Pound, Eliot, Williams, etc., broke with traditional metrics they knew what they were doing, what they were departing from, in breaking, for a time at least, the hold of the pentameter. In retrospect it made sense, and especially in light of WWI, and all the social and political chaos that followed. Yet poets like Yeats and Stevens continued to write in the old forms and meters, and with outstanding success. I continue to follow Stevens in this, in a quote from his letters I have referred to a number of times:

> Poetic form, in its proper sense, is a question of what appears within the poem itself. It seems worthwhile to isolate this because it is always form in its inimical senses that destroys poetry. By inimical senses one means trivialities. By appearance within the poem itself one means the things created and existing there. . . .

I don't think anyone since has stated the problem of poetry in our time more accurately.

We need to consider also the widespread abuse of language in our time—the use of language, of speech, to persuade, to sell, to coerce and promote. Imagine the effect of this misuse on people for whom it is standard from the time they can hear, speak, or read it. There is only one effective counter to this, and that is the example of good writing, of great writing and clear speech; of speech and poetry that serves us with its honesty and accuracy, its fidelity to the truth.

MC: You've gathered your poems in a collected volume, gathered various forms of nonfiction in your most recent collection *Fables and Distances*. What's next?

JH: As long as one feels the impulse, the need to continue writing, there will always be that something next, even when, as is sometimes the case with me, one enters a period when he feels he has little new to say.

But to be more specific, I seem always to have a number of unfinished poems, pieces of writing, some begun many years before. From time to time I will return to one or two of them, find the right place at which to begin, then revise and finish it. Just recently I was able to complete a poem begun in 1971, "In the Cave at Lone Tree Meadow." Why this required so long a time I frankly do not know, but feel that the wait was worth it.

And then there are totally new things I've begun and continue to think about and work on. For me the process can be long, and fortunately I seem to have been gifted with the necessary patience for it. I also usually refrain from talking about work in progress. I sense a sort of contract with the muse, in which certain secrets are not to be given away or talked about too freely. I have in mind a sort of collected essays, combining the best of *Living Off the Country* with *Fables and Distances*, and whatever else I may write in the meantime. But for the moment I'm in no rush about it. I've thought of some short fiction, a story or two I've had in mind for many years, and perhaps another autobiographical episode. For the moment, at least, I have little to add about Alaska, though there are a few themes or subjects I may return to at some point. There are plenty of younger talents here, busy with one aspect or another of the "last frontier," and I'll leave it to them.

WILLIAM CARLOS WILLIAMS

"My Dear John Haines"

Williams Carlos Williams (1883–1963) suffered a severe stroke in the summer of 1952 and could no longer read and comment on the numerous manuscripts and packets of poems sent to him by young, aspiring writers. His wife, Florence, monitored his mail and brought to his attention only those items she believed her husband would find of interest. One of these packets came from a young poet in Alaska "which struck me as being worth calling to Bill's attention." After typing his own thoughts to John Haines, he told his wife to further caution the young poet. "Widen your scope," she cautioned in a handwritten note accompanying her husband's typewritten letter. "Don't be satisfied with being labeled regional.*"*

April 21, 1953

My dear John Haines:

I'm certainly glad you wrote and sent me your poems for by doing so you revealed the most authentic talent for verse that I have encountered in your generation. Don't let's get swelled headed about it for you may have far to go to come out a finished artist but your very lack of success in selling your verse so far is a good omen. Continue as you are going, read, read, read all the examples of the verse you admire—and some that you do *not* admire—and you'll be in another ten years, if you have what it takes to survive, top dog.

Everything about your writing is properly placed. I use the term in the same way as one speaks of a singer's voice as being well placed. That is pure accident but a fortunate accident for you. You have besides the gift of making your page come alive in every detail. This comes from the meticulous honesty of your reporting. But this would all go for nothing if you did not instinctively know what and what *not* to report. This you cannot be taught. But these are virtues of the prosist [*sic*] and of writers in general, rare but not perhaps distinguished qualities in themselves.

The thing that makes you stand out as a poet is your unaffected sense of rhythm and your intelligent sense of how to make it an organic part of your composition. That is a rare gift indeed and a still unwritten chapter of the history of verse. You have a chance to write the next chapter in the history of verse—but you're going to get kicked around a lot before you come to that eminence.

Measure is the secret of that advance how to measure your verse (without strain) so that you can control it consciously and with ease. Instinct is not enough for the master of his craft. Free verse is not enough.

Well I leave it in your hands as the best pair of hands that I have encountered in a generation, at that I may be wrong but I don't think so. At least when Flossie read me your verses at the breakfast table this morning we neither of us wanted to stop until every word on the pages had been greedily swallowed, a rare occurrence in this household.

Send your verses to *Imagi* with my recommendation that they be printed, but be careful of offending the proprieties at least while you are young (write what you want but put it aside for the moment)—there are many places to send your verse. I'll try to have Flossie make a list of them but don't expect quick success.[1] Just keep writing and use your head and your eyes and concentrate just as much as you can into every word and clause and sentence. The rest is up to you.

Sincerely yours,

W. C. Williams

---

1. In a handwritten note accompanying her husband's letter, Florence Williams provided John Haines with the address of *Imagi*, in Baltimore, along with the addresses of *The Kenyon Review*, *Poetry Chicago*, and the Golden Goose Press, in Sausalito.

ROBERT SCHULTZ

Introduction at the 92nd Street Y, November 2, 1992

John Haines began writing poetry after moving, in 1947, to Alaska, and his work is crucially marked by the experience of homesteading there for twenty-five years. He has sometimes been praised as one of our most important regionalist writers, the first to register the experience of Alaska's wilderness and frontier in English. But we should be aware of the slightly dismissive tone of the label "regionalist," and remember the formulation of William Carlos Williams, who said: "The classic is the local fully realized, words marked by a place."[1] And even Wallace Stevens, with his willfully cosmopolitan imagination, agreed when he stated: "A mythology reflects its region."

If Haines' poetry was ever *merely* regionalist, it becomes more than that with his fourth and fifth books, *Cicada* and *In a Dusty Light*. In them his style tightens and concentrates, giving it an elemental quality that allows it to be at once fiercely local and universal. In these poems Haines' lines repeatedly drive us back to what he calls, in one poem, "the straw-filled cave of beginnings." In "By the Ocean," for instance,

> The sea voice is old in our ears,
> and fire is old in the
> salt white roots of the tree.

Such moments of contact with the elemental world are prized, but just as often humans are blind to the natural verities they cannot escape. In "The Tree That Became a House," the house speaks,

1. From the 1929 essay "Kenneth Burke" in the collection *Imaginations* (New York: New Directions, 1970), p. 356.

remembering the tree it was, and measuring the distance between its human inhabitants and its own former life "with finches, wind and fog—." The spectacle of human settlement is often dispiriting. In "News from the Glacier," Haines writes:

> We are awake
> in our own desolate time—
>
> clotheslines whipping the air
> with sleeves and pockets,
> little fists of plastic bags
> beating the stony ground.

And so the present is elegy to a past of rock, tree, ice, moose, owl. And the poet's apology for what he calls "our own desolate time" is to shape poems that follow the contours of the ancient elements, seeking, paradoxically, to render in words "wordless images / the earth gives up" ("Hunger"). His task is to speak to other people the way nature speaks to him, to find words that are not only marked by a place, but are themselves the very markers, at once eloquent and mute. As he says in a later poem:

> To prayer and petition
> God speaks the simplest words:
> *sun*, *rain*, and *frost*.
>
> ("Of Michelangelo, His Question")

The ideal, for nature's poet, is to speak with that same elemental authority.

But that, of course, is beyond humans, fallen out of undivided being into language and culture. And so the dominant note in Haines' poetry is elegiac. With a glacial sense of time and its epochs, he documents our evanescence. And with his characteristic imagery of wind and ash, he often writes like a prophet out of the wilderness. Not an angry Jeremiah, but more like the world-weary poet of Ecclesiastes, he perceives vanity in the passing show of human striving. Monopolies and cartels make him see "careers in the wind, / so many tradesmen of dust" ("In the Forest Without Leaves").

But what finally lasts? Driven by this question which, like an undercurrent, gathers strength through the career, Haines' work has, since 1980, grown more meditative, taking on the character of an enquiry almost philosophic or religious. What lasts is not in nature—even the elements abide in change—but the permanent may be, in Haines' poetry, something human, after all: not things themselves, but right knowledge of them, and the equilibrium that brings. Over and over, the poems dip back to imagine a lost and possibly recoverable wholeness. In the important recent sequence, "In the Forest Without Leaves," a speaker recalls "the round and roadless vista . . . when I had myself entire."

This romance of wholeness, as much as anything else, drives Haines' poetry. It is the quest that lasts.

John Haines and Vocation

When John Haines came to my campus two years ago to do a reading, I put him up at the same local motel where we lodge all of our visiting writers. Behind the front desk when we walked into the office was the clerk, who gave Haines the keys to his room and a remote control for his TV. Haines took his keys, then picked up the remote and stared at it. "What's this?" he asked. The woman at the desk looked at him, this elderly man with gray hair and glasses who held the remote as if it were a moon rock, seeing him for the first time.

"Why, it's a remote for your TV," she said.

Haines stared some more, until the function of the plastic object in his hand clarified; then he handed it back to her. "I won't be needing *that*," he told her. Now she was the one holding the remote with a baffled expression.

It was comic, this standoff between John Haines and the motel clerk, but serious as well, underscoring the life Haines had lived apart from technology and its dependencies, and taking me back to the poet I discovered long before in a prose volume called *Living Off the Country*—one of the most significant books I read as a younger writer. Arriving on the American literary scene after years of homesteading in Alaska, years spent developing on his own as a poet, the Haines of that book asked questions about things the poetry establishment had long taken for granted. How was it possible, given the emphasis on careerism and the winning of prizes, for poets to achieve their full maturity? Was the graduate school workshop the best place for a young poet, needing solitude and his own period of gestation? Where were the ideas in contemporary American poetry? And what was one to make of the resemblance between the contemporary poem and the technological device—each a lifeless object, each replaced the next year by another, slightly altered model? Shouldn't a poem be more than a gadget like—well, like the remote for a TV? It is no wonder that John Haines' book, and some of its essays when they originally appeared, caused consternation in an establishment sure, as was the clerk in my local motel, that what it had to offer was what anyone would want to have.

But *Living Off the Country* did not offend me; I identified with it. Drawn to Haines' book after reading his early poems, I had never been to the wilderness of Alaska, but my own location of North Sutton, New Hampshire, often seemed as far outside the poetry loop as his was. My first exposure to the literary scene came in the early 1970s when, as a teacher in the English department of a small junior college in nearby New London, I perused the regional poetry magazines my office mate was then publishing in—ragged journals with names like *The Small Pond* and *The Puckerbrush Review*—finding poems that felt willed and incomplete. Once, my office mate lent me a book called *The Young American Poets*. Was it me, or were these poems, too, mostly bad? I wondered. I had nobody, really, to ask, and nobody to tell me later on, when I traveled to the Poetry Room at Dartmouth College, which of the national magazines displayed there might be the best outlets for my own poems. As it turned out, I needn't have fussed so much in making my choices. The journals to which I submitted my early poems most often rejected them; worse still, while my office mate turned out poems left and right, my own output was aggravatingly slow. I couldn't seem to find a subject that satisfied me or an approach that would lead me from one poem to the next. Raising four children and spending my summers in graduate school, I had little time for writing, in any case. My notebooks were full of poems I could not finish.

In its commentary about what poems are, the process by which they are created, and the trajectory of the true poet's development, *Living Off the Country* provided a context for my initial struggles as a writer and gave me something to strive for. Most of Haines' readers probably did not notice that just beneath the book's controversy was a set of precepts about the poet's vocation, but I did, and I heard in the voice that enunciated them a rocklike authority that I clung to. Rereading *Living Off the Country* today, I am still struck by that voice—its sense of a speaker saying what he means, and of meaning fastened deep in the page. In every line, there is the feeling of character, and I realize now that this character, evident in all the prose Haines has written since, influenced my attitude toward poetry in my formative years as much as any particular remark he made.

My first reading of *Living Off the Country* began with Haines' review, reprinted from *kayak*, of the book I had seen a short time before, *The Young American Poets*. I still remember how bracing that review was. Preparing to be told I was wrong in my negative assessment of the book, I discovered Haines and I were in agreement. Furthermore, he explained his views about the book's poets in a way that showed me the value of my own struggle with uncertainty, even honored it. The trouble is, he wrote, that few of the poets

> know what a poem is.
>
> What is needed for good poems, besides exceptional talent, is patience, and a willingness to live, if necessary, in some solitude and obscurity while one's life and talent mature, even if that takes many years. . . . People instinctively wise know this and do not attempt to force their work into the open before it is ripe. And it is just this solitude that American literary life, with its magazine pages to be filled, its reputations to be made, its prizes to be given, so easily destroys. (*Living Off the Country*, 82)

I soon learned that the subject of solitude was an important one for this poet who had spent so much time by himself in Alaska. Nearly all of the essays in *Living Off the Country* touched on the subject in some way, and each reference seemed addressed to me alone, especially the passages that linked solitude with place. For like Haines, I myself had written poems about the north—that is, northern New England—and I was increasingly involved with my own place's meaning. "I think," he said in "The Writer as Alaskan,"

> that there *is* a spirit of place, a presence asking to be expressed; and sometimes when we are lucky as writers, and quiet in a way few of us want to be anymore, a voice enters our own, becomes mingled with it, and we speak with a force and clarity not otherwise heard. (*Living Off the Country*, 19)

This way of speaking through place and for it could only result from a long and observant residence, Haines said, after which the poet might find "another place" inside himself, describing, in the end, all places. As a student of American literature, I was familiar with such ideas; in fact, I had even read the text Haines cited in his essay, D. H. Lawrence's *Studies in Classic American Literature*. But the awareness I had was still an intellectual one. Haines' real-life experience with place helped carry what my head had known into my hands and feet, the American tradition now ready for use.

In "Roots" Haines spoke of a "ferocious transience" that swirled around the poet, making rootedness the more necessary. The essay's model was Robinson Jeffers, a poet who combined his life with his vocation, building his own house on the shoreline of Carmel, California, stone by stone in the same deliberate way he made his poems, with their own hold on place. Without some similar means of "standing aside," Haines warned, poets would only write verse that imitated the quick change and confusion of our technological society. Elsewhere, he spoke about the value of a literary tradition in providing steadiness and constancy. Put aside the fashion of graduate school poems, he implied in his essay "The Hole in the Bucket," recommending that poets learn from past writers how to combine the contemporary with the ancient:

Innovations in style, strange, disordered syntax, unusual images, idiomatic explosions—these soon pass, or are means to an end. Only that remains which touches us in our deepest, most enduring self. Behind every word is the memory of another, spoken a thousand times; in the intonation of the voice, in the rise and fall of the syllables, memory does its work and reconciles the poet and the reader to a world difficult and strange. (*Living Off the Country*, 71)

As he had in his description of place's influence on the poet, Haines referred in this passage to a deeper and clearer way of speaking in poetry. Surely no one has expressed more eloquently the value of the literary past to the poet.

In another essay, "Anthologies and Second Thoughts," John Haines wrote a paragraph that still bears the signs of my excited discovery more than fifteen years ago, its words underlined and surrounded by stars. The paragraph had special value, I see now, because it put into one place all the advice to young poets I had found scattered throughout Haines' book.

[Poets] . . . must find ways to be still in themselves, to listen and to silence the noise about and within them. Forget, if you can, about success in the market, ambition, career—all that is merely in the way. Read as much as you can, learn as much as you can, see as much as you can. Read the earth around you, as well as books. Don't be content to imitate your contemporaries and have their approval. Seek out the poets who exemplify the real tradition, one that goes back thousands of years, surviving every disaster. And keep to yourself; don't expect schools to do much for you; lasting poems are not likely to be written in a graduate seminar. Remember that all of our great poets in the past rose by their own efforts out of their own environment. (*Living Off the Country*, 94–95)

As meaningful as this advice was to me at a crucial time in my development, I now understand that it is timeless, relevant to young poets or older ones anytime, anywhere.

One of the things I anticipated most about John Haines' visit to my college in Maine two autumns ago was the chance to let him know how much his poems and *Living Off the Country* had meant to me and still meant, all those years later. In fact, this was what I told him shortly after I picked him up from a nearby campus where he'd given a reading the night before, adding my admiration for his new book of essays, *Fables and Distances*. For the rest of our trip, Haines did not, like other visiting poets, talk about the literary scene. He was interested in the place he had come to. How early did it snow? he wanted to know. What kinds of deciduous trees grew here? Where were the state's mountains located? When we arrived in Farmington—on our way to the local motel where Haines would ask still another question, about a TV remote—I stopped in the parking lot outside my campus building, leaving him in the car while I went inside to get a handout of his poems my classes had been studying. To my surprise, he wasn't in the car on my return, or anywhere around it. Then I spotted him exploring a nearby wooded area, exactly where I should have predicted he'd be: by himself, away from the noise of arriving and departing cars, reading the earth.

HELEN FROST

A Gas Mantle Lights the Darkness

The Stars, The Snow, The Fire is subtitled "Twenty-Five Years in the Northern Wilderness" and that is a modest claim. The time spanned within the memoir goes back forty-two years, to 1947. And the book includes stories told by men who were old-timers when Haines was a young man learning to survive his first Alaskan winter, making the historical scope of the book even greater.

But the book is not written as a chronological history, and its richness derives in great part from that fact. The book ranges over the years, as memory does, dipping in for a story of a man whose cabin burns down in the middle of a winter night, and the people who receive him hours later and thaw his frozen legs; or a detailed description of the life surrounding traplines; going on and returning later to a tale of a probable murder, which requires our understanding of the passions which traplines can arouse.

We travel over the years with the author, appreciating the dramatic moments and the meditative silences, and even ranging forward, in a dreamlike way toward a time when the landscape may be quite different, as in this passage:

> Sometimes there may come to us in a depleted world, the old hunter's dream of plenty. The rich country, full of game, fish and fur, bountiful as it once was. The bear, the moose, and the caribou. The woods are thick with rabbits; the marten crossing and recrossing, their paired tracks always going somewhere in the snow under the dark spruces. And carefully, one foot before the other, the round, walking track of the lynx: they never seem to hurry. Beaver in the ponds, a

goshawk beating the late winter thickets like a harrying ghost; and now and then the vague menace of a wolf passing through.

This, or its sometime shadow: the country dead, and nothing to see in the snow. Famine, and the great dream-passing.

The landscape of the book is painted throughout with this sort of light and contrasting shadow—a gas mantle lighting the shadows of a cabin, or the memory of a youthful adventure lighting the face of an old man, or the excitement of trapping animals clouded by the precise knowledge of their dying.

Because such knowledge is faced head-on, and never sentimentalized or rationalized, there will certainly be some readers who will find it objectionable. But I think most readers will appreciate the author's honesty in describing the world we share with animals not only in terms of the tender moments (there are plenty), but also when "It is rank, it smells of blood and killed meat, is compounded of fear, of danger and delight in unequal measure."

Though almost entirely masculine, the book is not antifeminist. Women were simply not often present in the times and places central to the life described here. But women readers will not feel excluded as an audience. The tales of encounters with bears, the description of wolves "singing" across the Tanana River, the thoughtful discussion of the presence and absence of bats—all this will draw in readers of any age and gender, whether or not they have ever been to Alaska, and hold them from the first page to the last.

The author's love for his subject—the land, the people, and the time he has known them, as well as the elements named in the title— is large and expansive. The detail and precision of his language, in this prose as in his poetry, brings to us the gift of a life lived with integrity and observed with sensitivity. The book will be remembered as Haines remembers people he has known through the years in Alaska: "When I think of them now, it is of something hugely tender and forgiving, akin to a healing thingness in the world that assures the soil of its grasses, the earth of its sun."

I hope for this book a wide readership to carry its memories and message toward whatever future awaits the world.

DONALD HALL

Stony John Haines

Winter News appeared in 1966 out of the heroic first decade of the Wesleyan University Press's poetry series. Many people noticed. When, in 1982, John Haines collected *News from the Glacier: Selected Poems, 1960–1980*, it did not receive enough attention. His new collection,[1] elegantly designed and produced by Story Line Press in Oregon, begins its life by winning a Western States Book Award; maybe people will notice again.

Haines writes lines that look on the page like the poem of our moment—visually or superficially common in the number of syllables in the line, in the number of lines in a poem. But Haines differs from others in the care of his language. He writes with a hard instrument on a hard surface: no disposable verses here. For the most part this book assembles sequences, an older man's accrual of experience and vision. In *New Poems*, take these lines from the fifth part of "Rain Country" (separately issued by Mad River Press):

> Remembering, fitting names
> to a rain-soaked map:
> Gold Run, Minton, Tenderfoot,
> McCoy. Here Melvin killed
> his grizzly, there Wilkins
> built his forge. All
> that we knew, and everything
> but for me forgotten.

1. That collection is *New Poems: 1980–1988* (Brownsville, OR: Story Line Press, 1990).

If there is someone who doesn't yet know: John Haines homesteaded for many years in Alaska; I had hoped to review him without mentioning Alaska.

The poem above, for anyone familiar with Haines, draws familiar water. Better to show his quality of care and scrupulosity, his stone-incising, by quoting him on matters we do not always associate with his name. Here's the first part of "Days of Edward Hopper."

> These are the houses that stand,
> broken and entered; these
> are the walls written by rain,
> the sparrow arches, the linear
> stain of all that will one day
> turn to smoke in the mind.
>
> Brick dust was their pigment,
> mortar and the grit of brownstone
> ground underfoot, plaster
> flaked to the purity of snow.
>
> And out of these we entered
> the glass arrangements of wind,
> became the history of sunlit,
> transient rooms, domestic shades;
> a substance volatile, so thin
> the light of stations burning
> at the roadside consumed us . . .
>
> And out of that, the stillness.

Note, please, how beautifully Haines paces his sentences over the line-breaks, varying the speed of the turn—drawing out a long *these*; flipping quickly past *thin*—and note, above all, the stony phrase-making that presents us, durably visible, "the glass arrangements of wind . . . ".

PART THREE
Alaska

WENDELL BERRY

There is a place you can go

There is a place you can go
where you are quiet,
a place of water and the light

on the water. Trees are there,
leaves, and the light
on leaves moved by air.

Birds, singing, move
among leaves, in leaf shadow.
After many years you have come

to no thought of these,
but they are themselves
your thoughts. There seems to be

little to say, less and less.
Here they are. Here you are.
Here as though gone.

None of us stays, but in the hush
where each leaf in the speech
of leaves is a sufficient syllable

the passing light finds out
surpassing freedom of its way.

I Travel with John Haines in Alaska

I stand on Denali Road at midnight so cold
the black breaks off in pieces, shattering
when hitting the ground,
chimes of broken ice.

A voice beside me, deep as the dark surrounding
a viola bow tuning its strings,
rasp the ice crystals away
from our cold feet

while making me smile
when resonating the differences
of cousins, cabbage and cauliflower,
and which he'd rather be

stirring the camp fire
watching the flames light the lanterns
hanging beneath horns exploding the brush
circling us

past the old man sitting in a chair
holding his rusty rifle, smiling a memory
hearing the viola declare
it's not good to be poor

Vera Thompson, breathing dirt
in the cemetery at Eagle, Alaska.
It could be me.
John Haines left me there.

JAMES HOPKINS

self-portrait

fifty miles north of fairbanks
the asphalt gives out
the gravel begins
and there's six hundred miles to go.

here's where you start to see
yourself from above—
tiny red pickup in a sea of fir,
the upper left corner of the world.

and a hundred miles later
it's the arctic circle
and even the a.m. radio dies.
only satellites peeking out from the lid of the sky,

and then wide-eyed but groggy at 1 a.m.
you slog into coldfoot for gas—
brand new boots ankle-deep in mud
as soon as you jump from the cab.

grilled cheese for 5 bucks
in a room full of stares,
a john haines paperback safe and dry
inside your gore-tex jacket.

here the red-eyed waitress
hates them bastards in washington,

will never, she swears,
go back to america.

by 3 a.m.
the road straightens out—
the dodge casting shadow
but the headlights still a habit.

here's where you wonder
about tire irons and water,
blink back grizzly and caribou,
sing crazy about summer.

a few fir trees scraping antlers
and fish full of river,
whole mountains like dogs
howling at the light.

and no sound but the truck
fighting through gravel—
an eye opening up for you
ghosting through night.

then here's where you stop
at the edge of the tundra.
the engine still running,
the door open wide.

you're outside in the cold
blowing on fingers,
setting camera on granite
with its tiny red light.

you've taken off running
like some drunken astronaut,
across the mossy planet
rising and sinking.

running and falling
and running and falling,
waiting for something
like the whole thing to blink.

GREGORY ORFALEA

A Walk in the Snow

John Haines was my teacher at the University of Alaska in the fall of 1972 and the spring of 1973. It was his first university class. It was also, unfortunately for UA and John, his last one there. He had only recently left his twenty-year subsistence life as a hunter, trapper, and fisherman at the homestead at Milepost 68 on the Alaska-Canada Highway, known in that stretch as the Richardson Highway. He spoke very low and appeared to mumble or grunt at times, the result, perhaps, of a hearing loss in his homestead days. We students didn't quite know what to make of him, though we knew we were in the presence of someone who had already lived an extraordinary life, one few if any would live again, and that he had brought back from his life in the northern woods some precious poetry. So we strained our ears and listened, especially for even the remotest indication that our work might be worthy.

How crass we were! It was said at our get-togethers in various cabins around Fairbanks that if John Haines made a grunt you were making progress. One of his classic indications of dismissal was, "There's a poem in there somewhere." On the other hand, if said with a more favorable lilt, that very same phrase might portend favor. As I say, we all cupped our ears.

Why I ended up in Alaska to do graduate study in writing is still not entirely clear to me. I had always had a fascination with the north woods, even as a boy in California, and the cabin our family had in the lower Sierra Nevadas was more magnetic to me than the beach. I was also revved up on Jack London and a TV show called *Sergeant Preston of the Yukon*. There had been a fair amount of wanderlust in our tribe; my two immigrant grandmothers had been mountain women in Lebanon. So though there was plenty of heat in my background, there was also this tradition of planting yourself in a cold, snowy spot in that heat. A good temperature to write at, I might add.

In truth, I was rejected by the workshop at the University of Iowa, a thing not entirely inauspicious. In those days, there were only seven Master of Fine Arts (MFA) writing programs in the whole country (about the right amount, now that I think of it—there must be well over a hundred now) and Alaska was my backup. After doing time on a newspaper writing obituaries just after graduating from Georgetown, I think it is a fair thing to say that I was burnt out on death. Tired of the Capital. Finished with the bottomless tragedy of Vietnam and the pomposities of the protest era, too. Politics in toto frosted me at that point (funny how these things come full circle— they frost me now, too). I may be one of the few people ever to have gone to Alaska to warm up.

William Stafford was poet-in-residence at the Library of Congress in 1971, and during an interview for my Georgetown literary magazine we shared our fascination with the Far North. That is when Stafford told me about John Haines coming out of the woods to teach. It must have stuck in my mind.

It snowed the first week of September when I arrived in Fairbanks. At first I lived in one of the college dorms, but when the opportunity came up to rent a cabin at 12 1/2-mile Nenana Highway for $100 a month, I took it. It was pretty good-sized as cabins went in those days—it had two rooms and a sauna stained brownish red with the blood of a slaughtered moose. It also had electricity, but no running water, and soon I had the inimitable experience of hustling to an outhouse at 50 below zero. My landlord, an odd bug who had left a crossbow under the bed, was wintering in Florida, so I pretty much had the run of the roost. The "roost" was set right on top of a hill with a view to the Alaska range, two hundred miles to the south. On a clear day, I could make out Mt. Foraker.

For about a week, I had a roommate who used to shoot his rifle out the cabin's front door, at what I am not certain. He might have been trying to bag a snowshoe hare or even a ptarmigan, but more likely he was just pumping away. His shells would land in my type-writer. Thank God he was soon gone back to the dorm in town, and I was alone out there on that hill—excited half the time, terrified the rest. The nearest human being was a mile away, Fairbanks itself 12 miles off. It was a great place to begin the life of a writer, and to commence reading *Winter News*.

I must admit at first I thought—with the arrogance of the young—that John Haines' haunting volume of poetry about life as a homesteader in the far north was too simple. I was not alone. One in our workshop dubbed it *Winter Snooze*. In the late sixties and early seventies, the bravado, playfulness, and linguistic boldness of poets such as Ferlinghetti, Ginsberg, and Neruda held sway over young, would-be poets. We credited excess, thinking, as Blake, it would lead to wisdom. Haines was entirely other. His poetry made that of William Carlos Williams, his father imagist, look arcane. But over time, *Winter News* sank in. Up on that hill I found, for example, I had memorized, without trying, "Poem of the Forgotten," that began "I came to this place, / a young man green and lonely," and ended

> and awoke
> in the first snow of autumn
> filled with silence.

Many mornings I awoke in the dark above Ester and its abandoned gold mine, and the silence I had once thought simplistic was now awe-full. In short, I think I was living in my own limited way a bit of the life Haines lived for many years, and in doing so came to appreciate the shuddering beauty and pathos of his voice.

We had an interesting bunch up in Fairbanks in those days, from all ends of the compass. Poet Bob Hedin had come newly wed with his beautiful and spunky wife Carolyn from southern Minnesota, likewise nonfiction writer John Hildebrand from Detroit. The three of us shared an office as the graduate teaching assistants of the place, and we became fast friends and have remained so for over a quarter century. We were constantly jibing each other, wiping out whole literary traditions in a word, poking fun at the bizarre characters in our bizarre department and our fate to get a graduate degree out in the frozen middle of nowhere (Hedin once said, apocryphally, our diplomas would be "hollows in the wind"). Hildebrand was nicknamed "Duke," as he liked to hunt and fish like his idol, Hemingway. In fact, I helped him build his cabin near Healy one summer, a gorgeous spot near a creek in the Alaska Range that ultimately repelled his first wife into leaving ("There's nothing to do here"), catalyzing Hildebrand's classic, heart-rending account of his solo journey to understand what became of his own personal—and in a sense, our shared—dream of the Far North: *Reading the River: A Journey Down the Yukon*. Hedin was dubbed "the Preacher" for his dour manner and rapier-like judgments. In fact, he possessed one of the best senses of humor I have ever come across. He was also the most mature writer of our gang and the first to land a book, *Snow Country*, a complete illumination that meant a great deal to us and which owes something to John Haines.

Among other characters in our workshop were Gordon Emmanuel Massman from Corpus Christi, Texas, who hauled north with a sheaf of ballads about somebody named Tommy (not the rock opera) and new wife (also Carolyn) from whom he would try and run away only to nearly freeze to death before hitchhiking back to his heater; Lee Leonard, who was writing a northern version of William Gass' story, "In the Heart of the Heart of the Country"; the brother of a published poet, Leon Stokesbury (a true misfortune—there is almost no history of brother poets anywhere on the planet jointly succeeding); Jon "Godball" Lyman from Boston, so nicknamed because there was absolutely nothing this man had not read, and he found a tradition—very generously, in my opinion—for just about everything we spewed forth; lastly, there was J.J., the only woman in our small workshop, whose face resembled a blanched kewpie doll's, and whose poetry, if I recall correctly, was either minimal or minimalist. Of the six or seven of us who secured the graduate degree, four went on to publish several books each, a percentage, I'd wager, that would stand up to Iowa. The outriders had done fair enough, under the tutelage of one grand outrider.

And this brings me back to our subject. John Haines did some interesting things in that workshop, things it took me a while to appreciate. He was convinced American poetry suffered from myopia, and he had us translating European and Latin American poets, and imitating them to some extent. I remember choosing to do Alexander Blok's poem which begins "Midnight. Streetlamp. Carriage stop. Drugstore." He also had us studying American Indian verse. But perhaps the biggest effect he had on all of us was the series of lectures that became his landmark essay, "The Hole in the Bucket," which starts out, "American poetry lacks ideas." It made us do an intellectual double-take at both the Beats and the dry crusts in the Academy, as well as at *Winter News*. It challenged us to be bolder in our thinking in poems, and to embrace a wider universe in general—of politics, history, anthropology, geology, etc.—than poets were taught to embrace at that time. In those days it was image, image, image. But Haines was beginning to challenge his own mentor, William Carlos Williams, who pronounced "No ideas, but in things." I think Haines had seen more things, more cold things, than an American poet had ever imagined. He was beginning to come "out of the woods of self" himself and he was asking us to do the same. This outward reach was not always successful (some of the poems in *The Stone Harp*, the volume published at the time, came off as too polemical). But it was an interesting admonition from someone who had plumbed solitude about as far down as a man could. As anyone who takes even a cursory look at his work, he is no romanticist of nature. In shooing us toward life in our work, it was as if he were warding us off from too-long a stare at the abyss, a stare, I hazard, he never completely shook. ("The Abyss" took on deified proportions up there, as did "The Dark," a phrase that appeared in the poems of someone named Brower no less than fifty-nine times.) For Haines, the stare later blossomed into the complex and fearful meditations on a crystal skull, a forest without leaves, and Edward Hopper that won him overdue awards, for *New Poems*. They were new in that they were long, intricate, and mental, but the stare was old, older even, than our old teacher and the earth he loved, and therein the terror.

John Haines had an effect on me as a writer in that he steered me toward the authentic, raw experience, plain (and not so plain) honesty with its attendant risks, patient evocation of the best detail, rather than ten close hits—and away from the crowd of my youth's love of staginess, self-dramatization, and verbal wildness. He knew if you were going to capture the real wild, you were going to have to underplay it. Thus it was that my natural inclination to elaborate, to extend, was tempered by this man's cold water.

His encounter with the Other in poems affected me perhaps more than anything else. I can think of no poem set in nature simultaneously more Grecian and Christian than "House of the Injured." Its agon is breathtaking. His great concern for what will abide (not much) and what will pass away in our civilization owes a lot to Cavafy and Shelley, perhaps, and unique in our poetry he combines an intense personal voice stripped of artifice with almost tribal authority. It can be chilling. But it can also be sad and touching as in "Rain Country." Haines also gave us all a strong example, an extreme one certainly, of writing done for the sheer pull of it, the courage of a vocation, rather than a career. Above all, he was against synthetic verse, such as that of the so-called New York School. But, frankly, his personal life was a walking cautionary tale.

When I think of John I think of the tremendous cost of a life of poetry. I don't mean one that is commonly lived—the brandied life of university tenure—but the life of an American given over to poetry alone. For by temperament or circumstance—little family or occupational supports—this has been his lot. I can think of very few American writers who have carried that steep a loneliness and isolation: Edgar Allan Poe, certainly, Thoreau to some extent. (Russian poets of the Silver Age, such as Fyodor Sologub, come to mind, as does the Norwegian Edvard Munch, though his poetry came forth on a canvas.) These put unique pressures on the man and on his friends. Over the years I remember several encounters where these pressures surfaced.

In my cabin in Fairbanks one night, after a dinner I had cooked for him, the subject turned to women. At one point, John just looked up and shook his head, "I fucked it all up." He was speaking specifically of his failed second marriage to Jo, the painter, with whom he had lived at the homestead, but I think he meant more than that. He may have been talking about a complete alienation from the future. Poets are manifestly creatures of the present; the future exists for them primarily as a concept, not a practical reality. And with one wedded so exclusively to poetry as John, it was no surprise, perhaps, that the future would present such peril when it became present.

Sometime later, in Pacific Grove, California, my sister and I stopped off and visited John and his third wife, Jane. There was a stilted formalism between the two—it was clear they were no longer close. I recall John sitting in a shaft of late sunlight, paging through a book. This was to be the one house in his life where there were children—not his, but loved. I think that was a very hard house to leave. Through the years, John would remember that visit and always inquire about my sister, whose mind was just beginning to go at that time.

After we had lost touch for some years, he resurfaced, coming in 1991 to teach in Washington, DC, where I had started a family and was working in the government. At first, I found him to be in bad humor—once at dinner he thrust a round wicker basket at my wife and demanded, "Anymore bread here?" On another occasion, as I was chopping wood out back, he spoke out of a deathly depression, and I begged him no, saying (selfishly perhaps) one person subtracting herself from a life was plenty, thank you. I also talked him into getting rid of his gun.

Though guarded at first, over time we warmed to him, and he to us. I recall with great pride our second son, Andrew, ably reading poems of Robert Frost at age nine to a group of neighbors huddled around the fireplace on a snowy night, with John Haines in the rocker rocking approvingly. It was a scene he often recalled to me with pleasure. I remember him helping to clear the heavy snow of '96 in front of our house. After a while he took to cooking a delicious frittata each visit to our culinary expert eldest son Matthew's approval. We'd meet at Roma's on Connecticut Avenue, where they used to mash grapes with their feet. We took walks together in Meridian Park, with its statues of Joan of Arc and Dante. He drew close to our third son, Luke, who has learning disabilities. He gave me a boosting quote when, at last, my first book of poems was published, and took an avid interest in my World War II history, *Messengers of the Lost Battalion*. He has been a steady friend and correspondent for many years now, showing special concern during a hard time when I was out of work due to a government layoff.

As there are a couple of hermits in my family, I have studied hermits. It is commonly thought that hermits are hard, antisocial, cold folk. My brother, however, startled me once with an interpretation of an uncle of ours who surfaces about once every ten years. He said he thought that what makes a human being withdraw from normal human contact is not hardness, but softness. In short, a hermit may be one who feels too much, rather than too little. He is someone who cannot deal with the quotidian disagreements, emotions of all kinds, and daily humiliations of living and working in society and so pass-

ALASKA

es up the benefits, as well. This wisdom may or may not obtain with John Haines. We know that solitude is a hydra-headed thing, that it is positive when one is at relative peace with oneself, and negative when one is not. I have a strong hunch that a stone of solitude was embedded in John before he ever went to Alaska. If anything, Alaska provided a more reliable companionship—at least for a time—than he appears to have known in the Lower Forty-Eight, a community of quirky isolates he describes with such devotion and power in the book I think will last longer than any, his memoir *The Stars, The Snow, The Fire*. That community died off, for the most part, and John's agonizingly slow departure from Alaska may have come from his refusal to admit that fact. These days, John's need for and interest in others—from his various outposts—has been made manifest to me.

But what I remember best and fondest of our encounters was a walk in the snow in Fairbanks twenty-six years ago. I had hosted the University of Alaska workshop to my cabin for a dinner of grape leaves cooked on my wood-burning stove. In attendance, too, were John Haines and our guest-of-honor, William Stafford. Stafford and Haines—so different in their fates, personalities, and poems—were friends along the poetic northern trail, Stafford in Oregon and Haines in Alaska. Stafford was something of a spiritual vagabond, and took a keen interest in the real vagabond that Haines was. In turn, Haines clearly envied Stafford's settled family and university life, writing about the Bard of Lake Oswego in "The Whale in the Blue Washing Machine." Stafford was a conscientious objector in World War II, while Haines served in the Pacific with the Navy. Yet they unmistakably shared some themes: the relentlessness of fate, the grim beauty of nature, life's stubborn limits against which the heart beats, often senselessly, a feel for the underdog, genetic, societal, or otherwise. Death. They shared a fascination with death, though Stafford had a way of dancing with or away from it that Haines did not. (Yet Haines has outlived Stafford, who was felled by an abrupt heart attack in 1993.)

That night in January 1973, it snowed incessantly. I had antici-
pated this and had asked a plower in town to come out that night
and plow the steep road up from the highway to the cabin, a road
down which I often cross-country skied and tumbled to get to school
and work. After the last drink was drunk and the last dance to Zorba
the Greek music in bunny boots was kicked, people began to leave
and it was evident that my plow man hadn't made a dent in that
snow. There must have been at least a foot of snow that night added
to what was already there, and he just kept slipping on my slope.
Someone had been smart, however, and parked all the way down on
the highway, about a mile walk. I was given the keys to that car. We
were most concerned for Stafford, and both he and Haines looked at
me and said, "Let's walk it."

So there I was, twenty-two years old, in a silent crunch downhill
between two literary lanterns just shy of the Arctic Circle. I listened
to their heavy breathing and watched it turn mortal. Along the way
we spotted a snow ptarmigan lift off into the dark, drawing a col-
lective "Ah!" from two veterans of beauty—and its cost—and one
neophyte. For what else is poetry but the record of the fallout of
beauty, as well as the precious moments before the Fall? That sad
duet of the Human and Time.

Haines' beard filled with ice and Stafford's lips, cheeks, and nose
turned purplish with cold. I don't recall either of them saying any-
thing profound, just that each of us stumbled some, but not much,
and that my breath visibly intertwined with my teachers' for a few
seconds forming a triadic question mark before the stars asserted
themselves.

I must say I felt called, well-guarded, at the brink of this per-
ishable writing life. We stared into the difficult imperishable. No
surprise like Stafford and Haines I was a late bloomer, publishing
my first book at thirty-eight (Stafford's was done at forty-six,
Haines' at forty-two). They were telling me: "Don't wait for Fate, or
the plow man. Descend! Descend in the cold!"

I walked back up the hill I had grown to know well. How could I know Hildebrand would end up happy the second time around in a small Wisconsin town, Hedin down a longer private road back home in Minnesota than he had been on in Alaska, Massman somewhere in Colorado, and I in the place both Haines and I had fled long ago, lodged with the luck of a beautiful family in a warm neighborhood in the false Capital. All I knew was I was alone after a great party and walk and had a hill to carry. I had entrusted the keys and road to Haines, who drove Stafford back to town. Stafford knew town. Haines knew the road.

JODY BOLZ

A Figure in the Landscape

When John Haines published his first book of poems, *Winter News*, in 1966, there was something new in the world of American poetry: a book with its own weather, each page a footprint filling with snow. It was wondrous and eerie, a vision of "a country," to use his own words, "both specific and ideal." Here was the Richardson homestead outside of Fairbanks—forest, tundra, river. And here was a figure in the landscape, willing to attend to it fully. Here was sunlight, and here too was dread—of predator or ice storm or starvation, the face of God—a dread known for millennia in the wild, not the toneless dread we feel now, well fed and sheltered.

For a reader, it was an imagined landscape, a dreamscape. Still, the poems left me feeling homesick. I read *Winter News* in 1974 when I was living in Wyoming at the edge of another great wilderness, trying to find a "country" of my own. I was twenty-five years old. My friend Pam Rich, a conservationist who'd gone to college in Alaska, gave me the book, knowing I wrote poetry. I picked it up with casual interest and opened to "Poem of the Forgotten":

> Well quit of the world,
> I framed a house of moss and timber,
> called it a home,
> and sat in the warm evenings
> singing to myself as a man sings
> when he knows there is no one to hear.

I kept reading, blindsided by the beauty of this book, this wilderness. I ordered more copies from the local bookstore and sent the news east to family and friends, eager to share the discovery.

A few years later, I was working in Washington, DC, as a writer and editor for The Wilderness Society. The Alaska lands campaign (the congressional effort to protect 100 million acres of Alaskan wilderness under the terms of the Alaska Native Claims Settlement Act) was in full swing, and we were giving the last frontier as much coverage as we could. In 1978, I contacted John Haines, whom I'd never met, to ask if we could publish some of his poems about Alaska in a double issue of our magazine, *The Living Wilderness*. He said he didn't have any unpublished poems for us just then, but he'd been writing some essays. Would we like to see them? I wrote back to say we'd look forward to seeing whatever he could send—but the truth is, I was disappointed.

Funny to look back at it now: it was something like asking William Blake for a print and having him mention he wrote verse as well. (*Well, I suppose we can take a look. . . .*) John sent me an essay that was clearly another kind of poetry, a piece called "Moments and Journeys." We published it and asked for more. Not long after that, he came to Washington for a visit, and we met. My ex-husband Hugh Phibbs and I spent the day with John at the National Gallery of Art looking at David Smith's sculptures and other exhibits. John's training as a visual artist, which I hadn't known about until that day, animated his conversation with Hugh, a painter himself. Afterward, we went out for soup and beer at a pub nearby with some local writers who admired John's work. I remember trying to reconcile my image of the person across the table—a sophisticate, an aesthete, a trim man in a sweater who disdained chilled beer and national politics—with the solitary figure I'd confronted in the poems and essays. Even John's voice, sometimes stern on the telephone, almost curmudgeonly, seemed different now—tempered by a wry raised brow, an ironic smile. When he laughed, I was startled by the careless whoop, the head thrown back. Maybe he wasn't entirely at ease with us, maybe he was used to being alone or being with one loved person. Still, he was having a pretty good time. What had I expected?

During the next few years, our correspondence, which had been established around details of editing and publication (I was able to publish another of his essays in the early '80s once I moved over to the Nature Conservancy), grew into a fuller exchange about our lives and our writing. We were slouching toward a friendship despite what divided us—the twenty-five years between my age and his, the contrast between the clamor of my home life (I was remarried, raising children) and the often-troubled stillness of his, the conflict between my why-choose attitude about art and life and his early conviction that sacrifices must be made.

In 1991 John was selected as the Jenny McKean Moore Writer in Washington, a visiting position at George Washington University, where I'd been teaching part-time for ten years. By then I'd left conservation journalism, although I'd kept up with John. His adjustment to city life was difficult, even harrowing during the first few months—a psychological jolt compounded by the fact that his homestead north of Fairbanks, the wilderness he'd explored and mapped with a lifetime of writing, was up for sale by its present owner. It struck me as ironic, even heartbreaking, that the homestead might be razed or transformed or subdivided that very fall, just as John's memoir, *The Stars, The Snow, The Fire,* was being widely read, making that landscape vivid and necessary to a new generation of readers.[1]

John had left Alaska, but he couldn't cut himself loose. He missed it and dismissed it, unable to imagine himself there or *not* there. During the year he lived in Washington, once he'd recovered from his sense of dislocation enough to joke about it, he boasted he'd told strangers that the wilderness imagery in his books was pure fantasy—that he'd spent his life driving cabs in Manhattan. I don't know that he really tried to fool anyone, but this lie was semi-serious. He resented being categorized as a nature poet, a wilderness

---

1. Even now, after years of negotiations, the future of this historic site is in question, though there's reason to hope it will be preserved.

essayist, a recluse, an animist priest, even though he *did* (and does) see himself as an Alaskan writer: as Alaska's writer.

It's true, of course, that the far North wasn't and isn't John Haines' only subject. He's written about literature and culture generally and specifically; he's written about his life, his migratory childhood, his youth, his forays into wilderness outside of Alaska; he's made translations, written reviews. Yes, it's true, of course, that he's been interested in a multitude of topics, practical and intellectual, and that he has produced a complex body of work. But he has claimed his territory in Alaska with his books as surely as Thoreau claimed Walden Pond. He wrote in an essay called "The Writer as Alaskan":

> The homestead at Richardson provided a place of departure from which I might go out into the world forearmed. On the evidence of my own experience, I believe that one of the most important metaphors of our time is the journey out of wilderness into culture, into the forms of our complicated and divided age, with its intense confusions and deceptions. (*Living Off the Country*, 13)

In his poems and in his essays, John has registered the spirit of wilderness with painstaking integrity and patience. He has been a student of changing light and freezing rivers, a "scholar of snow." However often he moves, his address as a writer will always be Mile 68, Richardson Highway, the loneliest address in American letters.

The Stars, The Snow, The Fire ends with a short narrative called "Richardson: The Dream." Here is an excerpt that includes the final sentences:

> The figure of a man approaches, walking west on the road, toward Richardson. . . . His face is hidden within the hood of his parka. A stranger, and yet he knows his way. . . .

He mounts the open porch [of a roadhouse], kicking snow from the steps. He stands before a door, he knocks and listens. There is no sound in answer; no dog barks, no light comes on within. . . .

The man stands on the porch and listens. The rough and peeling signboard creaks on its wires overhead. There is no other sound but the wind, quiet with snow in the forest. No stars can be seen, there are no lights anywhere in the distance. The entire landscape seems dark and empty, the vast Interior a place of snow and silence.

The man turns away, pulling his parka hood around him. He walks again on the road in the direction he came from, into the wind, toward Tenderfoot Hill. He disappears in the darkness. Snow closes around him, filling his tracks as he goes. (*The Stars, The Snow, The Fire*, 181–182)

This passage spooks me each time I reread it, conjuring a shadow I sensed years ago in *Winter News*. John may know who the hooded figure is—it was his dream—but I have no interest in asking him. I think I recognize the stranger who knows the way: the *reader* who has entered this stark, sacred landscape and means, somehow, to stay. Wasn't that what blindsided me about John's work from the start? Wasn't that what made the poems urgent and exciting? I'd become a person on the threshold of a dream, trying to go home to a place I'd never seen.

SHEILA NICKERSON

Listening at the Table of Silence

Much will continue to be written about the poetry of John Haines—
its symbolism and its significance in regard to sense of place.

What I would like to record is this: One morning, while John
sat at breakfast in our house in Juneau, our cat brought him a vole.
Alexander is a discerning and elegant Abyssinian. Now twelve, he
has never before or since performed such a service. He sensed in John
a being who lives, like him, in direct connection with the natural
world. He wanted to acknowledge and honor that connection.

Although I lived in Alaska for many of the years John was here,
I never visited him at Winter News Cabin at Mile 68 on the
Richardson Highway, nor in Fairbanks. I saw him on occasion in
Anchorage and many times here in my house and elsewhere in the
world.

On a spring day in 1986, John joined my husband, Martin, and
me while we were visiting our son Tom at Berkeley. Tom, a fresh-
man, mentioned that he was taking a course—somewhat by accident
of difficult registration procedures—on Babylonian Legends and
Myths and had been studying the Gilgamesh epic. John knew
Gilgamesh, of course. He was able to enter into a conversation with
Tom that I was blocked from joining by ignorance.

Once we were all together in England. John came to visit us at
my mother-in-law's cottage in Woodborough, a hamlet in Wiltshire.
John slept on a small couch in the living room and was awakened by
the children, to whom he spoke most kindly. We visited Aunt Lucy
Judd at her house near Salisbury, and there John helped plant some
trees on the banks of the little river which is a branch of the Avon.
We went to Stonehenge. That was in 1977, in the days when it was

still possible to climb on the stones. Our three children did. Walking away from the monoliths in the late light of a summer afternoon, we stopped, and looked back. Mostly, we looked at John, in awe. He would make the definitive statement, and we would all understand the mystery. After some silence, he said: "Big stones."

Just as, at Poulsbo, Washington, while we gazed out at the enormous tideflats, he said, "Big mud." John wasn't going to make life easy for us.

And once, even earlier, when John looked at some poems I had written, he said, "These seem to have been written in a hurry." How right he was. He was supportive—he always has been—but he wasn't going to let me get away with hurry. I did not live in a cabin in the wilderness. I lived at a busy intersection in the capital city with a houseful of children, pets, and hourly demands. But that was no excuse. Poetry is poetry and it demands focus.

I was introduced to John's work on the Alaska State ferry *Malaspina* on my way to Juneau in early October 1971. I was moving there from Boulder, Colorado. Carol Beery Davis and her husband, Trevor, one of Juneau's earliest settlers, were among the few other passengers and took me and my two young children under their wing. Martin had gone ahead two months before. Carol showed me *Winter News.* (She traveled with John's work and spoke of it constantly, to whoever would listen.) It has always been my favorite of his books. As with the work of Yeats, I settled in early with the early poems, forming a permanent attachment. Maybe it is because of the circumstances—*Winter News* handed to me as the map of a new, inscrutable home. Here was a chair "in which nothing but the wind / was sitting." Here were silence, desertion, and cold, lonely journeys. Best, here were the spirits, dreams, and sounds of animals. I felt I belonged in these poems, or, rather, that these poems were pointing me to where I belonged. "The immense sadness / of approaching winter" became my milieu. But the poem that defined me was "Listening in October." That was—is—my Alaska:

In the quiet house
a lamp is burning
where the book of autumn
lies open on a table.

There is tea with milk
in heavy mugs,
brown raisin cake, and thoughts
that stir the heart
with the promises of death.

We sit without words,
gazing past the limit
of fire into the towering
darkness . . .

There are silences so deep
you can hear
the journeys of the soul,
enormous footsteps
downward in a freezing earth.

Soon after I disembarked in Juneau, Carol Davis had me busy
with the Alaska Poetry Society, and I heard and learned a good deal
more about John. At the time he was serving as Alaska Poet
Laureate—the fourth to do so since Carol established the position
through legislative resolution in 1963. I remember society meetings
and dinners at the home of Dick and Mary Peter, across the street. On
at least one occasion John was there. On other occasions he was dis-
cussed. There was no question, even then, that John had become—
and would continue to be—Alaska's finest writer and most important
voice. We knew he was setting a standard of integrity and dedication
that would challenge us, both as poets and as people.

In 1985, when I was hired by the Alaska Department of Fish and Game, I became John's editor—at *Alaska Fish & Game* (later, *Alaska's Wildlife*). For my first issue of the magazine, in November, I ran "Shadows"—vignettes of a fox, a coyote, a woodchuck, and a lynx; and later there was a continuation with a piece on bats. These were all animals John had seen and observed. He belonged in this magazine where biologists and lay readers came together to celebrate in concrete fashion the wildlife resources of Alaska. In a more perfect world, he would have been in every issue.

John, through the kindness of Carol Davis, gave me a compass as I entered the state that was to be our shared experience for many years. Alaska was to give us natural beauty on a scale of grandeur sometimes marred by human activity on a scale of smallness hard to fathom. We saw the oil boom and the bust. We experienced the *Exxon Valdez* spill. We saw the forests slashed. We ran afoul of politics and pettiness, and much of it hurt. Now John has left, and I am leaving Alaska, too. I am leaving for different reasons but share his sadness and wonder. What is this thing called "place"? And how will we be able to find our way outside the place which became our heart's magnetic pole?

We will find it in our journeys through silence: at the moment when we know, truly, that "the only poet is the wind." Alexander the cat knows. Scholars and critics refer to silence in the poetry of John Haines as symbol and as threshold to mysticism. I will leave such thoughts to them and remember John Haines accepting his gift from the cat, John Haines bent into the fierce icy wind of Juneau, John Haines walking an English lane between hedgerows woven with singing birds. If mysticism is direct connection with God, then the poetry of John Haines is direct connection with the physical manifestations of God. It opens the door into forest and river bank and gives us news of the great breathing tundra.

My only argument with John is that the book of summer lies open as well as the book of autumn and that the journeys of the soul are *upward*, too, in a thawing earth. If I could walk into Winter News Cabin today, a place now locked in history, I would approach the table where the lamp is burning and reverently turn the page. See, John, I would say: Here is where we gathered who love you, even when we were far away, scattered over the world, listening, listening. . . .

TESS GALLAGHER

Bullet Holes and Hideouts:
A Letter from Syracuse

This letter was written to John Haines after I left Missoula, Montana. I'd taught a year at the University of Montana, covering classes in poetry writing for Madeleine Defrees and Dick Hugo. This would be the longest I would be in proximity to John, although we've had a correspondence and friendship ever since.

After I left Montana there followed a summer of fateful solitude at a place near Port Townsend, Washington, called appropriately "Discovery Bay"—a cabin overlooking water so beautiful I never wanted to leave, but which I did leave after Raymond Carver crossed the country to convince me to go back to El Paso with him and start a life together on the first of January of 1979.

One of the last things that happened to me before this in Missoula was inviting John to a celebration dinner. I had gotten a Guggenheim on the first try, and John was terrific company for really savoring this unexpected prize. It seemed like getting a jump on the mysterious process of such selection, to slap out a wad of the money on a big feed with John, especially and only John, as he had applied several times and not received a Guggenheim at that point, and was senior enough to me to have deserved it long ago, by anyone's estimation. Anyway, he was happy to "eat out" on the Gugg, despite being amusingly droll about his own fortunes with the fellowship machinery.

What I didn't tell John then was that I had a hideout one floor above him at the Missoula Hotel, a dilapidated building from Missoula's days before it turned into the LA of the Northwest, with business strips blasting the small-town homey feel of street names like Betty and Helen. I recall vividly passing the office of this hotel one day and spotting a bullet hole in the plate glass window. I liked it that no repairs were made so the bullet hole stayed at eye level, a reminder of something random and deadly that could find one at any moment.

John had chosen to live in this place whereas I went there for refuge. I had another address where I really lived, in the rented basement room of a house where other roomers entered like real ghosts through my sleeping space at early hours of the morning. I came to my room at the Missoula Hotel to write, to cinch my space up into a knot of what power I could manage then. And to sleep without giving quarter to anyone.

When I'd done my work in this rather bleak hideout, I sometimes wanted chatting company around 10 p.m. and John would also have been at it, writing away in his quarters below. I liked to think of him there, and that he didn't know I was so near, also writing, doing this reaching out beyond ourselves, past present time, discovering what we were going to say in poems and essays.

John companioned me in an interior sense that gave support and made the way friendly, such as it had not been for me in a long while. I was raw and skittishly wild from the collapse of my second marriage. John was a loner. We were loners together, and more important, apart. His moodiness and interior reserve suited me just fine. We were pals, I think one could say. This being the case I would go down the staircase we both used and outside in the worst weather to a phone booth and ring his room and say, "John, can you come out? Meet me at the Turf." There would be a nice hesitation while John considered all he was going to leave undone, and then he'd always say, "Sure." The Turf was one of those old plush mahogany red-velvet type bars with lighting left over from campfires and lanterns. It later burned down, I heard.

John and I walked places together in snow, talked poetry and life and love, drank a rough whiskey called Early Times and maybe an occasional Old Turkey. But we were not real drinkers. Two whiskeys was our limit. Another thing, we didn't have money. We had hearts getting wizened on the trail. We had a great desire to find out what and who mattered in a life. We had poetry, poetry, poetry—that pungent narcotic of the soul's bloodhound—searching.

There was something intimate and taciturn then and now about John that made his laughter golden when you were able to say something that amused him. Also a sweet outcast quality he wore like a cocked fedora with the kind of common-man dignity my father had. He could be near morose, melancholy, wry—what a cocktail!—and all chased down with a steadiness, a keenness of mind and intuition, that made even his asides terse abatements of the general dark. In fact, he seemed to talk in asides, some hyphenate code for tiptoeing out of his closely held inner room of contemplation and ruminatory diligence, so as to leave it undisturbed or unoffended by his sneaking off for human company.

Once I met John head-on as I tried to carry my bicycle up the stairs to put it in my room and foil the town's bicycle thieves. I was appalled at the prospect of accidentally getting my cover blown and invading his territory and mine. I stood clutching my handlebars and lied. I was on my way, I said, to talk to a student who lived upstairs. John seemed satisfied, like a sleepwalker who has met a doorknob and known not to turn it. Only years later did I confess to being so close a neighbor, sharing the same ruined hotel.

After Missoula, my cabin on Discovery Bay seemed an outpost of all those stories John had told me about Alaska—where I had not been at that time. I had a wood-burning kitchen range and a fireplace that heated an uninsulated room between cedar walls. I split alder wood every day with the same ferocity I went to my poems, thinking of at least one other individual on the planet who loved such a life as intensely, as passionately as I did—John, whose friendship I nurtured by just holding a place for what Ray would later call, in his poem for John Gardner, "the going to what lasts."

Oct. 24, 1980
[Syracuse, NY]

Dear John,

So glad to get your reminder about the pictures, snap-
ping me back to consciousness of the outside world. As you
may have guessed it has been tremendously challenging to
get this program going with few clues from anyone, Geo.
Elliot's ghost having said little and Philip Booth giving
some good advice via phone and Hayden threatening not so
seriously but nonetheless worrisomely to pack his bag (the
first week of school!) and heading for Vermont. (Qualms
about teaching of writing and University life, etc.)

He is of course well loved by all here, including myself,
and I would be deeply disappointed if he weren't here or
were to leave. So a good bit of energy has gone into letters,
notes, the baking of apple pies (this has worked the best!)
and generally keeping things out of his way, assuring that
I'm going to send my very best students on to him next
term from the undergrad. class. So Hayden has cheered up
under my onslaught of good attentions and of course the stu-
dents think he's wonderful though I think he has his hands
full because they all want to show off for him, and to get
him on their side they do outrageous things, little mean-
nesses to each other that he has had to work to counter.

Now you, dear fellow, are another matter. These por-
traits of your immortality . . . Well I have been passing
them around to my cute undergrads to stimulate their
muses. They are all buying snowshoes and saving their
money for sled dogs in the hopes of making it to Alaska to
build their cabins (hopefully there are a few empty plots
near yours!) out of gold tailings and the bones of old

Klondikers. I hope you can be of help to them, teach them how to build a few fires, etc. One of them is studying Eskimo and will be willing to travel to outlying villages she says. She is an ex-gradeschool librarian, newly divorced and she loves to write sonnets and read Edna St. Vincent M. aloud to her kissing geronomies.

As you see you have a lot to look forward to. Actually I've had these pic. around some time but as I say, gone crazy here with it all. I went up for promotion this month and just found out that I got it, at least as far as the department is concerned, and will be promoted to Assoc. Professor. It's a great vote of support from the people I teach with here and Ray and I are very very happy tonight. I'm drinking a little Irish and wishing you were here with me as per our night out when I got the Gugg. Ray is drinking ice water, but somehow it isn't the same.

So anyhow, yr a handsome critter, and Leslie is a lucky gal as she well knows and you luckier still, you rascal, for that sweet one. I have saved a set of pics for myself. Isn't Ted Hughes something! We really loved meeting him and hope it isn't forever until we see him again.

That's great news that Don Hall is going to include your book of essays in his Michigan series!!! Great. I can hardly wait for that. I'll be teaching you soon then, in *prose* and poetry.

Are you heading back to Missoula? I forget your scenario. Let me know so I can write. I promise to do better. Sounds like you're living off the land and getting the kind of solitude that makes for a reservoir of sanity in this break-neck world. I envy you, have some days I can't figure why I'm doing this. But I am getting writing done. I've written four stories in the last four weeks and have worked on revisions of poems done in the summer. Ray loves the stories and is encouraging me. So I'm very happy, all considered, though I do miss my walking-around-while-dreaming self which has suffered a grand assault from all it's taken to get settled here, start the program, teach full-time and write and yes, remember my friends.

John, much good love to you. I wish you were closer. I really don't get much time to make friends here, so I'm out in memory a lot to those I've cared for and miss now. Sorry to have been so slow in getting back. I'll do better now that I don't have to type my vitae twenty times and hunt for copies of my publications for such things as promotion. Ray sends love as well. We still tell everyone about our Alaska adventure. My dad has still such memories of your reading and his having been a hero in mine and being interviewed on radio. Please, if you're in touch with those we met there, please give them our greetings. I haven't written to anyone these days, except Madeline and now you.

Love, hugs—
Tess

The time of my letter to John where I talk about Hayden Carruth comes when I undertook to run the writing program at Syracuse University. Luckily I didn't consciously realize the place was a bastion of male power-mongering in which no female writer had ever held sway, and there I was, charged with running things, a ridiculous enterprise at best. Hayden was a longtime friend of John's which turned out eventually to be a warming of the nest for me, since Hayden was the porcupine-centerpiece of the program. Every time you wanted to do something you had to brave his quill-threat. Only when I realized this was camouflage to a soft and generous interior did I begin to let down my guard and enjoy knowing him. My drawing of Hayden in the letter was an attempt to share some of the fun of my initiation with John, who knew Hayden well. John was our bridge. "Have you heard from John?" Hayden and I would say to each other in the halls and be affably domesticated in the prospect of his having spoken to one or the other of us in the mail.

At Syracuse I was in my second year living with Raymond Carver. He had carried me across the threshold of our house on Maryland Avenue and we were like newlyweds, greedy for life, writing and teaching together, doing everything fast and in big gulps of sky like two crazed swallows. John also knew Ray and would visit us in our B. Street house out in Port Angeles later. There is the smell of wood smoke to that memory of the three of us on B. Street—for we heated the house with a woodstove. Maybe wherever John goes woodstoves just appear. Like how a master cellist must attract cellos, even in the subways of Bucharest. Woodstoves appear because they make you want to tell stories, to sit still, to pass the thought through the mouth in a waking dream. John's voice belongs next to a woodstove, a fire that has to be made and kept with human hands, a voice like fine muslin around an onion—I can still hear it. He's telling me something dry and thrown away, like onion skin before you reach white meat. Voice silky and fine-tuned as a small pink mouse-nose, but with a bagpipe drone or an old gramophone—acknowledging woe and the need to endure much that would be silly and wrong and possibly demeaning of human prospect.

Letters after this are a pitiful respite, at best—but John's good company for the journey is preserved in them to remind me of those Montana times and bullet holes, that Wild West form of refreshment where something deadly in maybe both our lives left its near-miss mark, and we went on. Long friendship, John, in this kind of woodstove thing we make. Letters, written and unwritten, both on the backs of invisible trees.

MARCELLA WOLFE

An Open Letter to John Haines

January 1998

Hello John:

I wanted to write immediately because of the sadness
I sensed in your letter about your leaving Alaska. I realize
what the place means to you as a writer; and as a soul. After
more than fifty years there, I can understand that. You said
you felt that leaving would mean closure to part of your
career as a writer. Don't think this way; it's just a transition.
You've always been able to write no matter what the circum-
stances. This is one of the things I admire most about you.
Even when you were going through those turbulent times
last year leaving the homestead and moving to Anchorage,
you were writing new poems and publishing a book.

One good thing about leaving Alaska is that it should
help you leave behind some of the sadness the place has
caused you. Sometimes in your letters, I sense a melancholy
as desolate as I imagine the white Alaskan landscape to be.
I can understand the alienation you've felt about never
being offered a position at University of Alaska Fairbanks.
Believe me, I can't understand why they wouldn't want
someone who has introduced so many people to the state,
more the beauty of the wilderness and the spirit of the land
than the state proper, but you know what I mean. But,
you've never needed that & institutional backing to create.
In fact, not having it has probably helped you. Where
would you be with your tenure? Somewhere in academia in
a leather armchair growing fat and complacent.

While I know the lack of stability you've faced has

been hard on you at times, I remember you telling me how it has also brought a sense of forced alertness to your life. That being forced to confront the world, more or less face to face, not simply talking about it in the classroom safely removed from the consequences, is essential for a writer. I don't think you would have written all that you have without it. I don't think you would be who you are without it.

After living so many places while growing up with your family—Long Beach, Washington, DC, Puget Sound, and later in New York as an artist—I guess having your homestead in Alaska did at least bring you a sense of rootedness in one place. It is something I struggle with myself here in Washington. I'm from here and love my life here. Despite the politics that obsess people here and the overabundance of self-important and unpassionate wonks, I've found most everything I need here for a happy life. Yet, something makes me too want to make myself a home in a place more rural.

I remember what a special place Washington holds in your heart. I loved our trip to the Navy Yard that day and hearing of your memories of the place when you lived there as a child. And our visits to Rock Creek Park. I was amazed at the many types of mushrooms you could identify during our hike there. And the ones you picked for me to take home to eat. I have to admit though, I felt a bit uneasy eating them because they grew so close to the road. Guess I have little in common with the Russian women you said you had seen gathering mushrooms and herbs along railroad tracks on the Kenai peninsula. I'm the typical city dweller who cringes at found food forms. Foraging in Rock Creek Park is not like it is in the tundra up there. Rock Creek Park becomes a commuter highway during the week, not a moose trail. They only close the park during the weekends, so urban nature freaks like me can go up there to forage. I'm sad to tell you I didn't eat the mushrooms. They're petrifying in a wooden bowl in my kitchen, a souvenir of our walk that day.

I remember your essay-writing workshop at George Washington University. You had us go out into nature and sit observing a single thing; a rock outcropping, a stream, or a tree, then write about it. I picked the creek in Rock Creek Park. In addition to my essay, the opportunity to be alone in nature silent and calming my busy mind, gave me a better appreciation for the creek that runs just yards from my front door, and the calming effect it has on me. It's made me more aware of the power nature can have over us even in the city. I'm much more aware of bird songs, which, with a quiet mind and listening ear, you can hear almost anywhere in the city, a canopy permeating the sounds of trucks and busses and chatter.

Our many discussions and your letters have also helped me be a little happier about the fate of the Earth. If you remember a few years ago, when I was in the fledgling DC Green Party, you made me aware of the pessimism I always expressed over the environment. How the Earth was dying and even if people started working to stop this today, we would never reverse our impact, let alone stop it from continuing its downward spiral. You told me that the Earth is not dying and that it was crazy to think that way; it is stronger than even the human imagination can fathom and will endure when we are long gone. I hope you're able to apply that hope you've given me in our friendship to your own situation now as you face this major transition. I know it will work out for the best.

I must close now to work on a poem with what's left of the day. Thanks for the support you offered in your last letter about my frustration at not yet having pulled all my disparate poems into a collection. It was encouraging to hear you were in your forties before you published your first book. Knowing you and the long, productive life you've had has helped me be less impatient with the overly gradual process of developing a writing voice. And, I need this—with all the other deadlines in my life, being a poet is the hardest thing because it just won't succumb to a nice, neat, linear time frame. Although your words of support meant a lot, you didn't tell me that long before you published your first collection that William Carlos Williams wrote to you in 1953 which I guess put you in your early thirties, around my age to say "and I'm certainly glad you wrote and sent me your poems, for by doing so you revealed the most authentic talent for verse that I have encountered in your generation." I read Williams' quote on the back cover of your book, *At the End of This Summer*, the collection of your early poems. True, it may have taken you time to get your first collection together, but you were surely getting some pretty strong encouragement along the way. And, I think you're pretty modest for not sharing this with me. I'll bet Williams didn't send notes like this to every young poet he read.

Take care and send more news when you arrive in Montana.

Sincerely,
Marcella

MIKE DUNHAM

No Place for the Poet:
Alaska's Most Honored Writer Can't Find a Job at Home

In the short history of our small state, only one Alaskan has achieved a national reputation as a genuine literary lion. Wherever serious authors are seriously discussed, in the pages of prominent journals and between the covers of major anthologies, John Haines is cited as one of America's greatest living poets and Alaska's finest writer. Forty-nine years ago, fresh from war duty in the Pacific, Haines came to Alaska and staked a homestead. Polishing his art while he subsisted off the land, he developed a strong and original voice that won instant and enduring admiration from the East Coast poetry establishment. Neither poetry nor subsistence nor the part-time jobs Haines has taken over the years come with a retirement plan. Elsewhere, poets of his status are typically hired to teach at universities. But not here.

Over the course of twenty years, neither the Fairbanks nor Anchorage campus of the University of Alaska has been willing to find a place for Haines. Today, the former poet laureate of Alaska, who turns seventy-two next month [in 1996], finds himself with no savings, little income and no real prospect of working in Alaska. Haines once hoped to stay on his former homestead for as long as he was physically able to face the hardships and keep working in the place where his muse first came to him. But in 1994 he lost his lease on the property. Since then, he and his wife, Joy, have lived an unsettled life among books and boxes in small apartments in Fairbanks and Anchorage. He picks up a few extra dollars by conducting workshops for aspiring writers in the basement of Cyrano's Bookstore and local living rooms.

One night recently, sitting straight-backed in a folding chair, he ranged over subjects from Chaucer to surrealism in clear, resonant tones. Even with the top two buttons open, Haines' wash-and-wear shirt seemed too small for his homesteader's chest, built up from years of carrying heavy loads. He told his students that a single poem can take twenty-five years to write. He spoke of the state and future of art, the summits and abysses of creative life. "Anybody who dedicates themselves to poetry is taking a chance," he said with a cold smile. "It's a daunting business, and I don't recommend it." He added that he'll have to accept any reasonable teaching offer that comes his way, even if it means leaving Alaska forever.

Many Alaskans may not appreciate what one of their own has achieved in the rarefied world of belles lettres. But respected experts Outside are eager to explain it. Bill Wadsworth, executive director of New York's Academy of American Poets, and University of Michigan English professor Richard Tillinghast, a contributor to *The New Republic* and *Partisan Review,* compare Haines with the most famous American poet of the century, Robert Frost. "He has probably won more important awards in the past five years than any other serious writer in the whole country," said Dana Gioia, literary critic for *The Washington Post.* The Western Arts Federation Poetry award, the Poets Prize and the $10,000 Lenore Marshall/*The Nation* Award were all won by Haines' 1990 collection, *New Poems.* Gioia said Haines' fame will transcend time and geography. "The Scandinavians and Germans are starting to read him. He writes magnificently about fundamental, important human issues, and that's the type of writing that has a good chance of being read in a hundred years."

Kevin Walzer, co-editor of *The Wilderness of Vision*, an anthology of scholarly criticism about Haines' work, said, "He has moved beyond the designation of 'Alaskan' and into the company of the most important poets of the 20th century. There are very few poets who do their best work late in life, but consider them—Stevens,

Williams, Yeats and John Haines." This anthology, due out this month, documents a national interest in Haines' work, going back thirty years, with analyses by luminaries including Pulitzer Prize—winning poet Anthony Hecht and pioneering nature writer Wendell Berry. Haines is not slowing down. He has recently produced what many feel is his best work. His new book, *Fables and Distances*, came out last winter and received quick praise from *Publisher's Weekly* and *The New York Times*. William Kittredge, scriptwriter for the movie *A River Runs Through It*, said Haines has earned a place in history: "At a time when the center of power was in the East, he showed that, if you stuck to your guns, it was possible to make it. That's the great gift he gave a whole generation of writers in the West."

Haines is perhaps the last in the line of self-taught, rustic American savants that includes Ben Franklin, Henry Thoreau, and John Muir. The son of a naval officer, he did poorly in school. He only received his high school diploma, he said, because he joined the Navy in 1943 and "they gave it to me as a patriotic gesture." When World War II ended, he came to Alaska and homesteaded 30 miles north of Big Delta on the Richardson Highway. After one winter, he returned to Washington, DC, to study sculpture and painting. One of his pieces received a prize from the Corcoran Gallery, one of America's premier art museums.

In 1954, Haines returned to his cabin with oils and brushes. He supported himself by hunting, trapping, gardening, and gathering, supplemented with a few odd jobs. The Interior cold made painting impractical, so he turned to his second love, poetry. He spent thousands of nights thinking, reading, and writing by the ocher glow of an oil lamp. After ten winters, his works began to see publication. It happened at a time when urban America was becoming emotionally aware of environmental issues. Haines' intimate descriptions of wilderness attracted modern readers as something new, a vivid rediscovery of the natural world. In 1964 he received the Jennie Tane

Award for Poetry from *Massachusetts Review*, the literary journal of the University of Massachusetts and associated colleges. The journal has published works by W. H. Auden, James Baldwin, Joyce Carol Oates, and Nobel laureate Joseph Brodsky. The next year he won his first Guggenheim Fellowship. In 1966, his first book of poetry, *Winter News*, came out to widespread notice. That year Russian poet Yevgeny Yevtushenko paid a visit to Haines' homestead. Yevtushenko, already famous for needling the Soviet government with "Babi Yar," had just brought out his first major collection, *Bratsk Station*. He toured America from New York to Nome and announced that the only Alaska poet he wanted to meet was John Haines.

In 1969, Haines sold his homestead for $7,000. He regretted the act almost instantly, and leased it back for many years. Still, the sale freed him to travel, write full-time, and accept temporary college teaching jobs. None of those jobs, however, turned into full-time work with a cushion for his senior years. Having arrived at those years, Haines doesn't want to talk about his personal finances. But friends familiar with the situation say it is grim. Essayist and story-writer Barry Lopez said he attended a dinner of literati in New York at which Haines' money worries became the main topic of conversation. "I don't know of another major American poet who is as financially pressed as John," Lopez said. "You can make money in fiction," said Kittredge. "But with poetry, you have to have a job, usually with a college." Bill Wadsworth expressed the feelings of several non-Alaskans when he said, "It bewilders me that your university system has not treated him as a star."

Haines has tried to get work with UA for years. He provided the *Anchorage Daily News* a desperate-sounding letter he wrote to UAF creative writing professor Peggy Shumaker in 1994: "I will be 70 years old this summer; I have no retirement . . . no pension, and, lacking occasional and always uncertain invitations to teach at a university elsewhere, I have at this time no income." Cynthia Walker, head of the English department at UAF, and Ronald Spatz, head of the creative writing program at UAA, said their programs could not afford to give a full-time job to Haines. Kittredge said that Alaska should be able to do for Haines what the University of Montana—with an enrollment one-third that of UA—did for him: establish a regents professorship with salary and benefits. "It wouldn't cost that much and would give a lot of prestige to UA," he said. "It's just a matter of what their priorities are." Sheila Nickerson—former instructor of creative writing at the University of Alaska Southeast and another former Alaska poet laureate—said UA remained flatly unreceptive to proposals from herself and others who hoped to create a position for Haines, even when the dollar amount was minuscule. "I'll tell you how penny ante it got," she said. "We were talking about a $5,000 stipend and benefits. We got absolutely nowhere."

Kittredge speculated that the unspoken truth might be that Haines is too old. "John has the publications and the awards. That stuff looks great on your *vita* if you're forty-two. The universities today want younger people, people ten years out of grad school." John Murray, an assistant professor of English at UAF between 1988 and 1994, heard colleagues cite the infirmities of age as an argument against hiring Haines. He said members of the creative writing faculty told him Haines was unfit to teach, in part, because his hearing aid and dentures made it hard for him to understand students and vice versa. Shumaker dismissed those allegations as "rank gossip." The real problem, she said, was Haines' personality. "He has the impression that it would be within my power to create a job for him, which is not true. When I've told him that, he's called me a liar. The fact is that John wishes to be employed here, and he is not, and this makes him quite upset. He has written hate mail to me and John Morgan (another UAF professor of creative writing) for many years, filled with accusations and insults." Haines said Shumaker also had written demeaningly to him, insulting his character and denigrating his teaching ability. Tom Sexton, current Alaska poet laureate and former head of the creative writing program at UAA, acknowledged that Haines can be a curmudgeon, but added, "That has nothing to do with being a good teacher or writer."

Haines taught at UAF in the early 1970s and, in 1988, received an offer to teach one class for $3,000. It came in a lean period when, he said, "I was about to sell my car to buy food." He turned it down because, at the same time, Ohio University offered him a one-year visiting professorship paying $40,000. Shumaker said Haines was never offered a position after that because, in part, "the demands of a full-time professorship would not be appropriate for John." Those demands include serving on committees and supervising students, Morgan said. "We have a substantial additional amount of committee work and John is not willing to do it." But Sexton said Haines works hard. "I had him down here (at UAA in 1972–1973) as a writer-in-residence. He had a hell of a rigorous schedule. He was here a couple of days a week, then flew to Fairbanks and taught." Sexton also praised Haines as a teacher who "influenced a lot of students who have since wound up as very successful writers." And yet, said UAF English professor Russell Stratton, UAF creative writing staff told him Haines was ineffective as a teacher. All the same, he invited Haines to address his honors class three years ago. "He had those kids enthralled. That business about him not being able to teach is a smoke screen for something else."

That "something else," according to UAF English professor Roy Bird, is "good old professional jealousy and academic politics." Nickerson said, "It's ironic that UAF gave John an honorary doctorate (in 1983) but refused to provide him any kind of real job, all because they feel threatened." Stratton agreed. "Haines is the only (writer) in the state with a national reputation. They think letting him in would reduce their own sense of influence." But Shumaker sharply disagreed. "We have good writers here. We don't have to be weak simply because he is so strong." Haines said he made one last try to get on at UAF in 1994. He submitted a proposal to teach a semester seminar, but "no acknowledgment, no response was forthcoming from anyone, not entirely surprising to me."

After that Haines moved to Anchorage and applied for a position teaching poetry at UAA. As editor of the *Alaska Quarterly Review*, Ron Spatz has published some of Haines' award-winning writings. Yet as head of creative writing at UAA, Spatz hired a younger, out-of-state poet. Spatz said that Haines' application was not considered because he does not have a master of fine arts degree. Asked why the degree was so crucial, Spatz answered he was following national guidelines. "Once you say in the job advertisement that you're looking for someone with a terminal writing degree, you have to stick to it." But Wayne Miller, dean of the UAA College of Arts and Sciences, said that degrees don't matter in cases like Haines'. He said exceptions are made every year. He also said no one in the college ever had formally proposed to him that UAA try to hire Haines. Spatz said he has proposed a paid lectureship and three-credit class he hopes Haines will teach in 1997. Such positions pay little, however, and carry no benefits. Haines said it wouldn't be enough to support him.

"It's hopeless," Nickerson said. "John wanted nothing more than to live out his entire life in Alaska. Now he feels he has no option but to take the first decent offer that comes from the Outside." Haines recently returned from readings in Ohio and Washington, DC. He has offers from as far away as England. The Berg Collection of the New York Public Library—the Valhalla of American writers, where the papers of such literary giants as T. S. Eliot, Virginia Woolf, and e.e. cummings are housed—is in the process of acquiring his working papers. "My days as a wanderer in the wilderness are over," he said. Although he realizes it's late in life to start an out-of-state job hunt, "I could hardly be worse off, . . . and the years are beginning to make things even more difficult." "John's always lived in a pure kind of way, unconcerned about money," Gioia said. "Now he's being punished for it. In the rat-filled world of academic literature, he's a figure of real integrity. It's a shame to see him in need." "If John had left Alaska in the rear-view mirror and relocated in Massachusetts twenty years ago, he wouldn't be in the position he's in now," Kittredge said. "The poetry world is quite Byzantine, and John is not a Byzantine-type person." "I wasn't very smart," Haines said. "I didn't know how to play the game. If I had been more savvy, I might have pursued some of the positions that were open back when universities had more money." He recounted invitations from the Lower 48 that he turned down in the 1970s and '80s. "Good schools, and I think they really wanted me. But I was bound to come back to Alaska. I didn't realize it at the time, but it was inevitable. I don't regret that choice. It's been painful and difficult. But that's just the way it is."

CAROLYN KREMERS

The Essential Things

I.

To see what is here, right in front of us: nothing would seem easier or more obvious, yet few things are more difficult.

—John Haines, *Living Off the Country*

September 1993

I drove 75 miles southeast from my cabin outside Fairbanks to John Haines' homestead on the Richardson Highway. God offered a brilliant Sunday morning—sky cloudy-bright, trees green and gold, cranberry leaves and bearberry leaves red as blood. The drive was easy—flat to North Pole, past the McDonald's, the gas stations, the Santa Claus House . . . through rolling hills . . . past Harding Lake with its boat trailers, motorhomes, and weekenders casting for fish.

"Go nine miles beyond Birch Lake and look for a mailbox on your right," John had told me, over the phone. "It says HAINES in red letters. The homestead is just past that, on the left. If you get to the scenic-view turnout with the little blue camera sign, you've gone too far."

The two-lane, paved highway dropped down a hill to the banks of the Tanana and curved with the mighty river. One of my favorite views in Alaska stretches here: wide braids of the silty Tanana; long gravel bars and islands; huge spruce stumps stuck in log jams, whole trees floating past; and, in the distance, the sharp snowy peaks of Deborah, Hess, and Hayes.

Tanana (*Tan·ə·nah*), the anglicized pronunciation of the Koyukon Athabaskan Indian name, Tene No', means "trail river." The traditional people of this part of interior Alaska, though—the Lower Tanana Athabaskans—called it Tth'itu (*Tth·ee·too*): "major river, straight water."

I had never realized that this was where John Haines lived.

Just past the mailbox, I turned left at a dirt driveway and stopped. A bright yellow FOR SALE sign hung crucified on a spruce tree, and a 55-gallon barrel blocked the way. I spotted John's dark blue, four-wheel-drive Toyota parked by an outbuilding and knew I was in the right place.

Walking up to the small frame cabin, I saw that it was painted green, with lavender trim. The door was closed. A three-by-five notecard hung on the door frame, attached with a clear plastic push-pin. In neatly typed letters, the white card said:

ANY MORNING OR AFTERNOON:
If I am not at the house, I will be at the writing studio. Follow the footpath past the sheds, and look for the path uphill to the right.
    You will see the studio a short distance up the hillside.
                                                John Haines

I smiled and set out.

Sharp smells of ripe high-bush cranberries and wood burning filled the air, and a breeze riffled the yellow leaves falling all around.

"Come down to the homestead," John had written several times in postcards, since we had met in Sitka a few months before. He'd mentioned the traffic—"those blasted RVs and all those diesel trucks barrelling south"—but still, I was surprised at how close to the highway this 160-acre homestead was.

Now I stood on the porch of the writing studio, raising my hand to knock, and I knew I had entered a fairy tale—the enchanted forest, the wicked witch, the frog turned into a prince. Already, nothing seemed real.

I knocked, and the door opened to a square, white room with windows on all sides. John shook my hand and, looking as fit and patrician as I remembered from Sitka, invited me to sit down. He wore nothing wild or bohemian—tan trousers, an open-collared white cotton shirt, a hearing aid. His wavy gray and white hair, gold wire-rimmed glasses, pocket-watch fob, and slender stature evoked an air of distinction. He was sixty-nine. Born in 1924, the same year as my mother, John had been described by a friend of his and mine as "the poem becoming night."

As John and I talked, I glanced around the studio, and he showed me some of its features. Solar panels on the roof collected energy for the storage batteries that provided electricity to the room. John's desk—a board laid between two file cabinets—sat by the window to the south, with an electric lamp and electric typewriter arranged on top. A short bed hugged the east wall, and a tin airtight stove put out heat in the corner by the door. Beyond the windows, sun played on aspen leaves. Light, light, light. I got a sense of freedom, looking out. The highway snaked out of sight and could not be heard.

John told me about this sanctuary—how a friend had helped him build it, that it wasn't finished, and that, perhaps, the writer within was beginning to run out of energy. Not for writing, but for fighting to stay at the homestead.

"What are you writing now?" I asked, noticing sheets of paper lying neatly about the room.

"A book-length poem about wax museums," John said. "It's grim and ironic. Perhaps a bit humorous, too. . . . And a third book of essays."

I thought of John's other two nonfiction books—*Living Off the Country: Essays on Poetry and Place*, published in 1981, and *The Stars, The Snow, The Fire: Twenty-Five Years in the Northern Wilderness*, published in 1989. The first book reinforced my own desire to write truthfully about Alaska and about what matters, and the second book—stunning work about John's memories of his years on the homestead—had drawn me to read it again and again, reminding me that nothing stays the same.

John traded his slippers for tennis shoes and checked the fire. Then we walked out the door, down the stairs, and back on the path.

He showed me the shack that served as his workshop—a gold-rush cabin he had dismantled and moved from Banner Creek almost forty years before. The shack was filled with tools. I could see: this man values handmade things.

"Tell me more about the homestead," I said. I was confused about who owned it and why John was unable to live in such a magical place as long as he wished. I had heard only pieces of the story, secondhand.

John said that he had sold the homestead—"Foolishly, for a pittance"—at a time in his life when he needed a change and some money.

"There was a new professor at the university in Fairbanks," he explained, "a fellow with an MFA from North Carolina. He and his wife needed somewhere to live, and they seemed genuinely to like this place. It was 1969, and I wanted to move to California. I thought I would never come back.

"The professor was fired after two years but didn't want to leave Alaska. He and his wife started an adult learning center in Fairbanks. Then he died of a brain tumor, and the deed passed to her."

I was intrigued to hear how John had chosen this land—and how he hadn't chosen it, at all. He'd come to Alaska "on a lark" in 1947, driving up from Washington, DC, with a friend. Both men were young (John twenty-three), and veterans of World War II, and they drove from DC to Iowa to Montana—"Where we loaded up with a lot of tools and supplies," John said—and on to Alberta, Canada, and the Peace River, finally joining the Alaska Highway in the Yukon.

"It was a muddy, narrow road in those days," said John, "with frequent delays and washouts, and small ferries where, now, there are bridges."

His friend left at the end of the summer, returning to a wife and child in DC, but John stayed.

"I couldn't find land to claim around Fairbanks, though," he said. "That land had all been taken."

He drove south on the Richardson, a dirt road that had been a dogsled trail and stagecoach route connecting Fairbanks and the port of Valdez. A local had told him, "Go down and look along the bluffs of the Tanana River. That's beautiful land down there—big, open country."

John had come to this hill forty-six years ago—before I was born—when the trees were short and thin. He told how he pulled into this clearing.

"I'd been working a job in Fairbanks, and I had a truck at the time. I spent the night in the truck and the next morning looked over the country. I decided I liked it, and that was that."

John shook his head. "There was a lot I didn't realize back then," he said. "I knew nothing about building or about gathering food. But when you have to do things in order to survive, you learn."

The more I listened to John's stories, the more fortunate I felt to have bought land myself, at last, and a cabin—a small log cabin in a location not as stunning as this, without so much sunlight and on two acres, not a hundred sixty—but a cabin and land, nonetheless.

What is it that draws us to places we could never imagine, root-ing some of us here, some there? Who can predict where a life will lead? And who is to judge the decisions we make—to buy a piece of land or sell it, to live with someone else or alone, to do what it takes to cut trees and plant a garden, build a sled or a boat or a green-house, raise a dog team, haul water and wood, shoot a moose, snare a lynx, love a place maybe more than a person?

Back in the cabin after a walk to the waterhole, and along a path to pick mushrooms, and uphill to "the meditation bench" and a spectacular view of the river and the Alaska Range ("John, you live in a paradise," I said, and meant it, knowing too that none of us does or can, and maybe never will), John showed me small black-and-white photos of all these things: things he chose to do with his life, "when I was young and loved to work and had energy to work all day. Work, work, work." He showed me photos, too, of his first wife and his second—1950s and '60s snapshots that reminded me of my mother when she was young, with brown hair instead of gray, her body slender and full of the energy John spoke of, the energy that older people remember and marvel at, amazed at who they once were.

It puzzled me that, after all this hard work and hard loving of hard things, John had nothing—and everything—to show for it. He had no wife and no biological children or grandchildren. He owned no land or home. He had no retirement pension, no job, no steady income, and no idea what the winter might bring.

John said he hoped that someday this homestead—or part of it—could be bought back from the woman he sold it to.

In 1983, a representative from the State Historical Society and a state legislator from Fairbanks had led an effort to purchase the homestead with state funds to be matched by private donations. But the project failed. Eight years later, in 1991, the professor's wife put the property up for sale, asking $125,000.

According to John, the place was appraised at only about $85,000. Peter Scholes of the Trust for Public Land and other interested people formed the "Save the John Haines Homestead Committee." Their hope was to raise funds and to get the United States Congress to enact legislation that would acquire the homestead as a National Historic Site.

"It is likely," the committee's mission statement said, "that no site in the bush or homestead anywhere [in the United States] has been so thoroughly documented by a person of such consummate literary achievement."

Sponsors of the effort included well-known writers such as Hayden Carruth, Dana Gioia, Edward Hoagland, William Kittredge, Philip Levine, N. Scott Momaday, Molly Peacock, and William Stafford. The group received pledges totaling $100,000, but the professor's wife would not lower the price.

Now, two years later, John continued to lease the property, mailing a check each month to Fairbanks and paying for improvements himself, such as the writing studio. He took jobs "Outside" when he could—visiting writer, guest editor, distinguished speaker.

"You live more frugally than I, John," I said, not without embarrassment. I was humbled at how little he seemed to own. His cabin had no electricity, running water, or telephone—certainly no VCR or TV. His furniture was utilitarian and inexpensive: a full-sized bed with a headboard; a bookcase behind it; a small wooden table, draped with a dark green cloth and flanked by two unmatched wooden chairs; a soft couch covered with a maroon India spread; homemade wooden shelves for more books, and dishes; a calico curtain across the five-gallon "slop bucket" that collected water from the sink.

"Where do you keep your clothes?" I asked, not seeing any.

John smiled. "Didn't you see the closet in the entryway?" he replied. He explained that his winter clothes were stored in boxes in the storage shed and that recently he'd taken several bags of old clothes to the Salvation Army in Fairbanks.

"I have way too much," he said. "Too many clothes, too many shoes, too many *things*. But one wears different clothes in different places. What I wore in Washington, DC, was different from here. . . . That's the beauty of having a small place. There's no room for extravagance. You have few things, because you have no place to put them."

John told me his cabin had been broken into twice during the past three years and that the most recent break-in had been especially upsetting. "They took the stereo and the quilt my stepdaughter had worked on for a year, and they broke the windows and strewed stuff all over the floor. At least they didn't take the stove."

The stove was an elegant, half-barrel, black iron woodstove embossed, to my surprise, with the name L.L. BEAN. John said the door had come from the catalog company in Maine, but that he had built the rest of the stove himself, using a 30-gallon oil drum and other parts bought locally.

"I worked a good part of the summer of '81 on that stove," he mused, adding that the original woodstove—the one he'd begun using in 1948—now heated the workshop.

His wryness returned. "Of course, whoever broke in here left the books. The devils probably couldn't read."

I did not envy this man—this friend and inspiration—who lived alone in an isolated place within yards, now, of one of Alaska's two main highways. I knew how it felt, though, to have one's personal space violated. I told John that a man had almost broken into a carriage house I had rented in Denver one summer, and that afterwards I was so angry I decided to take karate lessons. I studied long enough to learn to break a board with my foot. I didn't say how I imagined aiming a swift kick at a face, if ever again I awoke in the night to a faint clicking sound and discovered a man hunched over, snipping wires in the mesh of a screen door, making a hole to reach in.

John had a pistol now. He pointed to it—on the bureau near the bed, by the door. The pistol was black and small. It looked almost like a toy. I figured it was loaded. John said he would probably get rid of it soon. He wasn't as jittery now as after the last break-in.

Time heals.

The trails that John cut decades ago were passing back into the forest, into the "woodlands," as he called them (a New England term to me), into the alders and downed birches and aspen, the mushrooms, cranberries, and ferns. We did not walk beyond the spring-fed waterhole, and John said it was getting hard to find the path to the meditation bench overlooking the river.

Wandering along the creek with me, he pointed out remnants of the bridge that had been part of the Old Richardson Road. Some of its timbers had become part of his cabin. He showed me cans rusting under alders, cans that people used to pour fuel into their Model T Fords on the bumpy ride from Valdez to Fairbanks, in the days when there were no gas stations and people packed their own fuel.

"This creek just happened to be at a convenient distance between settlements," John said. "People stopped here to fill their cars and trucks with gas, and then they threw away the cans. That's how this creek came to be known as Gasoline Creek."

The root cellar John dug outside the cabin had caved in, the garden he cleared above the house was returning to wild plants, and the greenhouse was now a skeleton of silver-gray timbers, an open-air cathedral for birds.

Beneath those timbers, lettuce and broccoli grew in planters among weeds. A few wild raspberry bushes had also taken root. John cut two stalks of broccoli for me and plucked some lettuce. I set the vegetables on a sawhorse in the yard, with the paper bag of mushrooms we had picked. This was the first time I had ever gathered mushrooms, and I was enchanted with their variety—their colors, textures, shapes—and with how much John did and didn't know about them.

"This is a chanterelle," he had said, as we walked in the forest, looking. . . . "This is a boletes. . . . This looks like an amanita. Poison, yes . . . Here's a meadow mushroom. . . . This red cap with the white stalk is called a *Russula*. It can make a person sick, if eaten. . . . And these are the hedgehogs I've been waiting to pick with you. . . . This one—I'm not sure. It smells good. The gills aren't white. I think I'll try it, after I check it again in my book. I won't try it on you, though."

At the table in John's cabin, over tea, he showed me his three books about mushrooms. Mushrooms grew at my cabin, and now I was eager to collect some. I had seen amanitas on my land, the white-spotted red ones—the ones that are poison. But what else?

"I suggest you find a copy of the *Audubon Guide*," John said.

Like his writing studio, mushrooms pulled me into the fairy tale. They were what they were made of, and more. The way they grew, apparently, from nothing. How John or I plucked them from the ground, and there were no roots. How they grew from spores. How different mushrooms popped up under different kinds of trees. And how there were hundreds of names for them—and colors—in books.

How the meadow mushroom flourished in the lawn outside Sophie's Station in Fairbanks, where John kept an apartment and where he might have to live the next winter, though he didn't want to. And how no one seemed to gather mushrooms from the lawn but John.

I was struck by how the mushrooms on John's homestead grew sturdily each year, in different places and in the same places, surprising John—and me: one who knew the country like the back of his hand, one just beginning to learn. How the mushrooms turned black and rotten, full of worms, and how they got trampled, then seeped into the earth, like liquid, only to come up again in forests and marshes, tundra and cities, at homesteads and over the world.

And how one gathered each mushroom in wonder, inspected it carefully, and dared to eat it—sautéed in a small skillet and stirred with a wooden spoon . . . butter, garlic, a dash of pepper.

II.

From the first day I set foot in interior Alaska, and more specifically on Richardson Hill, I knew I was home. Something in me identified with that landscape. I had come, let's say, to the dream place. . . . I think such a recognition must be rare, and I was extremely fortunate to have it happen in the way that it did. Such a purity of feeling, of joy and of being in the right place, I have not often felt since.

—*Living Off the Country*

October 1993

John visited my cabin for the first time, yesterday afternoon for dinner. He brought some mushrooms to sauté and a bottle of red wine. I'd made vegetarian lasagna, a Greek salad with olives and feta cheese, and sourdough chocolate cake.

The first thing John wanted to do, though, was walk on the land. He asked where the boundaries were—I don't know exactly, since they're not marked—and he agreed it's good that the west end of the property borders a 90-acre parcel of roadless land. It's unlikely that area will be developed soon, for it slopes steeply down into a bog, and a road would be expensive to build and maintain. And anyway, the land faces northwest, not south.

From my cabin I can see no one else's house except one bit of white, to the east, through the trees, where my neighbor Susan's frame cabin sits. In winter I like to drive home down the snow-packed, four-wheel-drive road and notice whether Susan's lights are on. Their yellow glow feels friendly in the dark.

John and I walked over much of my land. He identified some mushrooms and the fungi attached to downed trees. I showed him the wild raspberries and wild roses, the cranberries and Labrador tea, the horsetail ferns, dwarf dogwood, and felt leaf willows, growing in different parts of the forest floor. He told me that these hills around Fairbanks were once covered with spruce, that the miners had logged the forests to get wood for shelter and fuel, and that the trees which grew back were the deciduous birch and aspen.

"Eventually," John said, "if left in its natural state, all this hillside will be covered again with white spruce. The birches you see will grow old and fall down or be displaced by the sun-and-moisture-stealing conifers. See? Look at these trees. At first glance they appear to be birch, but scattered among them are spruce seedlings."

I nodded, surprised at what he could read.

"And look at this. Now here is a fine old birch. It must be seventy years or more—as old as I. Part of the old-growth forest, no doubt, missed by the miner's axe. Imagine what this fellow has seen."

John thumped the trunk. "It sounds solid. Yes, this one should last another decade or more, unless lightning strikes it, or bugs. A magnificent tree. . . ."

We climbed up the rickety back steps of the cabin to the narrow deck, walked its length past the picture window that looks out on the big birch, and I opened the plywood door to the screened porch. On the porch, out of habit, I leaned my knee and shoulder against the thick inner door and pushed.

Inside the cabin—built with six-inch, three-sided logs—John smiled at the traditional, low-beamed ceiling a foot above our heads.

I showed him the shower installed the month before, between the kitchen and living area. He asked the make of the black iron wood-stove in one corner of the room—a Resolute—and I pointed out the electronic, Monitor oil-stove beside it. Unlike John's cabin, mine is not heated solely with wood, and I have added running water—a kitchen sink and shower—but not a septic system. The outhouse is cheap, and fine with me.

The cabin is one room—18 feet by 20—with an angle of wooden steps leading up to the loft. The kitchen sink divides the room, with the stairs behind it. A thousand-gallon tank, buried underground outdoors, connects to a pump and water heater in the root cellar, and the sink and shower run with water, hot and cold.

Upstairs, John raised his eyebrows at my Macintosh computer and laser printer, placed on a door between two file cabinets. Soft light from the south-facing dormer windows touched my papers, and the birches outside—some curving over the roof—could be heard rustling their dry leaves. A queen-sized futon mattress, covered with a flannel quilt my mother had made, lay on the floor where the roof sloped down.

"This cabin is darker than mine," John said. "It faces the wrong direction. You can't wake in the morning and see the sun streaming in, or the river just out your window."

I felt as if slapped, but said nothing. Perhaps John's comment masked pain, I thought. Or something hard. Surely it wasn't meant as it sounded.

Homestead. The word evokes the Homestead Act of 1862, which Congress used to grant settlers 160-acre parcels of federal (that is, Indian) land for the purpose of farming. The word also signifies the land, house, and outbuildings that make a family's home. When John honored my bought cabin and two acres with the word *homestead*, though, he was acknowledging their spiritual dimensions, I think. He was affirming the way living with one piece of ground and sky—year after year through the cycle of seasons, protected from the vice of winter by just a membrane of wood and glass, and the heat from a single stove—can teach humility and joy, stillness and attention, and a grounding that doesn't go away.

Each of us does what we can. This cabin on these few acres at the bend in this dirt road—seven miles from the university, on the side of Chena Ridge where the northern lights play in winter and the moon sails high to spill in windows, where moose browse on willows, snowshoe hares leave tracks, and spruce grouse cluck with their young in spring—this was what I could afford after resigning from the job in Bethel. This land and cabin are sanctuaries, much like John's. Surely he must know that. Or if he doesn't, perhaps he will soon.

Back downstairs, we sat at my small table and opened the red wine. I used the corkscrew on my Swiss Army knife. The sun was setting, salmon-colored, and slanting in the picture window.

As John poured the wine, he seemed to relax, and I felt thankful—for this homestead, this friendship, this chance to share what can't be sold.

III.

To the extent that it was possible for me, I entered the original mystery of things, the great past out of which we came. I saw the midwinter sun sink in a cleft of the mountains to the south, and I felt I had learned a great secret.

—*Living Off the Country*

May 1997

"Never sell your homestead," John said, on that first visit to my cabin, and he has repeated it several times since. I listen. I won't give up my homestead, if I can possibly hold on.

I'm sitting on the back deck of my cabin, nine-fifteen on a Saturday night. The sun is moving across the opposite ridge. The sky hangs blue, translucent, and the birch leaves shimmer that startling, chartreuse spring-green. A wood thrush sings, and faint sounds of the Parks Highway float up the valley—diesel trucks, cars, an occasional RV. I'm wearing plenty of clothes—my purple fleece jacket, jeans, socks, running shoes—and the red box of STRIKE ANYWHERE wooden matches sits by my side, ready for lighting a coil and a citronella candle. So far tonight, though, there's been only one mosquito.

I just finished talking on the phone. I needed the address of a poet-friend and no one seemed to have it, so I called John in Anchorage.

It's always so good to hear John's voice. His writing and his *life*—those many years on the homestead and now, in Anchorage, an exile in his own state—mean a lot to me. He probably has no idea. I think I understand how much he would like to have served on the permanent faculty of the University of Alaska.

"Of all the places I've ever taught," John has said, "the University of Alaska seems the most confused. It has never been able to decide what it is for."

I have to admit, sometimes the school has also seemed that way to me.

I'm glad that John has married again, and I hope that he's happy with Joy. I remember their wedding, in 1994, at the homestead. It was June 29, John's seventieth birthday. Two days before, during a dinner party at my cabin—with lettuce from the homestead and potato-salmon pie—several of us had mused about the things we love and the difficulty of trying to honor those things and still make a living. Eyes sparkling, John had turned to me and said, "Just remember, if everything else fails, you open the gourmet café and I'll tend the cash register."

At the wedding, half a dozen friends stood in the grass outside John's cabin, as Joe Enzweiler, a poet from Fairbanks, led the ceremony and co-signed the marriage license. Joy, who is my age—almost thirty years younger than John—looked radiant in sandals, a simple dress, and her long brown hair.

There were wildflowers and flash pictures and a feast of food: John's eggplant ratatouille with Parmesan cheese; chips and salsa; sourdough bread and olives; salad from the skeletal greenhouse; wine and beer. I'd made a cheesecake and brought last summer's blueberries, cooked in a sauce. There was a store-bought chocolate cake, too, with blue lettering: JOY & JOHN. And champagne and a sixteen-year-old Scotch.

It was hard when, two weeks later, John was evicted from the homestead.

I think I will never forget driving to Richardson that morning, not knowing what I might find but hoping that John's friends and Joy could get him to leave before the State Troopers arrived. I had a vision of the poet with his watch fob and gold-rimmed glasses, barricaded in the smokehouse with a loaded shotgun in his hands—and I knew it was not far-fetched.

When I arrived, though, everyone was hauling belongings—furniture, tools, boxes of dishes and clothes—from the cabin out to the yard.

The rest is a blur to me now. Somewhere in my journals are notes scribbled later—about the books on the shelves and John's wry remarks as he took down each volume, one by one, two by two, blowing the dust away, and about the note he left tacked to the cabin door. What remains, also, is the bottom half of a pale-blue glass bottle that John placed in my hands—an old bottle, he said, from the days of Fred Campbell and Melvin.

That evening, I covered the raw rim with Scotch tape, and now the glass sits on the yellow counter in my cabin. I keep wooden spoons in it, and spatulas. Tools for making things. It feels good to have something old and hard and clear from the Richardson homestead, serving a purpose in mine.

Over the phone, John gave me our friend's address, then asked how I'd been. We talked, and he said he came up from Anchorage last weekend and drove with friends—Dan O'Neill and John Kooistra—to the homestead. It's owned by a Fairbanks dentist now—a woman who cares about the place, John says, and cares about his writing and his love for the land.

John said the woman gave O'Neill the keys, and the three men went down and "sort of camped there. There's no furniture in the place now, to speak of," he said. "It was sad, of course, to be there. But we had a good visit. We stayed up Friday night, drinking whiskey and talking. We recited some poems and this and that, and on Saturday we walked around. I told Dan about the history of the place, and he took notes and shot some photos. There's almost no one left who remembers these things, now. So it was alright. . . . The place needs a caretaker, though."

"What about your writing studio? Was it doing okay?"

"Oh, yes. No one has bothered it. It's tucked away back from the road, you know. And there's nothing in it to steal. I checked, and it seemed to be fine. I miss that place, of course. Anchorage has never felt like home. "

We spoke a few minutes more, and John said he'd heard I was moving to Spokane.

"Yes, I'm going down to teach in the Creative Writing Program at Eastern Washington University. I'm driving out in late August. I'll be back in summers, though. I've rented my cabin to a friend for the winter."

We talked about the Interior, how it's our *home* and hard to leave.

"It's good to visit other places, though," John said. "Especially for a writer. I always enjoyed my stints at Ohio and DC, Tennessee, and so on."

"I promise to become a better correspondent," I said, to this master of postcards and neatly typed letters.

John chuckled.

After hanging up the phone, I felt pensive. How much I have learned, these eleven years, about myself and Alaska—this place we love until it breaks our hearts. How much wiser I am now than when I first came . . . to Tununak, the Yup'ik Eskimo village that changed my life. How many people I know, all over the state, and how much I understand, now, about land. Not just the soil but the Earth and all that lies above it and below.

I glanced around the cabin. How different my experience in Alaska has been from John's. He lived a subsistence lifestyle for many years, and I have not. Yet I've had a richness of experience with Native people and with villages in the bush, things he never had.

John cleared part of his land and built his cabin himself, where-as someone else built mine. I remember digging in the soil that first June, though, and several times since—how the black top-soil is crumbly and mixed with dark birch leaves, tangled with tree roots and flat, mica rocks. How the mud below is brown, wet and slippery like clay, and hiding more rocks. And how everything below the surface feels COLD through thin garden gloves, COLD from being frozen and buried in snow.

"Never sell your homestead," John says.

I'm beginning to understand. Never give up this refuge-connection, with and against all that is hard in the world.

IV.

It's still a place I go back to, in mind and in spirit, though it seems I cannot return to it fully in fact. The material it gave me is still part of my life, and I go back to it in poems and in prose, trying to understand as well as I can the significance of what happened to me there. The experience was so powerful that it has influenced everything else I have done. Probably I measure everything else against it. Of all things I have and am, it is something I do not lose.

—*Living Off the Country*

June 1998

I'm headed home for the summer, home to Fairbanks after my first year teaching in Spokane. Over the last ten months, my memories of Alaska—of Tununak and Bethel, the Brooks Range, my cabin—have given me strength, and hope that I'm doing the right thing, and faith that I'll always return.

In the last four days, I've driven a thousand miles from Spokane to the Stewart-Cassiar Highway in British Columbia, and another thousand miles to the Yukon-Alaska border. Trickster, my companion—my silver Subaru—is running well. Only 350 miles to go.

A half hour north of Delta, I start watching for John's homestead. Last September, he moved with Joy from Anchorage to Montana, but I know part of him will never leave.

Here is the turnoff for Tenderfoot Pottery, an artist's studio I've yet to visit. Here is the old Richardson Roadhouse, destroyed by fire years ago. Here is the sign for Banner Creek, and the bridge. And here is the Tanana.

Tth'itu. "Major river, straight water."

The view is stunning, as ever, huge black and white thunderclouds billowing and tumbling on top of each other, crowning the braids of silver-gray water. A ragged edge of spruce-tops marks the horizon and, in the foreground, gravel bars and islands hug trapped, dead trees.

Somewhere up on my right, on that hillside, is a meditation bench—a small bench made of boards, set on the sod beneath the quivering aspen. Whenever I drive this stretch of road, I imagine a man sitting on that bench, someone thoughtful and wise, who knows how to synchronize with the view.

And last September, besides moving to Montana, John flew to New York, where he received the sixty-third annual fellowship of the Academy of American Poets. He was proud, like this hillside, and honored and pleased.

I'm watching for the dirt driveway and the hand-painted sign on the gate made of hard metal poles:

RICHARDSON HOMESTEAD
EST. 1947

Here is the gate, padlocked, just as I saw it last fall.

I park the car and duck under the poles. I feel a need to check in.

Gingerly, I walk across the untouched grass to the cabin window and peer through. Not much to see but the sink and a white plastic chair. *Never sell your homestead.*

I step back and turn in a circle, looking at all the rest. It's early evening. The sun shines yellow, and the outbuildings seem peaceful and intact, the sawhorse ready for someone to cut wood. A bit of moldy canvas, dangling from a roof-beam of the skeletal greenhouse, twirls in the breeze.

I've brought my mushroom book to Spokane and back again. It's a pocket-guide: *Alaska's Mushrooms* by Harriette Parker. Not the one John recommended, but it's given me a start—collection tips, safety rules, recipes. Photographs of thirty-four species, "from edible to DEADLY."

I scan the area for mushrooms, but see none.

I have an urge to walk up to John's writing studio. I don't care what the legal documents say.

That's sacred ground, though. I won't walk there. It's private property—John's private property—and the only thing to do, the essential thing, is wish it well.

JOHN MURRAY

Out of Alaska

Sixty miles south of Fairbanks, the road edging the dark muscular waters of the Tanana River, I pulled over at the homestead of John Haines, poet laureate of Alaska. Two log cabins and a storage shed stood near the road. On the hill above the rough-hewn cabins there was a greenhouse and beside it a large vegetable garden. Further back in the woods was his writing cabin.

I got out of the car and stretched and then made a quick reconnaissance to see that everything was secure, as I had promised John back in town. Haines had chosen the place carefully, when he first arrived at the age of twenty-three. This was just after World War II, Haines a Navy veteran. He was an independent young man and not suited for the military career of his father, who commanded a submarine in the war and later retired as an admiral. Haines had tried studying art for a while at the Hans Hoffmann School, hadn't liked it and so had somehow wound up homesteading along the Tanana River, which was at that time (the Alaskan Highway unpaved and barely five years old) truly the end of the world.

If nothing else, I admire the man's courage.

All in all, John Haines did an excellent job with the land, especially considering he was not born on it. The main cabin faced south, so that the windows would catch the sun early in the spring and late in the fall, and the surrounding hills protected him from the worst of the elements. There was an active springhead in the ravine, and an endless supply of kindling on the hundred and sixty acres behind the place. Back of the homestead boundary was the trackless wilderness, the gently forested slopes and rolling tundra domes where he spent the better part of forty-five years hunting, fishing, dogsledding, camping, hiking and picking berries. Even now, you would have to hike north on a straight line one hundred and twenty miles to cross the first road. Beyond that gravel highway it would be another four hundred roadless miles to the first polar bear.

I sat on the steps of his cabin, the door padlocked by the new owner, and reflected on the man who built it.

John Haines is, above all, the bard of the boreal forest, the lyric voice of the Great North Woods. In that capacity he is a poet sui generis. I can't think of anyone to compare him to. Robert Service? Not hardly. Service never lived what Theodore Roosevelt called "the strenuous life" of a pioneer, the decades in the bush, the winter nights with the wife reading Elizabethan poets beside a lantern, the dogs howling at something in the dark. What Robert Service did was to affectionately rhapsodize about the outback in fireside ballads that for some reason a surprising number of people adore. After one of his surgeries Ronald Reagan surprised Nancy and the doctors by reciting, in toto, "The Cremation of Sam McGee." Shakespeare the general populace cannot recall, but Service they can recite from memory.

While Haines is not widely known as a writer, his work is well regarded among other writers. Edward Abbey once called Haines' book *News from the Glacier* the finest book of poetry from Alaska because it was "about ordinary things, about the great weather, about daily living experience."

I think that sort of judgment means more to him than having the reputation of a Jack London, who visited the frosty north for less than one year and approached it just as the miners of his generation did—steal as much as you can and get out.

Haines often writes of autumn, the season poets of all cultures and times, from Wang Wei ("October in the Mountains") to John Keats ("Ode to Autumn"), seem most inclined to praise. Haines writes of the yellow sandbar willows and the final run of sea-run salmon, the cutting of the wood and the training of dog teams, the rut of the moose and the melancholy Vergilian calm on the land. His watchful eye notes the grand sweep of the season, the "even, majestic tread" of fall passing over the north country, as well as the minute details: "The deep, shaded mosses have stiffened, and there are tiny crystals of ice in their hairy spaces" (*The Stars, The Snow, The Fire,* 139). Haines once wrote an entire essay on ice, describing how it slowly forms in the upland ponds and major watercourses as autumn progresses:

> I bend over, looking at the debris caught there in the clear, black depth of the ice: I see a few small sticks, and many leaves. There are alder leaves, roughly toothed and still half green; the more delicate birch leaves and aspen leaves, the big, smooth poplar leaves, and narrow leaves from the willows. They are massed or scattered, as they fell quietly or as the wind blew them into the freezing water. Some of them are still fresh in color, glowing yellow and orange; others are mottled with grey and brown. A few older leaves lie sunken and black on the silty bottom. Here and there a pebble of quartz is gleaming. But nothing moves there. It is a still, cold world, something like night, with its own fixed planets and stars. (*The Stars, The Snow, The Fire,* 145)

There are no others like him, nor will there ever be, for the wilderness of which he sang no longer exists. I speak here of the true wilderness, where a man or a woman can go wherever they please, whenever they want, and do whatever they want. When Haines arrived in 1947, there were only three national parks or monuments in Alaska: McKinley, Glacier Bay, and Katmai. Now almost all the land has been placed in some category of state, federal or native corporation land management. Gone are the days of the self-reliant homesteaders, the free-ranging prospectors, the independent trappers. Men and women who lived where the mountains and streams were too young and numerous to name. Some would say the change is good. Others would disagree. I would say it is simply history. The same process of converting virgin land into tax-producing townships occurred in Massachusetts three centuries ago, in Missouri two centuries ago, in Montana a century ago. Wherever civilization appears, the wild is doomed.

One late August day a few years earlier I spent the afternoon at the homestead with John, then in his sixty-eighth year. He was a man of average height and build, with a strong, surprisingly youthful face, and a full head of steel gray hair and eyes that saw what you are thinking. He had none of the stiffness and frailty you see so often in senior city dwellers, but moved with the vitality and quickness of those half his age. In fact, he was about to marry a woman of forty summers. He laughed often and loudly, and told funny stories, and gossiped freely, none of which you would guess from his writing, which is restrained and deliberately worded as utterances meant to endure usually are. We sat outside for a while, talking about things—literature, the woods, the season—and then he showed me around the grounds. It was quite unlike being taken on a tour of a house or yard. This was a landscape that was an organic part of the man, and of his writing. He showed me where the blueberries grew in a woodland clearing, and how the raspberries flourished on a particular sunny bank, and he rooted around in the reindeer moss beneath a birch tree and pulled out an edible mushroom, happy for the addition to his dinner salad. Everything was familiar to him, every secret of the forest, and he was eager to share the bounty with anyone who cared to visit.

Over the course of the stay, John told me of building the homestead and of his life as a poet and nature essayist. It was not always a happy story, although parts were fascinating—the anecdotes of such luminaries as Dylan Thomas after a reading back east in the 1950s and Raymond Carver playing a practical joke in a bar somewhere (Carver dedicated a poem to Haines). I think it is a sacrifice to be a poet in any age; read Dr. Johnson's life of Richard Savage or Walter Jackson Bate's biography of John Keats and you can be sure of that. In our own time, though, with the dominance of the visual image and the popularity of song lyrics, the task of the traditional bard has been even more daunting. Put the poet on an obscure homestead in northern Alaska and Haines' achievement becomes even more impressive: eight influential volumes; several major awards; a secure reputation as one of the major voices of his generation.

Like most of his guild, John Haines fought a lifelong battle against poverty. Once, during a particularly lean time, he sold the homestead and then entered into an arrangement where he rented the cabins back from the new landlord. Eventually, and this was happening even as we talked that day, the landlord evicted him. She had decided to sell the place. The subsequent loss of the homestead nearly killed Haines, physically and spiritually. Many fault the university just up the road. If he had been given a teaching job, any kind of regular position, the situation would not have reached that point. The fact that the resident writers did not offer him significant employment, as with Wendell Berry at the University of Kentucky, or Gary Snyder at the University of California, or Edward Abbey at the University of Arizona, will not be forgotten by posterity. Haines has taught with distinction all over the country, but only briefly in Alaska. Today he and his wife reside in Missoula, Montana, living on Social Security and part-time work, in many ways Haines now a partial man without his beloved homestead.

Of all his poems with autumn as a theme, my favorite, "The Turning," speaks to the great cycles of nature, the turning wheel of the seasons, of fruition and transformation:

I

A bear loped before me
on a narrow, wooded road;
with a sound like a sudden
shifting of ashes, he turned
and plunged into his own blackness.

II

I keep a fire and tell a story:
I was born one winter
in a cave at the foot of a tree.

The wind thawing in a northern
forest opened a leafy road.

As I walked there, I heard
the tall sun burning its dead;
I turned and saw behind me
a charred companion,
my shed life.

What I most remember from my visit with him that autumn
day is this. He pointed to a fallen aspen beside the cabin and told me
of his fondness for the tree, of how the mating squirrels once scam-
pered up and down the powdered white trunk every spring, and how
the mountain bluebirds built their twig and leaf nests in the green
boughs each summer, and how he watched the pulsing red northern
lights flicker among the branches on cold winter nights. A year ear-
lier, during a blizzard, the tree had blown down, coated in heavy wet
snow and battered by gusts. He hadn't the heart to make kindling
of its wood. "It would be like chopping up and burning a friend," he
said, "It would be unthinkable." He would leave the white-barked
giant there in the bracken ferns and cranberry bushes, to return to
the forest in its own time and way.

To see a man speak of a tree as a friend, and to mourn its loss as
most grieve the departure of a loved one, restored some of my faith
in humankind. In a world of hubris and violence, where cities are
destroyed in an instant and congresses are bought off by special
interests and presidents resign in disgrace, here is a man who has

spent his maturity devoted to the cause of nature and gentleness and love. His life is like that rocky cairn you see on the mountaintops, that marks the trail and leads you safely over the high pass into the next valley. Where would the world be without the honest souls who build those signposts, whether in a gallery full of paintings, a set of musical scores, or a shelf of books? Who have no other cause but to create things of truth and beauty in a world of ugliness and madness? In the autumn of my life, I find myself looking increasingly to my elders, to those of my father's generation. I study their lives and choices as I traverse a landscape where there are many routes and few reliable maps.

PART FOUR

Honoring John Haines

This book was originally intended to celebrate the life and works of John Haines on the occasion of his seventy-fifth birthday in 1999. It evolved into something much bigger than this yet a number of poems and brief memoirs collected for the book—what the Germans call a "Festschrift"—were always intended to pay tribute to John Haines as he reached that major benchmark in his life. The poems and memoirs written for John by his friends, fellow writers, and students, are collected in this section and are dedicated to him.

—S.B.R.

TOM SEXTON

Wolves

While his friends drag
a stringer of bright fish
up the trail,

a fisherman throws
dark salmon into
a slough from

his skiff.
They float belly-
up in opaque

silt. Overhead
small planes carry
hunters who are

dreaming of wolves
they will run
to ground from the air

before the kill.
I imagine you bent over
the last sliver

of open water. You're
looking for dog-salmon
to gaff before ice

and hunger set your table.
In dreams, wolves call
from their snow-

bound island, and you wake
and walk to the river
the moon's splayed paw on your shoulder.

JAMES A. GRIFFIN

The Ground of Death

Into this landscape: a hunter.

I see him drop down
from the hill
overlooking countryside
about to fall prey to houses and roads.
He moves with easy stealth
as though he knows his way:
ancient trails through colored woods,
high tawny grass turned by the licking wind,
wide fields whispering.
He knows places
only he knows
and the weather of particular skies,
the signs of game
and wilder animals.
He lives his wilderness
as did his fathers,
mapped in the blood,
the pulse passed down and on
in a land still tracked
with necessary ritual:
hunt, kill, and sacrifice.
He moves from field to wood
down steep ways
until in the evening air,
camp smoke curling sluggish

incense under pines,
the hunter's eyes
reflect fire, stare
half close, slowly
shut.

I see the hunter draw his bow
careful and deadly.
The buck thrusts his antlers
from berried brambles, a body of smoke,
ears high and taut,
eyes outstaring
speckled leaves where the strange shape
releases an arrow.
The deer bolts sideways,
blood spattering the brambles
as he leaps white tail high
through saplings,
one eye aslant, glimpsing
the shadow man,
then crashes toward
the deepest woods,
the leaves loud and scattering,
trees bruising him, his world bleeding,
trying to outrun
the pain inside, dodging
thick familiar hickory and oak,
trees merging and emerging
as the light drains from a cold sky,
his muzzle and nostrils
frothing foam and blood,
breath seething
like a wet fire. He falls

forward tasting earth,
rolls to his side
legs struggling to run, kicking . . . stop.
A single eye
stares.

I see the man
discovering his game
pause in his approach
as though afraid of death
or as if his quarry
were alive
with all the force and wonder
of a living thing
about to rear up
and gore him
in the hunt resumed.
The buck does not stir.
The hunter strokes the rough coat,
strange, brutal antlers,
looks at the seized eyes,
anticipates the ritual trophy.
He hangs the carcass head down, splays
the legs with a bough, then wields
the bright knife, hacks through belly and breast,
gropes beyond his wrists in blood and entrails,
tears out the gray bag of stomach, the bowels
saving the musky urine.
He finds the pink fisted heart,
prizes it out steaming like a birth and
throws it on the sliding pile of offal.
When he is done
the hunter washes

JAMES A. GRIFFIN

in the frigid water of a stream.
He lashes a rope to the rack
then girds it around his shoulders
and starts for home,
the carcass dragged behind.
It is very still.
A chill wind rises.
Soon a cold rain falls
followed by drifting snow
lightly
covering the ground.

I stand a long time.

JACK MATTHEWS

Traces

Fingerprints everywhere
ghosts of elm rings printed
from a regular school of stumps
the inscrutable woodcuts of sleep
where all is simplified but
crooked beyond the reach of houses
memories like a wagon track
through a field of brain clay
a congregation of old chairs
still warm from the passion
of cutting sanding oiling
done in a fit of making
the future laid like a cool hand
upon the craftsman's bow
love for all the various corpses
implicit in a forest of maples
prophecy in an echo of hallways
behind unbuilt stairs
the sound of saw and hammer
not even awakened yet in the aisle
where grouse sit in the wallpaper
and wait like paintings to grow
underneath some specific hand
called forth to the human task.

BIRCH PAVELSKY

Old Bridge at Gasoline Creek

Collapsed stanchions, chartreuse moss overlain.
Alders are crossing,
willows are crossing,
donating leaves, white or yellow
to the small water.
Grasses are crossing,
wasps are crossing.
As if looking for a future
every bridge member leans now
relapsing into the bed
of the creek.
Pearls of light are crossing,
obelisks of cool shadow.
Leaves hush down,
lay white side or yellow side
in the tea-brown water.

TAMLIN PAVELSKY

Moving Away

I'll never hear the owl's cry again,
echoing across the braided river
dampened by the slowly drifting cover
of icy mist, which tells me to unbend
my wings and fly to meet him there, so still,
perched on driftwood on a sandy island.
He'll call again, I'm sure, but only silence
will answer from the top of this bare hill
where I wait until the gray of morning
rises, as if a chord on some controlling
organ calls me downward, slowly tolling
out each heavy step I take in the warming
air. The cabin, mine for twenty years,
that waits below amid the ice-bent birches
is silent under the long moon that arches
from here to Asia through my naked tears.
All that's left is what I have to leave:
the owl's cry that tells me not to grieve.

NANCY SCHOENBERGER

Water Birches

In the blue heaven of birches
women stiffened and took root.
Hair shivered into wind.
White river, white where
the menace of stillness begins,
look for birches: listening,
rain-soaked.

The birch leans through seven
layers of light—ghostly, spare,
melancholy. Though the lemon-
throated finches on bare branches
are tolerated, crows speak
to the tree's heart.

It is August. The birches dream
of wooden boats, the long canoes
prepared for sleep.
In the fine driven rain
they bend, they murmur
their desires to the river.

Look for obedience, women
drifting into sleep.

Another Physician's Appreciation of John Haines

Some years ago I had the privilege of working in public health in Bolivia. I lived in La Paz and traveled extensively through the country. Bolivia had three distinct regions, the low land tropics of Santa Cruz, the middle level altitudes of Cochabamba at 9,000 feet, and the high altitudes of La Paz and the Altiplano at 12,000 to 13,000 feet. I had the opportunity to continue my interest in reading poetry, and came across the poem "Working in Darkness," by Thomas McGrath. The first stanza of the poem is

> I think of the ones like the poet John Haines,
> During those long years in Alaska,
> Working alone in a cold place,
> Sitting in darkness outside the pool of light:
> Ice-Fisherman facing the empty hole of the page,
> Patient, the spear poised, waiting for a sign.

This poem sounded true to me. Perhaps it was living close to the high Altiplano; its flat terrain, its immensity dwarfing the impoverished campesinos who worked the land, and the great Andes that ended the flatness that made me feel this poem had power. The cold, the starkness of the Altiplano, the reflected light of the mountains and the land, brought McGrath's poem to me with some force. The waiting, searching for signs, and the patience needed to do this was the converse of our consumer craziness, our flipping through days as if they were TV channels, our failure to focus and be of serious purpose. My six years in Bolivia gave me time to pause, to think of purpose, the strength of good writing, the silliness of much that is petty and self-serving.

It was in this context that I discovered the work of Haines. I recall staying in the way station of Patacamaya, outside of La Paz, and reading the beautiful poem from *The Stone Harp*, entitled "Wolves":

> Last night I heard the wolves howling,
> their voices coming from afar
> over the wind-polished ice—so much
> brave solitude in that sound.
>
> They are death's snowbound sailors;
> they know only a continual
> drifting between moonlit islands,
> their tongues licking the stars.
>
> But they sing as good seamen should,
> and tomorrow the sun will find them,
> yawning and blinking
> the snow from their eyelashes.
>
> Their voices rang through the frozen
> water of my human sleep,
> blown by the night wind
> with the moon for an icy sail.

This poem stuck to me. It resonated with truth and reflection. It made me pause, think of the signs around me, and brought mindfulness to the moment. As I explored more of Haines' work, I found his prose was sharp, critical, and helpful. His work was serious, had ideas I could use, and had little to do with the frivolous.

After returning from Bolivia, I began a correspondence with

Haines. I had the opportunity to spend time with him and his wife in May 1995. At our meeting we spoke of Giono, Broch, Musil, and Mann. I brought him a book by Erich Heller, and we discussed Heidegger. He read me a poem by Auden about Ernst Toller. Later, I sent him the introduction to Toller's autobiography, *I Was a German*. We have continued to write. He is the literature mentor of a lifetime. Haines is a poet who is versed in great literature, ponders the question of writing as a service, and sticks to his political guns.

Robert Coles, the child psychiatrist and literary critic, often writes of the importance of literature to physicians. To read great writers is to enter a silent dialogue with thinkers whose vision and art spills into everyday life, into the caring of patients. Poetry and novels allow one to enter subtle plots with character variations that reflect what physicians can see. In other words, it can heighten sensitivity, and I also believe, can enhance care. The same is true in public health. Literature can sharpen mindfulness, make one aware of the power of words and their often careless use.

In April of 1953, William Carlos Williams wrote to Haines: "The thing that makes you stand out as a poet is your unaffected sense of rhythm and your intelligent sense of how to make it an organic part of your composition. That is a rare gift indeed and a still unwritten chapter of the history of verse. You have a chance to write the next chapter in the history of verse—but you're going to get kicked around a lot before you come to that eminence." Haines has fulfilled that promise. He has a serious body of work that has the power to heal and renew. And, for that, I am deeply indebted.

RICK BASS

The Slower Cycles of Nature

It would be impossible to measure or quantify the effect John Haines' work has had on me; how his poems and essays combine with my own landscapes to see the world in a new or certain way. I'm very moved by his notions of routes and paths; as a hunter, the images and concepts in his work help grind and polish one of the lenses with which I see the world.

> To follow without hope
> Of turning, the animal-reek
> Of one's own track . . .

I love, too, how he speaks of the paths and sentences of rivers, and time; stones and boulders as words, and the whisperings of dust and dirt. I love the way John Haines sees the world, which is to say, I love the way the world is.

The great cycles of the world are celebrated in ways so powerful that those cycles seem revolutionary, rather than "ordinary." In "On a Certain Field in Auvers," he writes:

> 'And the clock of evening, coiled
> like a spring? . . . Who turned
> the stars in their sockets
> and set them to spinning?'
> It was I.

The slower cycles of nature, with their power dwarfing our own tiny cycles—all these things, and more, are not Haines'—they were the land's in the beginning, and will be after we are gone—but I know of no one who can observe, describe, translate, and interpret them even remotely like John Haines; and for this, I, his devoted reader, am most grateful.

JOHN HAINES

Last Words on the Poet

He owed his enemies a debt of gratitude.
Enemy or friend, those who could not see,
excused from failure by their nature;
those who saw a little way, by laziness
or habit unable to see farther;
and those who followed nearly to the end,
then in some latent disposition
turned aside before their eyes knew light.

Acquaintance or relation, loved or not,
in ignorance and fear they set up walls
before him, switched the roadway signs
and sought to mine the very ground
beneath his feet. Some beckoned
from a pleasant meadow, bidding him
stay awhile; and others merely laughed
to see him climb the barriers,
stumbling at the crossways, and hesitate
before the smile and languor of reclining
ladies. But he could not condemn them,
their fortunes and solace were not his,
and likely enough their hearts
would have rejoiced if they had understood.

They had all served; their walls and
misdirections, snickerings and enticements,
only served to set his foot the firmer
and slowly teach his eyes to fasten
on the troubled slope ahead,
as tooth and claw develop keenness
in a hungry winter season.

Though blind before it all, his enemies
were spurs, through that perhaps
his friends; and those who turned away
disclosed the road he was to travel.

A JOHN HAINES CHRONOLOGY

1924	Born in Norfolk, Virginia, on June 29, to John Meade Haines and Helen M. Donaldson. His father was a career officer in the United States Navy.
	Moves with his family to Vallejo, California
1926	Robert B. Haines, a brother, born in Vallejo
1932–1938	Haines and his family reside in Long Beach, California; Bremerton, Washington; Honolulu, Hawaii; San Diego, California; Newport, Rhode Island; and New London, Connecticut.
1938–1941	Family moves to Washington, DC, where they reside at the Washington Navy Yard; attends St. John's College High School in Washington, DC.
1943–1945	Serves in the United States Navy during World War II, first with a subchaser in the Atlantic, and then onboard the *USS Knapp* (DD-653), in the Pacific
1945–1946	U.S. Navy service. Discharged at San Pedro, California, in January 1946
1946–1947	Attends the National Art School, Washington DC
1947	Haines and fellow Navy veteran Gilbert Howard leave Washington, DC, for Alaska. There they part company and Haines homesteads on a piece of land along the Richardson Highway and the Tanana River.
1948–1949	Returns to Washington and attends American University where he studies art. He is awarded a prize for his sculpture *Visitation* by the Corcoran Gallery.
1949–1950	Employed as a statistical draftsman, Department of the Navy, in Washington, DC
1950	Moves to New York City and resides in Greenwich Village

1950–1952	Attends the Hans Hoffmann School of Fine Arts, New York City
1952–1954	Resides in Monterey, and in the Carmel Valley of California
1954–1969	Returns to his homestead at Mile 68, Richardson Highway where he hunts and traps and works as a general laborer
1964	Receives Jennie Tane Award for Poetry from the *Massachusetts Review*
1965	Awarded a Guggenheim Foundation Fellowship in poetry
1966	*Winter News* published by Wesleyan University Press
	Russian poet Yevgeny Yevtushenko visits Haines at the Richardson homestead
1967	Awarded a National Endowment for the Arts Fellowship in poetry
1970–1974	Resides intermittently in Pacific Grove, California, and in Alaska
1971	*Twenty Poems* published by Unicorn Press
	The Stone Harp published by Wesleyan University Press
1972–1973	Poet-in-Residence at University of Alaska, Anchorage
1973	Directs *Land-Bridge to Community: A Literary Response,* a conference about land uses and policies sponsored by the Alaska Humanities Forum
1973–1975	Serves as a judge for the Lamont Poetry Selection, Academy of American Poets
1974	Buys a small cottage in Indianola, on the Kitsap Peninsula of Washington State; Visiting Professor, University of Washington, Seattle
	Leaves and Ashes published by Kayak Press
1974–1980	Primary residence is Missoula, Montana
1974–1975	Visiting Lecturer in English, University of Montana, Missoula
1976	Awarded the Amy Lowell Scholarship and travels to England, Scotland, and Spain
	In Five Years' Time published by Smokeroot Press

1977	*Cicada* published by Wesleyan University Press
	In a Dusty Light published by Graywolf Press
1978-1979	Resides briefly in Indianola, Washington, before returning to Missoula
1979	Scriptwriter for *The River Is Wider Than It Seems*, a documentary on the Flathead River funded by the Montana Committee for the Humanities
1980–1994	Primary residence is the Richardson homestead, in Alaska (several brief visits to Missoula in the early years)
1981–1983	Teaches at Sheldon Jackson College, in Sitka, Alaska
1981	*Living Off the Country: Essays on Poetry and Place* published by the University of Michigan Press
1982	Receives Alaska Governor's Award in the Arts for lifetime service to the literary arts in the state
	News from the Glacier: Selected Poems, 1960–1980 published by Wesleyan University Press
1983	Awarded an Honorary Doctor of Letters from the University of Alaska, Fairbanks
	Revised edition of *Winter News* published by Wesleyan University Press
1984–1985	In residence at the Djerrasi Foundation, in Woodside, California, and at the Villa Montalvo, in Saratoga, California
1984	Receives second Guggenheim Foundation Fellowship in poetry
	Collaborates with composer John Adams on *Forest Without Leaves*—a cantata for chorus and orchestra, which premiers November 11 in Fairbanks
1985	Receives Alice Fay di Castagnola Prize from the Poetry Society of America
	John Haines, by Peter Wild, published by Boise State University as part of its Western Writers Series
1987	In residence at the Ucross Foundation, in Clearmont, Wyoming, and at Centrum, in Port Townsend, Washington

Receives Ingram Merrill Foundation Grant

1988   Recording of *Forest Without Leaves* released by Owl Recordings, Boulder, Colorado

1989–1990   Teaches at Ohio University, in Athens, Ohio

1989   *Meditation on a Skull Carved in Crystal* published by Brooding Heron Press

            Receives Western Arts Federation Award for *New Poems: 1980–1988*

1990   *New Poems: 1980–1988* published by Story Line Press

            Rain Country published by Mad River Press

1991–1992   Jenny McKean Moore Visiting Writer, George Washington University, Washington, DC

1991   Receives Lenore Marshall / *The Nation* Award for *New Poems: 1980–1988*

1992   Shares with Mark Jarman the Poets Prize for *New Poems: 1980–1988*

            Elliston Chair in Poetry, University of Cincinnati

1993   Chair of Excellence in the Arts, Austin Peay State University, Clarksville, Tennessee

            The Owl in the Mask of the Dreamer (collected poems) published by Graywolf Press

1994   Receives Lifetime Achievement Award by the Alaska Center for the Book

            Where the Twilight Never Ends published by Limberlost Press

            Gives up the Richardson homestead as his primary residence and moves to Anchorage

1995   Receives Academy Award in Literature, American Academy of Arts and Letters

1996   *Fables and Distances: New and Selected Essays* published by Graywolf Press

            The Wilderness of Vision: On the Poetry of John Haines, a collection of reviews, critiques, memoirs, and interviews, edited by Kevin Bezner and Kevin Walzer, is published by Story Line Press

A Guide to the Four-Chambered Heart published by Larkspur Press

1997   *At the End of This Summer: Poems, 1948–1954* published by Copper Canyon Press

1999   Turns seventy-five

2000   In residence at Centrum in Port Townsend, Washington, and at the Vermont Studio Center in Johnson, Vermont

Participates in a Rockefeller Foundation residency in Bellagio, Italy

2001   Poet-in-Residence, Bucknell University, Lewisburg, Pennsylvania

Moves to Missoula, Montana

For the Century's End: Poems: 1990–1999 published by the University of Washington Press

2002   Invited to give a public reading at an international Shakespeare conference in Vladimir, Russia. This conference was sponsored by the Russian Academy of Sciences and the Vladimir State Pedagogical University.

2003   Named Northern Momentum Scholar by the Northern Studies and Honors Programs at the University of Alaska at Fairbanks for the Spring 2003 semester. He is hailed as "the most prominent living writer associated with the state of Alaska."

JOHN HAINES: A BIBLIOGRAPHY

Winter News. Middletown, CT: Wesleyan University Press, 1966. (Another edition was published by the University Press of New England [Hanover, NH] in 1982.)

Suite for the Pied Piper. Menomonie, WI: Ox Head Press, 1968.

The Legend of Paper Plates. Santa Barbara, CA: Unicorn Press, 1970.

The Mirror. Santa Barbara, CA: Unicorn Press, 1971.

The Stone Harp. Middletown, CT: Wesleyan University Press, 1971. (Additional editions were published by Rapp & Whiting-Deutsch [London] and by the University Press of New England [Hanover, NH] in 1971.)

Twenty Poems. Santa Barbara, CA: Unicorn Press, 1971.

Ryder. Santa Barbara, CA: Unicorn Press, 1971.

Leaves and Ashes. Santa Cruz, CA: Kayak Press, 1974.

North by West. Seattle, WA: Spring Rain Press, 1975.

In Five Years Time. Missoula, MT: SmokeRoot Press, 1976. (Another edition was published by the University of Montana, Missoula, in 1976.)

The Sun on Your Shoulder. Port Townsend, WA: Graywolf Press, 1977.

Cicada. Middletown, CT: Wesleyan University Press, 1977. (Another edition was published by the University Press of New England [Hanover, NH] in 1977.)

In a Dusty Light. Port Townsend, WA: Graywolf Press, 1977.

The Writer as Alaskan. Tempe, AZ: Porch, 1979.

Minus Thirty-One and the Wind Blowing: Nine Reflections About Living on Land. Anchorage: Alaska Pacific University Press, 1980.

Living Off the Country: Essays on Poetry and Place. Ann Arbor, MI: University of Michigan Press, 1981.

Other Days. Port Townsend, WA: Graywolf Press, 1981. Poetry.

Other Days. Port Townsend, WA: Graywolf Press, 1982. Prose memoir.

Of Traps and Snares. Marina Del Rey, CA: Dragon Press, 1982.

News from the Glacier: Selected Poems, 1960–1980. Middletown, CT: Wesleyan University Press, 1982. (Additional editions were published by Harper & Row [New York] and by the University Press of New England [Hanover, NH], both in 1982.)

Stories We Listened To. Swathmore, PA: Bench Press, 1986.

You and I and the World. Ann Arbor, MI: University of Michigan Press, 1988.

Meditation on a Skull Carved in Crystal. Waldron Island, WA: Brooding Heron Press, 1989.

The Stars, The Snow, The Fire: Twenty-Five Years in the Northern Wilderness: A Memoir. Saint Paul, MN: Graywolf Press, 1989. (An additional edition was published by Washington Square Press [New York] in 1992. Graywolf Press issued a new edition in 2002.)

New Poems: 1980–1988. Brownsville, OR: Story Line Press, 1990.

The Owl in the Mask of the Dreamer: Collected Poems. Saint Paul, MN: Graywolf Press, 1993.

Where the Twilight Never Ends. Boise, ID: Limberlost Press, 1994.

Fables and Distances: New and Selected Essays. Saint Paul, MN: Graywolf Press, 1996.

A Guide to the Four-Chambered Heart. Monterey, KY: Larkspur Press, 1996.

At the End of This Summer. Port Townsend, WA: Copper Canyon Press, 1997.

For the Century's End: Poems 1990–1999. Seattle, WA: University of Washington Press, 2001.

ACKNOWLEDGMENTS

Rick Bass. "The Slower Cycles of Nature," copyright 2003 by Rick Bass. Published here, for the first time, by permission of the author.

Wendell Berry. "There is a place you can go," copyright 2003 by Wendell Berry. This poem first appeared in *The Sewanee Review* (Summer 2002). Reprinted by permission of the author.

Jody Bolz. "A Figure in the Landscape," copyright 2003 by Jody Bolz. Published here, for the first time, by permission of the author.

Raymond Carver. "The Cougar," copyright 1973 by Raymond Carver. This poem first appeared in *CutBank* 1 (1973), and subsequently in *Fires* (1983). Reprinted by permission of Tess Gallagher.

Matthew Cooperman. "Wilderness and Witness: An Interview with John Haines," copyright 1996 by Matthew Cooperman. Originally published in *Quarter After Eight: A Journal of Prose and Commentary* 3 (1996). Reprinted by permission of the author.

Robert DeMott. "'Close to Religious Aspirations:' Notes on John Haines' Poetry," copyright 2001. Originally published in *Literature and Belief* 22 (2002). Reprinted by permission of the author and *Literature and Belief*.

Mike Dunham. "No Place for the Poet," copyright 1996 by *The Anchorage Daily News*. Originally published in *The Anchorage Daily News*, May 12, 1994. Reprinted by permission of the author and *The Anchorage Daily News*.

Helen Frost. "A Gas Mantle Lights the Darkness." Originally appeared as a book review in the *First City Scene Magazine* of the *Ketchikan Daily News* (December 30, 1990–January 5, 1991), copyright 1990. Reprinted by permission of the author and the *Ketchikan Daily News*.

Tess Gallagher. "Bullet Holes and Hideouts: A Letter from Syracuse," copyright 2003 by Tess Gallagher. Published here, for the first time, by permission of the author.

James A. Griffin. "The Ground of Death," copyright 2003 by James Griffin. Published here, for the first time, by permission of the author.

John Haines. "Last Words on the Poet," copyright 1997 by John Haines. Originally published in *At the End of This Summer* (Port Townsend, WA: Copper Canyon Press, 1997). Reprinted by permission of the author and Copper Canyon Press.

Gregory Orfalea. "A Walk in the Snow," copyright 2003 by Gregory Orfalea. Published here, for the first time, by permission of the author.

Birch Pavelsky. "Old Bridge at Gasoline Creek," copyright 2003 by Birch Pavelsky. Published here, for the first time, by permission of the author.

Tamlin Pavelsky. "Moving Away," copyright 2003 by Tamlin Pavelsky. Published here, for the first time, by permission of the author.

Steven B. Rogers. "Stories I Have Listened To," copyright 2003 by Steven B. Rogers. Published here, for the first time, by permission of the author.

Donna Redhead Sandberg. "Individualists and Idealists: 'On a Certain Field in Auvers,'" copyright 2003 by Donna Redhead Sandberg. Published here, for the first time, by permission of the author.

Nancy Schoenberger. "Birches," copyright 2003 by Nancy Schoenberger. Published here, for the first time, by permission of the author.

Robert Schultz. "Introduction at the 92nd Street Y," copyright 2003 by Robert Schultz. Published here, for the first time, by permission of the author.

Tom Sexton. "Wolves," copyright 1994 by Tom Sexton. Originally published in *The Bend Toward Asia* (Chugiak, AK: Salmon Run Press, 1994). Reprinted by permission of the author.

Marion K. Stocking. "From A to Infinity: A Half-Century of Poetry," copyright 2003 by Marion K. Stocking. Published here, for the first time, by permission of the author.

Henry Taylor. "A Form of Patience: The Poems of John Haines," copyright 1998 by Henry Taylor. Originally published in *The Hollins Critic* 35, no. 5 (December 1998). Reprinted by permission of the author.

Clark Waterfall. "I Travel with John Haines in Alaska," copyright 2003 by Clark Waterfall. Published here, for the first time, by permission of the author.

William Carlos Williams. "My Dear John Haines" (Letter from William Carlos Williams to John Haines), copyright 2002 by Paul H. Williams and the Estate of William Eric Williams. Used by permission of New Directions Publishing Corporation.

Marcella Wolfe. "Open Letter to John Haines," copyright 2003 by Marcella Wolfe. Published here, for the first time, by permission of the author.

ABOUT THE CONTRIBUTORS

Rick Bass is the author of seventeen books of fiction and nonfiction, which explore the important environmental issues of our day, including the short story collection, *The Hermit's Story* (Houghton Mifflin, 2002); a novel, *Where the Sea Used to Be* (Houghton Mifflin, 1998); and an essay collection, *The Book of Yaak* (Mariner Books, a subsidiary of Houghton Mifflin, 1997). He has lived with his family in the isolated Yaak Valley of northwestern Montana since 1987.

Wendell Berry is a writer and farmer living in Kentucky.

Jody Bolz teaches creative writing at George Washington University. Her poems have appeared recently in *Ploughshares, Indiana Review, Gargoyle, River Styx, Sonora Review, Poet Lore,* and *The Women's Review of Books,* and also in a number of anthologies, including *Her Face in the Mirror* (Beacon, 1994) and *Knowing Stones* (John Gordon Burke, 2000). She received a writer's award from the Rona Jaffe Foundation in 1998–1999 and a scholarship to the Bread Loaf Writers' Conference in 2001. She has another career in advocacy journalism, working for both the Wilderness Society and the Nature Conservancy as a writer and magazine editor.

Raymond Carver (1938–1988) was born in Oregon and lived in Port Angeles, Washington. His first collection of stories, *Will You Please Be Quiet Please?* (McGraw-Hill, 1976), a National Book Award nominee in 1977, was followed by *What We Talk About When We Talk About Love* (Knopf, 1981); *Cathedral* (Knopf, 1983); and *Where I'm Calling From* (Atlantic Monthly Press, 1988). *Call if You Need Me: The Uncollected Fiction and Other Prose* (including five newly discovered stories), was published in 2000 by Havill Press. A poet as well as a short story writer, Carver received *Poetry* magazine's Levinson Prize in 1985, and his poems are collected in *All of Us* (Knopf, 1998).

Matthew Cooperman is the author of *A Sacrificial Zinc* (Pleiades Press, 2001), winner of the Lena–Miles Wever Todd Prize, and *Surge* (Kent State University Press, 1998), winner of the Wick Chapbook Prize. His poetry, essays, and interviews have appeared in such journals as *Field, Denver Quarterly, Black Warrior Review, The American Literary Review,* and *LIT.* A recipient of a writing fellowship from the Fine Arts Work Center in Provincetown, he was a founding editor of the exploratory prose journal *Quarter After Eight,* in which his interview of John Haines first appeared. He currently teaches writing at the University of Colorado in Boulder.

Robert DeMott teaches at Ohio University in Athens. His recent books are a collection of essays, *Steinbeck's Typewriter* (Whitson Publishing,1996); a bio-bibliography and memoir, *Dave Smith: A Literary Archive* (Alden Library, Ohio University, 2000); a collection of poems, *The Weather in Athens* (Bottom Dog Press, 2001); and an edited collection of interviews, *Conversations with Jim Harrison* (University Press of Mississippi, 2002).

Mike Dunham grew up in rural Alaska and has lived in Anchorage since 1967. He has worked for the *Anchorage Daily News* as a music critic, arts reporter, and editor. He has also published in *Opera News, Reason Magazine, Chamber Music America*, and *The Hopkins Quarterly*. He has made the music of Gerard Manley Hopkins an area of special study.

Helen Frost is the author of *When I Whisper, Nobody Listens: Helping Young People Write About Difficult Issues* (Heinemann, 2001) and *Keesha's House* (forthcoming from Farrar, Straus & Giroux in 2003). Her first book of poetry, *Skin of a Fish, Bones of a Bird* (Ampersand), won the 1993 Women's Poets Series Competition. She is the editor of two anthologies: *Season of Dead Water* (Breitenbush, 1990), about the *Exxon Valdez* disaster with a foreword by John Haines; and *Why Darkness Seems So Light: Young People Speak Out About Violence* (Pecan Grove Press, 1998); and the coauthor of a play by the same title (Pioneer Drama Service, 1999). She lived in Alaska from 1979 until 1991, and now lives in Fort Wayne, Indiana.

Tess Gallagher is a poet, short story writer, and essayist with numerous books to her credit. Her most recent book is *Soul Barnacles, Ten More Years with Ray* (University of Michigan Press, 2000). Her short story collection, *At the Owl Woman Saloon*, was published in 1999 by Simon & Schuster. She is currently working on a book of oral stories with the Irish painter and storyteller Josie Gray, entitled *The Courtship Stories*. In 1999 Ms. Gallagher received the prestigious Nancy Blankenship Pryor Award for unique contributions to the literary culture of Washington State. She continues to live and write in Port Angeles, Washington.

Dana Gioia is a poet, critic, and translator. He has published three books of poetry—most recently, *Interrogations at Noon* (2001, Greywolf), which won the American Book Award. His book of essays, *Can Poetry Matter?*

(1992) was republished in 2002 in a special tenth anniversary edition. He currently serves as Chairman of the National Endowment for the Arts.

James A. Griffin participated in the 1991–1992 Jenny McKean Moore Poetry Workshop taught by John Haines at George Washington University. His poetry has appeared in *The Midwest Quarterly*, *Poet Lore*, *The Maryland Poetry Review*, and in other periodicals and anthologies, including *The Next Parish Over: A Collection of Irish-American Writing* published by New Rivers Press. A journalist, freelance writer, political campaign manager, and sometime sailor in the Atlantic, he resides in Bethesda, Maryland.

John Haines was born in Norfolk, Virginia, in 1924. He studied at the National Art School, the American University, and the Hans Hoffmann School of Fine Art. The author of more than ten collections of poetry, his recent works include *For the Century's End: Poems 1990–1999* (University of Washington Press, 2001); *At the End of This Summer: Poems 1948–1954* (Copper Canyon Press, 1997); *The Owl in the Mask of the Dreamer* (Graywolf Press, 1993); and *New Poems 1980–88* (Story Line Press, 1990), for which he received both the Lenore Marshall Poetry Prize and the Western States Book Award. He has also published a book of essays entitled *Fables and Distances: New and Selected Essays* (Graywolf Press, 1996); and a memoir, *The Stars, The Snow, The Fire: Twenty-Five Years in the Northern Wilderness* (Graywolf Press, 1989). Haines spent more than twenty years homesteading in Alaska and has taught at Ohio University, George Washington University, and the University of Cincinnati. Named a Fellow by the Academy of American Poets in 1997, his other honors include the Alaska Governor's Award for Excellence in the Arts, two Guggenheim Fellowships, an Amy Lowell Traveling Fellowship, a National Endowment for the Arts Fellowship, and a Lifetime Achievement Award from the Library of Congress. He lives with his wife, Joy, in Missoula, Montana.

Donald Hall has published fourteen books of poetry, most recently *The Painted Bed* (Houghton Mifflin, 2002) and *Without* (Houghton Mifflin, 1998). Other notable collections include *The One Day* (Houghton Mifflin, 1988), which won the National Book Critics Circle Award, the *Los Angeles Times* Book Prize, and a Pulitzer Prize nomination; *The Happy Man* (Random House, 1986), which won the Lenore Marshall Poetry Prize; and *Exiles and Marriages* (Viking, 1955), which was the Academy of American Poets' Lamont Poetry Selection for 1956. Besides poetry, he has written books on baseball, the sculptor Henry Moore, and the poet Marianne Moore; children's books, including *Ox-Cart Man* (Viking, 1979), which won the Caldecott Medal; short stories; and plays. He has also published several autobiographical works, such as *Life Work* (Beacon Press, 1993), which won the New England Book Award for nonfiction. He lives at Eagle Pond Farm, in Danbury, New Hampshire.

James Hopkins holds a B.A. in French Language and Literature from Duke University, where he studied poetry with Deborah Pope and Joe Ashby Porter. He has received two Jenny McKean Moore fellowships for poetry, studying with John Haines and Anne Caston at George Washington University. He has served twice as the codirector of the Washington Prize for Poetry. His poems have appeared in *Minimus*, *WordWrights!*, and *The Federal Poet*. His chapbook, *The Walnut Tree Waits for Its Bees*, was published by Mica Press in 1997. Another chapbook, *Eight Pale Women*, will be published by WordWorks in 2003.

Carolyn Kremers lives and writes in Fairbanks, Alaska. She has taught creative writing at Eastern Washington University in Spokane, and at the University of Alaska Fairbanks and the College of Rural Alaska in Bethel. She is the author of *Place of the Pretend People: Gifts from a Yup'ik Eskimo Village* (Alaska Northwest Books, 1996) and *Upriver* (poems). Her essays and poetry have appeared in numerous publications, including *Alaska Quarterly Review*, *Creative Nonfiction*, *Indiana Review*, *Manoa*, *Newsday*, *North American Review*, and *Runner's World*. "The Essential Things" is from her book-in-progress, *Then Came the Mustang*.

Joel Kuritsky, M.D., worked as a medical epidemiologist in Bolivia from 1988 to 1994. It was during this time that he discovered the poetry of John Haines, while searching for writers who might help him reflect on both the incredible beauty and starkness of that country. He is presently the director of the Immunization Services Division, Centers for Disease Control in Atlanta and has served as a Senior Consultant for Public Health and Conflict Resolution for The Carter Center. He resides in Atlanta.

Michael H. Lythgoe is a retired U.S. Air Force officer who holds an M.F.A. from Bennington College. He studied with John Haines as a Jenny McKean Moore Fellow at George Washington University in 1992. His poetry chapbook, *Visions, Revisions*, was published by ROAD Publishers in 1994. His poems, reviews, and interviews with contemporary poets have appeared in several publications. He lives in Gainesville, Virginia.

David Mason is a native of the Pacific Northwest. He is the author of several books: *The Buried Houses* (1991), *The Country I Remember* (1996), and *The Poetry of Life and the Life of Poetry* (2000), all from Story Line Press. He teaches at Colorado College and lives in the mountains outside Colorado Springs.

Jack Matthews is Distinguished Professor of English Language and Literature at Ohio University. He is the author of twenty-two books, including novels, short story collections, essays, poetry, and plays. His book, *Schopenhauer's Will*, is scheduled to appear in a Czech translation, even though it has yet to be published in English. He resides in Athens, Ohio.

Thomas McGrath (1916–1990) was born and raised in North Dakota and attended the University of North Dakota at Grand Forks, where he earned a B.A. in 1939; and Louisiana State University at Baton Rouge, where he studied with Cleaneth Brooks. He was a recipient of a Rhodes Scholarship, but the outbreak of World War II prevented him from going to Oxford. He taught briefly at Colby College, in Maine, in 1940–1941, and then served in the military in 1942–1945. He taught at Los Angeles State University, from which he was dismissed following an appearance before the House Committee on Un-American Activities. He returned to teaching in 1960 at C. W. Post College in New York. He also taught at North Dakota State University at Fargo (1962–1969) and at Moorhead State University (1969–1983). During the last years of his life in Minneapolis, McGrath continued to write new poems for his work-in-progress, *Death Song*. He died in September 1990 following a long illness, and the manuscript was published by Copper Canyon Press the following year.

John McKernan teaches at Marshall University in West Virginia. He is the author of a chapbook, *Postcards from Dublin* (Dead Metaphor Press, 1999), and *Walking Along the Missouri River* (Lost Roads Publishing, 1979).

Wesley McNair is a recipient of grants from the Rockefeller, Fulbright, and Guggenheim foundations. He was awarded two National Endowment for the Arts fellowships and prizes from *Poetry*, *Poetry Northwest*, and *Yankee* magazines. His most recent books are a collection of poems, *Fire* (Godine); and a collection of essays, *Mapping the Heart: Reflections on Place and Poetry* (Carnegie Mellon Press), both published in 2002.

Miles David Moore studied with John Haines as a Jenny McKean Moore Fellow at George Washington University. An earlier essay on Haines, "A Mind in the Wilderness," was published in *The Wilderness of Vision* (Story Line Press, 1996). Moore is the author of two collections of poems, *The Bears of Paris* (WordWorks, 1995) and *Buddha Isn't Laughing* (Argonne Hotel Press, 1999). His poetry and essays have won awards from *Poet Lore*, *Potomac Review*, and *WordWrights!*

John Murray has published over forty books, including *Cinema Southwest: An Illustrated Guide to the Movies and Their Locations* (Northland Publishing, 2000), which won the Southwest Book Award; and *Mythmakers of the West: Shaping America's Imagination* (Northland Publishing, 2001). He lives in Denver.

Sheila Nickerson lived in Juneau, Alaska, from 1971 to 1998. Like John Haines, she served a term as Alaska's poet laureate. She is the author of *Feast of the Animals: An Alaskan Bestiary*, Volumes I and II (Old Harbor Press, 1987); *Disappearance: A Map* (Doubleday, 1996); and *Midnight to the North: The Untold Story of the Inuit Woman Who Saved the Polaris Expedition* (Tarcher, 2002). She lives in Bellingham, Washington.

Gregory Orfalea is the author of several books, including *Messengers of the Lost Battalion* (Free Press, 1997). He was in John Haines' first and last class at the University of Alaska, Fairbanks.

Birch Pavelsky has lived in Lincoln Creek, Alaska, west of Fairbanks, since 1982. His poems have appeared in *Bone Winter*, *Permafrost*, *A Good Crew*, and *The Ester Republic*. The poem appearing in this volume makes reference to an old abandoned bridge over Gasoline Creek near the Haines homestead at Richardson.

Tamlin Pavelsky has spent most of his life in Alaska, where he was born, and in California. He recently received a B.A. in geography from Middlebury College, in Vermont, where he also studied poetry under Jay Parini. He is currently pursuing a graduate degree at UCLA and continues to nurture his passion for both poetry and classical cello. Son of Birch Pavelsky, he has known John Haines most of his life.

Donna Redhead Sandberg is a freelance artist, poet, writer, and a long-time resident of Fairbanks, Alaska. She has studied at the University of Wisconsin, the Pratt Institute, and the University of Alaska in Fairbanks and holds degrees in English and Arts in Teaching. She currently teaches photography at West Valley High School in Fairbanks.

Nancy Schoenberger is a former director of the Academy of American Poets and the author of three books of poetry, most recently *Long Like a River* (New York University Press, 1998). She is also the author of the recent biography of Robert Lowell's third wife, *Dangerous Muse: The Life of Lady Caroline Blackwood* (Nan A. Talese Books, 2001). She teaches creative and nonfiction writing at the College of William and Mary and divides her time between Williamsburg, Virginia, and Los Angeles with her husband, the writer Sam Kashner.

Robert Schultz is the author of a novel, *The Madhouse Nudes* (Simon & Schuster, 1997) and two collections of poetry: *Winter in Eden* (Loess Hills Books, 1997) and *Vein Along the Fault* (Laueroc Press, 1981). He has been the recipient of a National Endowment for the Arts literature fellowship in fiction and the Emily Clark Balch Prize for Poetry from *The Virginia Quarterly Review*. He currently chairs the Department of English at Luther College in Deborah, Iowa.

Tom Sexton has lived in Alaska for more than thirty years, and is the founder of the creative writing program at the University of Alaska in Anchorage. He was Alaska's poet laureate from 1995 to 1999. He has known John Haines since 1968.

Marion K. Stocking is a scholar of the Byron/Shelley circle and most recently was the editor of *The Clairmont Correspondence* (Johns Hopkins Press, 1995). She has taught at the University of Maine, the University of Colorado, and for thirty years at Beloit College. She has been the editor of the *Beloit Poetry Journal* since 1954 and recently edited *A Fine Excess: Fifty Years of the Beloit Poetry Journal*. She lives in Lamoine, Maine, on the shore of Frenchman's Bay.

Henry Taylor is Professor of Literature and codirector of the M.F.A. creative writing program at American University in Washington, DC, where he has taught since 1971. His third collection of poems, *The Flying Change* (Louisiana State University Press, 1985), received the 1986 Pulitzer Prize in Poetry. His first two collections, *The Horse Show at Midnight* (Louisiana State University Press, 1966) and *An Afternoon of Pocket Billiards* (University of Utah Press, 1975) were reissued in one volume in 1992. Another collection of poems, *Understanding Fiction: Poems 1986–1996* (Louisiana State University Press) was published in 1996, and his collection of clerihews, *Brief Candles*, appeared in 2000 from Louisiana State University Press. His poetry and translations from Bulgarian, French, Hebrew, Italian, and Russian have appeared in numerous periodicals and anthologies. He has also published translations from Greek and Roman classical drama.

Clark Waterfall first encountered John Haines' poetry while attending a poetry class at the Fort Wayne campus of Indiana-Purdue University. He later participated in a campus workshop taught by Haines. He lives in Fort Wayne.

William Carlos Williams was born in Rutherford, New Jersey, in 1883. He received his M.D. from the University of Pennsylvania and returned to

Rutherford, where he sustained his medical practice throughout his life. Williams also embarked on a prolific career as a poet, novelist, essayist, and playwright. He sought to invent a singularly American poetry centered on the everyday circumstances of life and the lives of common people. His major works include *Kora in Hell* (Four Seasons Co., 1920), *Spring and All* (Contact Publishing, 1923), *Pictures from Brueghel and Other Poems* (New Directions, 1962), the five-volume epic *Paterson* (New Directions, 1963, 1992), and *Imaginations* (New Directions, 1970). Williams' health began to decline after a heart attack in 1948 and a series of strokes, but he continued writing up until his death in New Jersey in 1963.

Marcella Wolfe is a poet and freelance writer living in Washington, DC.

FROM THE EDITOR

This project was first conceived during the summer of 1997 while I was sitting at the kitchen table in our little lakeside cottage in Sabbathday Lake, Maine. I had just written a brief letter to John, and it struck me that two years hence he would be celebrating his seventy-fifth birthday. The original idea was to collect contributions from many of John's friends and colleagues and to assemble a Festschrift to commemorate this important benchmark in John's life. Fortunately, the response to my idea was overwhelmingly positive. Unfortunately, I was not able to complete the work before John's birthday came and went. Nevertheless, I believed it was still important to finish the task at hand—no longer a Festschrift in the general definition of the term, but an overall appreciation of John's life and his contribution to American arts and letters in the latter half of the twentieth century.

I want to thank all the people who have given me aid and comfort over the past four years as this project progressed from a fanciful idea on the edge of a New England lake to the book you see before you. First and foremost, I wish to thank John Haines for his friendship and wise counsel over the past decade, since our first meeting in the fall of 1991 when I was a Jenny McKean Moore Fellow in Creative Writing at George Washington University and John was Writer-in-Residence. This book is an appreciation of his life and work by his many friends and colleagues, but, more important, it is my own personal testament to our friendship, which will always mean a great deal to me. Without John's friendship, this book would have remained nothing more than a good idea.

I also want to thank the contributors to this rather eclectic collection of essays, reviews, memoirs, letters, and poems—not only for their kind permission to use their work, but also for their patience as I began to mold the collection into what it has become, and for their ideas and timely responses to my numerous inquiries and comments. I would like to single out Miles David Moore, who endured my many flights of fancy and endless grumbling in the early days, and who read the manuscript in its many drafts and offered his studied opinions. This is a better book for his time and attention. I would also like to express my appreciation to the editors and publications that have permitted me to reprint some of the selections appearing in this collection.

Robert G. Waite, my good friend and colleague, has been a valued confidant who has read just about everything I have written in recent years. We have discussed this project for hours and hours, and I thank him for his many good ideas and suggestions. I owe you one, friend.

Finally, I want to thank my new friends at CavanKerry Press—Joan Cusack Handler, Florenz Greenberg, Ellen Trama, Baron Wormser, and everyone associated with this fine new independent publishing house—who read the final manuscript and who understood what I was trying to do. I also wish to thank Helen Maggie Carr for her keen eye during the editing of the final manuscript, Sylvia Frezzolini Severance for her splendid design work, and proofreader Pat Jalbert-Levine and indexer Nora Harris for their contributions to the finished book.

I was sitting at the same kitchen table, in that small lakeside cottage in Maine, when I received the good news that CavanKerry Press had agreed to publish the manuscript. The dream has now come full circle.

Steven B. Rogers
Mount Rainier, Maryland
December 2002

A GRADUAL TWILIGHT

INDEX

Note: Authors of poems, essays and letters have been identified in parentheses following the titles of their works. All other titles are works by John Haines.

free verse, 41, 44, 63, 76, 143–144
Friedrich, Caspar David, 28
"From A to Infinity: A Half-Century of the Poetry of John Haines" (Stocking), 15–38
Frost, Helen, 159–161, 290
Frost, Robert, 214

G
Gallagher, Tess, 201–207, 290
"A Gas Mantle Lights the Darkness" (Frost), 159–161
Gasoline Creek, 228
    See also "Old Bridge at Gasoline Creek" (Pavelsky, B.)
George Washington University, 6, 191, 211, 280
"Gerontion" (Eliot), 20
Giacometti, Alberto, 69–70, 111–112, 113
Gilgamesh, 195
Gioia, Dana, 41, 51, 75, 131, 214, 219
Gogh, Vincent van, 22, 103–108, 114, 117, 118
Good Friday earthquake, 3
Goya, Francisco de, 17, 69, 115
Griffin, James A., 255–258, 290–291
"The Ground of Death" (Griffin), 255–258
Guggenheim Foundation, 216

H
Haines, John, 291
    abstractness in poetry of, 36
    academe, 6, 130, 131–133, 191, 218
    adjustment to city life, 191
    advice to young poets, 157–158
    aesthetic dimension of, 50, 87–88
    age discrimination and, 217–218
    as Alaska Poet Laureate, 197
    as an Alaskan writer, 191–192
    art, 21, 112

cats, 195
Chinese art and poetry, 139, 140
chronology, 277–281
creative process of, 52, 117
depression of, 184
early life of, 7, 40, 129, 215
early works, 26–32
effect of students on, 182
environment. See nature writing
essays and reviews. See individual titles under Haines, John, works by
homesteading. See homestead on Richardson Highway
influence of literature on, 128
influence of place on, 128–130
isolation of, 183
lyricism of, 17–18
marriages, 183, 234–235
meditative quality of poetry of, 44–45, 48, 151
memoirs. See individual titles under Haines, John, works by
morality, sense of, 86
mushrooms, 210–211, 229–230
nature, view of, 104–105
nature writing, 40, 50–51
poetics, 74–75, 82–83
politics, 75–76
regionalism of, 149
relations with children, 183, 184
relations with women, 183 (See also "An Open Letter to John Haines" [Wolfe]; "Bullet Holes and Hideouts: A Letter from Syracuse" [Gallagher]; "The Essential Things" [Kremers])
religiousness of, 85–86, 90
role of the poet, 106
romanticism of, 51, 92, 151, 182
unfamiliarity with technology, 153
Haines, John, works by
    "Admission," 30–31
    "Age of Bronze," 19
    "Alive in the World," 87

A GRADUAL TWILIGHT

ABOUT THE EDITOR

STEVEN B. ROGERS was born in Chicago in 1951 and has lived all over the United States. He holds a B.A. in German and English from Florida Southern College, a M.A. in German Literature from the University of Arizona, and a Ph.D. in German Area Studies from the University of Maryland. He was a 1990 Jenny McKean Moore Fellow in Creative Writing at George Washington University, where he worked with John Haines. He received a second Jenny McKean Moore fellowship in 2002, and worked with Suzannah Lessard. His poems, as well as his critical and historical essays, have appeared in a number of journals, broadsides, and anthologies. As a founding member of the Washington, DC, chapter of the American Literary Translators Association, he has completed translations from German, French, Latvian, and Estonian and he is currently working on German translations of John Haines' selected poems. He was the judge for the annual chapbook competition of the Georgia State Poetry Society in 1991, and for the past several years he has been a reader for the Washington Poetry Prize. He is a leading Thomas Wolfe scholar, having lectured and written extensively on Wolfe's relationship with Germany, and is working on a book on this subject. He is also completing a book on Frank Lloyd Wright and his designs for the campus of Florida Southern College. He serves as the president of the Thomas Wolfe Society based at the University of North Carolina at Chapel Hill. For the past twenty-six years he has worked as a historian in the Washington, DC, area where he resides with his wife.